WAR
WALKS

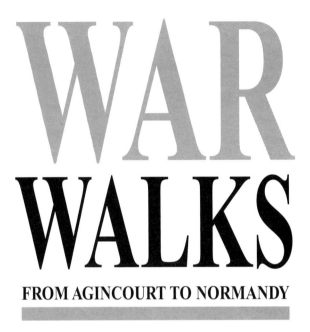

WAR
WALKS

FROM AGINCOURT TO NORMANDY

Richard Holmes

BBC BOOKS

Acknowledgements

The author wishes to thank Matthew Bennett, Stephen Burke, Tony Coutts-Britton, Mike Martin, Ian Pyecroft and Isobel Swan, whose knowledge has saved him from numerous errors: he is solely responsible for those that remain. Life is never much fun in the Holmes' household when a book is being written. On this occasion the author is more than usually grateful to his wife Lizie and his daughters Jessica and Corinna who had to endure an unusually bleak midwinter.

This book is published to accompany the television series
entitled *War Walks* which was first broadcast in 1996
Series Producer Mark Fielder · Producer/Director Steven Clarke

Published by BBC Books, an imprint of BBC Worldwide Publishing,
BBC Worldwide Limited, Woodlands, 80 Wood Lane, London W12 0TT

First published in hardback 1996
Reprinted 1996 (three times), 1997 (twice)
Paperback edition first published 1997

ISBN 0 563 38749 1 (hardback)
ISBN 0 563 38360 7 (paperback)

Photographic acknowledgements

Bankfield Museum/Calderdale Leisure Services 51 above; Bridgeman Art Library 30, 42-3; Crown Copyright Reserved, Public Record Office 35; Estate of Rex Whistler 1996 Dacs/photo supplied by the National Army Museum London 62-3, 194, 195; E. T. Archive 16, 34, 38-9, 51 below, 73 above; Imperial War Museum 89 below, 96 both, 102, 103, 109, 112, 131 (courtesy E. Shephard copyright holders), 117, 131, 136-7, 139 both, 152, 155 centre, 164 right, 173, 175, 178-9, 184, 202 below, 209, 217; Liddle Collection, University of Leeds 89 above and centre; MOD Pattern Room, Nottingham 51 below, 188-9; National Portrait Gallery 17 above; Robert Hunt Picture Library 202 above; The Royal Collection © Her Majesty The Queen 54-5; The Tank Museum 155 above and below, 164 left, 182; William Turner 121 above (courtesy Mr Marshall), 121 centre, 121 below (courtesy Mrs Hargreaves), 148 (courtesy Hyndburn Tourist Office); Victoria and Albert Museum 73 below; Wallace Collection 17 below; Welsh Guards 189, 195 (courtesy Colonel of the Regiment).

Designed by BBC Books and Andrew Shoolbred
Maps by Line and Line
Picture research by Anne-Marie Ehrlich

Set in Times New Roman
Printed and bound in Great Britain by Butler and Tanner Ltd, Frome and London
Colour separations by Radstock Reproductions, Midsomer Norton
Jacket printed by Lawrence Allen Ltd, Weston-super-Mare
Cover printed by Belmont Press, Northampton

Contents

Introduction page 6

CHAPTER 1

Agincourt 1415 page 16

CHAPTER 2

Waterloo 1815 page 50

CHAPTER 3

Mons and Le Cateau 1914 page 88

CHAPTER 4

The Somme 1916 page 120

CHAPTER 5

Arras 1940 page 155

CHAPTER 6

Operation Goodwood 1944 page 188

Introduction

If you want a book about strategy then you have already read too far, for this is a book about men, most of them very ordinary, and the ground they fought on. The battles included in this book are Agincourt, Waterloo, Mons and Le Cateau, the Somme, Arras and Operation Goodwood. They are all set in a few hundred square miles of northern France and southern Belgium, a space so confined that a single day's drive could take us across all our battlefields. Here, in what Charles de Gaulle called the 'fatal avenue' through which invaders have so often jabbed to the pit of the French stomach, the events of history intertwine like the braided knot on a hussar's cuff.

This book is intended to work at two levels. At one, it is narrative military history, slanted towards the view of regimental officers and men, and intended for the general reader in armchair, train compartment or airline seat. At another, it is aimed at travellers who intend to view the fields themselves. It is not a guidebook in the strict sense, for it will neither suggest where you might eat or sleep, nor attempt comprehensive coverage of the cemeteries and monuments that frost this part of Europe. Instead it identifies those pieces of ground best able to take us, like Dr Who's tardis, from the present to the past. Some can be reached by car but others cannot and, in any event, the texture of a battlefield is best felt by walking the ground, if only for a mile or two. The formula inevitably varies from place to place: the Somme, which lasted for four months, offers a greater range of walks than Agincourt, which was over in a couple of October hours. The suburbs of Arras have their limitations: in contrast, the forest of Mormal, between the battlefields of Mons and Le Cateau, is a beautiful setting for a quiet hour or two.

Each chapter is laid out in the same way, with an introduction which sets the campaign in context, a larger section of narrative, and then a description of a number of viewing-points – 'stands', as battlefield visitors are apt to call them – and the events that unrolled across them.

Many of the combatants whose paths we follow had crossed the languid Somme, sometimes in the footsteps of fathers or grandfathers. Other features of the landscape would have been familiar to soldiers across the centuries. The gradient of Vimy Ridge, glowering down over the Douai plain, probably drew as many oaths from the Duke of Marlborough's men while they jockeyed for position with Marshal Villars in 1711 as it did from Siegfried Sassoon's Harry and Jack, who grunted misplaced approval of their general as they slogged up to Arras with rifle and pack in 1917. One of the Durham Light Infantry battalions that attacked down the ridge in 1940 had prepared for battle in trenches dating from its Canadian capture in 1917, and was commanded by an officer who had fought over the same ground as a subaltern. As they tramped these haunted acres, soldiers were conscious that history was tugging at their sleeves: Le Cateau was fought on 26 August 1914, the anniversary of Crécy, a fact which helped some combatants to put their own perils in perspective that busy morning.

Architecture and artefacts alike mark the passage of armies. When Charles Carrington, an infantry officer in the First World War, revisited the battlefield near Péronne in 1923 he found a trench still full of the debris of war. He dug an old gun out of the mud and found, to his surprise, 'that it was not a modern rifle but a Brown Bess musket, dropped there by some British soldier during Wellington's last action against a French rearguard in 1815.' Péronne was the base for the French advance guard in the Agincourt campaign of 1415. Wellington's men took it on their way from Waterloo to Paris in 1815, the Germans cropped the towers in 1917, and the building now houses the Historial de la Grande Guerre, arguably the best First World War museum in France. In Mons, away to the north, the cast-iron figure of the Main Guard Monkey outside the town hall has had its shiny head patted, over the centuries, by Austrian, French, British and German soldiers, as befits a creature who squats at the crossroads of military history.

The Changing Weaponry of War
So much for space. In time we march from Agincourt in 1415, fought with weapons which might not have dismayed the Romans, to the break-out from Normandy in 1944, whose veterans still enrich Remembrance Day. In the process we touch many of the developments which have shaped the face of war. Cannon were first used in Europe during the Hundred Years

1	2	3
AGINCOURT 1415	**WATERLOO 1815**	**MONS AND LE CATEAU 1914**

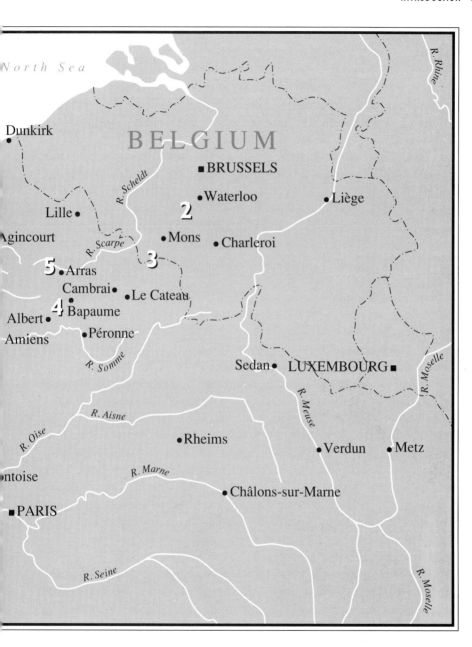

North Sea

Dunkirk

B E L G I U M

■BRUSSELS

R. Scheldt

•Waterloo

•Liège

2

Lille•

Agincourt

R. Scarpe

•Mons

•Charleroi

3

5•Arras

Cambrai•

•Le Cateau

4 Bapaume

Albert•

•Péronne

Amiens

R. Somme

Sedan• LUXEMBOURG■

R. Meuse

R. Moselle

R. Aisne

R. Oise

•Rheims

•Verdun

•Metz

R. Marne

ontoise

•Châlons-sur-Marne

■PARIS

R. Seine

R. Moselle

R. Rhine

4	**5**	**6**
THE SOMME 1916	ARRAS 1940	OPERATION GOODWOOD 1944

War, and in the First World War the inhabitants of Crécy and Azincourt (as Agincourt is now known) heard creeping barrages and lightning bombardments which would have horrified a medieval gunner as much as his smelly and unreliable cannon shocked the men of his own day.

For the men of Agincourt, battle centred on muscle-power, applied to bowstring or sword-hilt, for this was war in its first age. Waterloo saw war in its second age. Although raw muscle still played its part – cavalrymen hewed one another through steel and bone with a desperation that would not have surprised a medieval warrior – the real killer was flying iron or lead, impelled by gunpowder from the products of the Industrial Revolution. The process accelerated in the First World War. We might see the Somme as a contest of machine-minders, with gunners busy at their work stations on the giant assembly line that converted metal and chemicals into torn earth and dead soldiers, and the infantry part of their raw material. It was this unequal contest between flesh and metal that so impressed contemporaries. 'Somehow it makes one feel so helpless,' reflected a veteran. 'There is no chance of reprisal for the individual man. The advantage is all with the shell, and you have no comeback.'

The machinery of war grew more complex on the Somme. Tanks made their first halting entry on to the stage there on 15 September 1916, and in May 1940 they burst across it, heading westwards this time, to change the way men thought about war. In August 1914 the aircraft made its first real contribution to major war when an aviator from the Paris garrison saw that the Germans had turned in front of the French capital: the outflanking wheel of the Schlieffen plan had failed. A generation later, gull-winged Stukas provided German armour with flying artillery, while the preparation for Operation Goodwood in 1944 used strategic bombers to transform the landscape, up-end Tiger tanks, and transform languid Norman countryside into a latter-day version of the Somme.

The Changing Style of Command

It was not simply the tools of killing that changed. Styles of command and the technology on which they depend are rarely as eye-catching as weapons, but they are every bit as important. At Operation Goodwood we can glimpse the dawn of war's third age, as information technology began to dominate steel, just as that steel had supplanted raw muscle. Our first two battles show generalship in its heroic guise. Henry V, who led his men at Agincourt, and the Duke of Wellington, British commander at Waterloo, would have agreed that command in battle meant personal intervention, and that personal intervention meant personal risk. Indeed, the nature of their armies and the weapons they used gave them little choice.

Heroic generalship never ran smoothly: what might have happened had the French sword which lopped off part of Henry's crown bitten deeper, or if one of the bullets which decimated Wellington's staff had hit the duke himself? It was damaged beyond repair by the increase in the size of armies that came with the perfection of conscription in the late nineteenth century. When Henry shouted 'Advance banners!' he could see his whole host move off across the muddy plough at Agincourt. Although Wellington's army was much larger, he could gallop across the whole Waterloo position in a few minutes, and his knack of finding the battle's balance meant that he was always on hand to stiffen a shaky square or unleash those volleys that sent the Imperial Guard ebbing back down the slope.

In 1914 the old machine broke down at last. In that first year of the war it was difficult for a commander to be sure where he ought to be. Moltke, German commander-in-chief, was too distant from the battle, and isolation and responsibility imposed on his flawed character a burden it could never sustain. Joffre, his French opponent, was altogether more robust, and had taken the wise precaution of conscripting one of France's leading racing drivers who spun him between subordinate headquarters at a speed which Napoleon – no sluggard when it came to covering ground – would have envied.

As the First World War went on, senior officers felt compelled to stay back at their headquarters to command rather than to go forward to lead. And after all, what meaningful personal contribution could they make by scrambling about in trenches? Nonetheless, many generals displayed courage denied them by popular mythology and, in doing so, paid the supreme penalty. Of the first seven British divisional commanders who went to France in 1914, three were killed in action and one was wounded. Only one British divisional commander was killed on the Somme, and the battle's character was in part determined by a more remote style of command. It may be unfair to call it château generalship, but it was certainly command by telephone and typewriter. Technology and military logic alike conspired to draw generals into the rear, almost a foreign country to the glum heroes up the line, where they lost that demonstrative, risk-taking and risk-sharing quality which had hitherto been a matter of honour.

There were still times, even during the Second World War, when heroic leadership tilted the balance. Henry V or Wellington might have had little in common with Major-General Erwin Rommel, commanding 7th Panzer Division at Arras in 1940. Yet they could scarcely have disapproved of his instinct, as British tanks ploughed deep into his division, to position himself at the crucial point, animating a defence which might not have proved successful without his leadership – a quality ancient even when Agincourt was fought.

Crucial Campaigns
The battles we visit in this book differ almost as much in size or significance as they do in weapons or tactics. Some, like Agincourt and Waterloo, shunted history in a particular direction. A victory for the attacker might have had results that we can only guess at: in the first case, perhaps a bruising end to English ambitions in France, and in the second the long-term re-establishment of Napoleon as emperor. Much the same can be said of Mons and Le Cateau. They were tiny by comparison with many other First World War battles but it is hard to see how the British could have lost them and still won the war. A decisive Allied victory on the Somme might not have ended the war at a stroke, but it could scarcely have failed to alter its complexion. The British counter-attack at Arras and the attack in Operation Goodwood had more modest implications, but each helped to shape a crucial campaign.

Private and Official Accounts of War
Our journey across most of these battlefields is based on a rich mixture of source material. Wellington remarked that it was as difficult to write the history of a battle as of a ball: participants did different things at the same time, with subjective views of events and often no yardstick against which their own recollections might be measured. Nevertheless, if we are to see battles through the eyes of participants, we must start by listening to what they have to tell us. The personal accounts of twentieth-century combat stretch down the whole chain of command. Officers had long kept diaries and written to family and friends. One consequence of the rise in literacy, the availability of writing materials and the arrival of a cross-section of male population in the army was that the keeping of diaries spread throughout the ranks.

The more I work on the First World War the more I am struck by the quality of many of the accounts written by men serving in the ranks. In some cases this ought to be no surprise. Frederic Manning, author of *The Middle Parts of Fortune* and its expurgated version *Her Privates We,* was a poet and essayist who served in the ranks by choice. Ernest Shephard, on the other hand, left school at fourteen and went to sea before enlisting into the Dorset Regiment in 1909 at the age of seventeen. He fought in France as a sergeant and company sergeant-major and was killed as a second lieutenant in January 1917. He recorded his experiences in eighteen small pocket-books, clearly and descriptively written, and illustrated by sketch-maps of trenches. John Lucy was a corporal in 1914 but, as his memoir *There's a Devil in the Drum* demonstrates, was anything but the bone-headed NCO so beloved of scriptwriters. Shephard's diaries and Lucy's account have both been published, but there are hundreds of unpublished personal accounts (an increasing number on audio tapes) in private hands and public collections.

Armies generate paperwork in quantities which sometimes stun even those who ought to be inured to their bureaucratic methods, and a lot finds its way back to archives. The Public Record Office at Kew is an essential port of call for the military historian. In both World Wars units kept daily diaries, and these generally survive at Kew. They are of mixed value. If a unit was in the thick of action its adjutant or chief clerk, upon whom the writing of the diary usually devolved, might have his mind on other things. The important rubs shoulders with the commonplace: a battery diary might tell us how many shells it fired – but not what their targets were.

Official historians have a larger canvas to paint. The official histories of both wars are divided into volumes covering given theatres of war: the red-jacketed First World War series for France and Belgium consists of several volumes for each year, together with associated tomes of maps and annexes. Most were the work of Brigadier-General Sir James Edmonds, whose objectivity remains a matter of debate amongst historians. And here, of course, is the rub. The notion of official history has a whiff of 'officially sanctioned' history about it. Even if governments are right to maintain that the contents of such books are a matter for their authors and are not necessarily a reflection of any official view, official history is not generally entrusted to historians who harbour deep-seated suspicions of the Establishment. Thus even if an official history can devote space to telling the truth, it may not always tell us the whole truth.

Finding the truth becomes harder the further we retreat from the twentieth century. Waterloo is an exception, recognized as such even in its day. Contemporaries found it so obviously climactic that it inspired unprecedented interest, and it is no accident that the British struck a medal for soldiers of all ranks who fought there, although campaign medals were not generally granted at that time. Captain William Siborne assembled several hundred letters written in response to his appeal for help in constructing his massive Waterloo Model, and these were later published by his son. Moreover, the battle features in dozens of recollections, published and unpublished, which cover the Napoleonic period, and as far as this book is concerned Waterloo ranks alongside the Somme for the availability of detailed accounts.

Our study of Agincourt is supported by better contemporary accounts than is the case with most medieval and early modern battles but, even so, sources are tantalizingly thin and we cannot be sure of facts which would present no problems in any of our later battles. How were the English drawn up? Did the archers fight on the flanks of blocks of men-at-arms, between, or even in front of them? It is small wonder that Lieutenant-Colonel Alfred Burne developed the expression 'inherent military probability' when studying battles of the period, for there are moments when scholarship can inch its way no further and must take a leap of educated judgement.

Whatever our deductions about the way Agincourt was fought, we still lack that view from the past that illuminates our other battles. Ensign Gronow tells us what it felt like to be in a square at Waterloo, Corporal Ashurst gives us a snapshot of the sunken road at Beaumont-Hamel on the Somme, and Major von Luck describes defending Cagny against onrushing British armour. We have no answering voice from Davy Gam or Lewis Robbesard Esquire: the sands of time have choked them, and we must let the ground they fought on and the weapons they bore speak for them.

Visiting the Battlefields
The maps in this book are intended to enable the reader to make sense of the narrative and to locate individual stands or viewing-points; they are not designed for navigation across Shakespeare's 'vasty fields of France'. For this purpose it is hard to beat the 1:200 000 Michelin maps. Agincourt and the Somme lie on Sheet 52, Waterloo and Mons on Sheet 51, Le Cateau and Arras on Sheet 53 and Operation Goodwood on Sheet 54. The Commonwealth War Graves Commission (2 Marlow Road, Maidenhead, Berkshire SL6 7DX, tel. Maidenhead 34221) produces the Michelin series overprinted with the location of its cemeteries. The Commission will provide information on the place of burial of servicemen who have known graves, as well as on the Memorials to the Missing which commemorate those who do not. The Institut Géographique National 1:50 000 maps are considerably more detailed, and commend themselves to those who intend close study of a single battlefield.

The stands described here can be reached along roads or tracks that, at the time of writing, offer public access, although I cannot guarantee that this will remain the case. Visitors to battlefields do well to remember that one man's historical site is another's livelihood, and a little common sense often turns away a good deal of wrath. Finally, almost any visit to the fatal avenue confirms the fact that the products of the munitions factories of the superpowers of their day were fired into it. Tons of unexploded shells and mortar bombs are ploughed up each year – my friend Colonel Henri d'Evry, late of the Spahis, lost the back of his plough to a shell only two years ago – and are left in piles where farm tracks meet the road. Other items turn up on ground that thousands of feet must have crossed: I recently found a live Hales rifle-grenade, dating from the First World War, in the Durhams' assembly area up on Vimy Ridge. Leave such things well alone, for mustard gas corrodes the lungs as fatally in 1996 as it did in 1916, and high-explosive, even old high-explosive, is a killer. But enough for preambles. Let us set off and see how, in the words of the 'Agincourt Carol':

> Our King went forth to Normandy
> With grace and might of chivalry.

KEY
Military Symbols used on Maps

☐ Allied/British troops

◼ Enemy/French or German troops (depending on which troops are the enemy in the battle referred to)

Formation Symbols

☐ Army

☐ Corps

☐ Division

☐ Brigade

☐ Regiment

☐ Battalion

☐ Company

Types of Units

⊠ Infantry (so an Allied Infantry Battalion is represented thus ⊠ with an Enemy Infantry Battalion represented thus ◤)

◿ Cavalry (so a Cavalry Brigade is represented thus ◿ with an Enemy Cavalry Brigade represented thus ◥)

⬭ Armour (so an Armoured Division is represented thus ⬭ with an Enemy Armoured Division represented thus ⬬)

⊠ Mechanised Infantry

⬭ Armoured Reconnaissance

CHAPTER I

Agincourt
1415

Background

The young king rode a white horse. Like his men Henry V had passed an anxious night but, if the grey morning weighed as heavily on his spirits as it did on theirs, he did not show it. He rode along the front of his little army, telling his soldiers what they needed to hear. Their cause was just; the penalty of failure would be unthinkable; and he would fight alongside them to the end. He must have seen what a sorry spectacle his host, as a medieval army is properly termed, presented. There was rust on armour and mud on silken surcoats. The going was so heavy that many of his archers, who had long since discarded their breeches after repeated bouts of dysentery, were marching barefoot to keep their footing. After a long and dispiriting wait the French declined to attack but remained drawn up, rank on rank, at the far end of the field. The king ordered: 'Banners advance! In the name of Jesus, Mary and St George!' His men knelt, kissed the earth which they could soon expect to cover them, and stepped off across the plough.

The Hundred Years War (which lasted from 1337 to 1453) was an intermittent struggle between nations whose identity solidified as it went on; a coalition war, with the English often supported by Burgundians and Gascons, and even a civil war, whose combatants looked back to a heritage that was partly shared. Conflict between England and Scotland played much the same part in forming the English army of the Hundred Years War as the Boer War did for the British army of 1914.

We cannot be certain that this is a accurate likeness of Henry V,
but the face radiates the cold determination which characterised
him. The pudding-basin haircut was popular with knights who
spent much of their time cooped up in helmets like this basinet.
The cruciform-hilted broadsword was the classic knightly weapon.

Edward I (1239–1307) was known as 'the hammer of the Scots' and his experience in Wales and Scotland encouraged him to change the way English armies were raised. He disliked levying troops as an obligation of land tenure, when men who held estates from the Crown were bidden to appear with their followers for forty days' unpaid service. Often too few reported for duty, the end of their service might not coincide with that of the campaign, and their weapons and equipment might not be up to the task in hand. Edward began to raise soldiers by indentures or contracts, whereby a commander was paid to furnish specified troops for a set time at agreed rates of pay. In practice both systems co-existed for a time, and even when the indenture system was widespread a magnate, serving for pay, would ride to war with many of his feudal underlings behind him.

Fighting Tactics
The dominant military instrument of the age was the man-at-arms, a war-rior armoured from head to foot and trained to fight on horseback, known in popular shorthand as a knight. He might actually have been a knight, who had the standing to be eligible for knighthood and had undergone the formal ceremony. But he was as likely to be an esquire, a rank below the knight, or a man with no social pretensions but the ability to obtain and use arms and armour. The charge of the mounted knight was often decisive, but it had acute limitations where ground did not favour massed cavalry or where infantry was prepared to stand and fight. It was a blunt weapon, yet its appeal to a knightly class, bred to fight on horseback and despise spurless peasantry on foot, was enormous.

English kings found it hard to recruit knights and use them well. It was difficult to find men whose wealth enabled them to serve with horse, armour and attendants, while geography and opponents limited the effec-tiveness of those who did serve. Their charge sometimes succeeded in Edward I's forays against the Scots, as it did at Dunbar in 1296. At Falkirk two years later cavalry broke up the 'schiltroms' – close-packed masses – of Scots spearmen only after their ranks had been thinned by archery.

Edward II had not grasped the importance of combined arms tactics when he met the Scots on the Bannock Burn near Stirling in June 1314. He squandered his cavalry against four great schiltroms, masking the fire of his archers in the process. When the archers moved off to a flank and opened fire they were caught by the Scots cavalry and ridden down. The schiltroms then pushed on into the English infantry, left shaky by the retirement of the horse. As Scots reinforcements came into view, the English broke and fled.

Bannockburn helped to change English tactics, and early results were encouraging: when Sir Andrew Harclay's royalists beat the rebellious Duke of Lancaster at Boroughbridge in 1322 they fought on foot in the Scots manner. At Dupplin Moor in 1332 and Halidon Hill the following year, dismounted English men-at-arms and archers proved too much for even Scots spearmen, and the Earl of Northampton, supporting a contender for the Duchy of Brittany, saw off a larger French force at Morlaix in 1342.

The English learned other lessons in the north. A host crawled slowly across the landscape, trailing provision carts and baggage wagons. It took the field in the summer, when food for men and horses might be found on its march. As long as it moved it could bring fresh sources of supply within reach of foraging parties, but when it halted the most energetic 'purveyors', as its quartermasters were called, might find it impossible to match dwindling supply to ravenous demand.

The Scots, in contrast, were adept at staging raids which lived off plunder and supplies carried on pack-horses, and the English developed similar techniques which formed the basis for that important component of medieval strategy, the *chevauchée*. This large-scale raid sought to avoid battle but to inflict damage on the areas it passed through, weakening an enemy's economic base and moral authority. A *chevauchée* might be forced to fight, and the greatest English victories of the period – Crécy, Poitiers and Agincourt – took place when *chevauchées* were caught by superior French forces. Battles did not ensure that territory passed from vanquished to victor. To secure territory, a commander needed to take the key towns in it, and this usually demanded sieges which were costly in lives and time, and demanded specialist knowledge and equipment.

As a *chevauchée* moved through enemy territory there were great opportunities for profit. Michael Prestwich has identified 'patriotism, desire for chivalric renown, and hope of financial gain' as motives which led men to fight for Edward III, and points out that 'the hope of gaining wealth through plunder was a major incentive'. The chronicler Thomas Walsingham affirmed that 'there were few women who did not have something from Caen, Calais and other overseas towns; clothing, furs, bedcovers, cutlery. Tablecloths and linen, bowls in wood and silver were to be seen in every English house.' If humble men could feather their nests, their commanders did even better: ransoms paid to redeem captured noblemen enabled the brave or lucky to make a fortune at a stroke. Sir Walter Manny obtained £8000 for the prisoners he took in 1340, and the enormous ransom of £500 000 paid to free John II of France, captured at Poitiers in 1356, cemented English royal finances for a generation.

The Fighting Men

Royal preference for recruiting well-paid volunteers and the profit made from campaigning in France helped to change the character of English infantry. Most of Edward I's spearmen and archers were pressed men, recruited by commissioners of array who were not averse to accepting bribes to leave a man at home. By the time of Crécy in 1346 there were still pressed men aplenty: in 1347 one Robert White was released from prison, after his committal for 'homicides, felonies, robberies, rapes of women and trespasses', to serve at the siege of Calais. But alongside the likes of Robert White marched men of a very different stamp. Archers, first recruited in Nottinghamshire and Derbyshire, and then increasingly in Wales, Cheshire and Lancashire, had played an important part in the wars of Edward I.

By the time of Edward III growing numbers of archers were mounted, using horses for mobility on campaign and dismounting to fight on foot. Archers became men of recognized status, lower than knights but higher than ordinary foot soldiers. This was not enough to ensure that they would be captured rather than killed out of hand, for they ranked below the level at which the medieval laws of war offered theoretical protection. There was little point in keeping an archer prisoner because his family could not buy his release. So he might be killed, or so mutilated as to be militarily useless. The derisive gesture of waving two fingers at an opponent dates from this period, for the French would sometimes cut the forefingers off captured archers so they could not draw a bow. The defiant wave, made as an archer scampered for safety, showed that he was still in fighting trim and would be back with a bow in his hand and arrows in his belt. It was a gesture which typified the cockiness of someone who knew that across 100 yards (90 metres) of turf he was the equal of any knight in the land.

The longbow, source of this confidence, was a 6-foot (1.8-metre) stave, ideally of yew, although elm or ash would do, fashioned so that its belly, which faced the archer, was rounded and its back was flat. The bow tapered to the knocks, where the bowstring was attached. It was carried unstrung, and a knowing archer would keep his bowstring somewhere dry: in a pouch for long journeys, or under his hat or helmet if there was a sudden shower before battle. The 30-inch (75-cm) 'cloth-yard' arrow was made from a variety of woods, although ash was a favourite because its weight increased impetus. Barbed broadheads were effective against unarmoured men or horses, but for penetrating armour there was nothing to equal the unbarbed bodkin point. Arrows were usually fletched with goose feathers.

As many as four dozen arrows were carried in a quiver or tucked into the waist belt, and once an archer had taken up position he might stick arrows in the ground to aid speedy reloading. He could dispose of ten or twelve a minute, shooting to a maximum effective range of some 300 yards (270 metres). At this distance he might risk a 'roving shaft' at an individual target, although he would be lucky to hit it. It was never wise to take risks: when the English besieged Caen in 1346 some of the garrison bared their buttocks from the walls (a doubly offensive gesture at the time, because Englishmen were widely believed to have tails) and were killed by the shafts that followed. Long-range arrows were directed into the thick of the enemy's formation, archers shooting, as the chronicler Froissart wrote, 'so thick and fast that it seemed like snow'. It was not until the range was much closer that the archer would aim straight at his chosen target, the heavy war-arrow with its bodkin point smashing through most of the armour it hit.

The medieval archer drew to the side of his head, not the front of the face like a modern bowman. The power required to draw a bow varied from 80–160 lb (36–72 kg). And it was not a matter of brute force but of technique and strength combined, the result of long practice at the butts which developed arms and upper body. While a man could be easily taught to use a crossbow, by no means a contemptible weapon even though it was fragile and slow to reload, he had to be bred to the longbow.

The Causes of the Hundred Years War

Although in theory the Hundred Years War sprang from Edward III's claim to the throne of France, on the grounds that his mother was a daughter of the French royal house of Capet, it had wider causes. The English Crown held large possessions in south-west France, and each monarch had to pay homage to the French king for them, which resulted in regular legal wrangling. The great towns of Flanders were natural customers for English wool, and looked to England for aid against France. The Scots, conversely, expected French support against England. Edward loved pageantry and knightly accomplishments, and saw foreign war as an opportunity to strengthen a throne undermined by years of factional strife.

Fighting broke out in 1337, but it was not until July 1346 that Edward landed in Normandy to mount a *chevauchée* to join his Flemish allies in the north. The French blocked his path and although Edward managed to cross the Somme at Blanchetaque, between Abbeville and St Valéry, he was brought to battle at Crécy on 26 August. Genoese crossbowmen in French service were the first to taste the goose feather. As they faltered under the blizzard of arrows, wave after wave of knights spurred forward against the English. By nightfall the French had lost, by one estimate, 1500 knights and 10 000 foot soldiers. Edward marched on to take Calais, which became the chief English base in northern France.

Over the next few years the French experimented with attacks by men-at-arms, dismounted so that horses would not be maddened by arrows, combined with flanking thrusts by mounted men. In 1356 they caught a *chevauchée* under Edward III's son, the Black Prince, near Poitiers, but were badly beaten. Their king, John II, a prisoner in English hands, agreed to concede territory and pay a huge ransom, but his son had to be brought to heel by a *chevauchée* which encouraged him to con-clude the Peace of Brétigny in 1340, confirming Edward's possession of much of south-west France. John died, still a prisoner, before his ransom had been fully paid, leaving his kingdom in the hands of his weak and sickly son Charles V. In 1369 war bubbled up again. This time the French avoided battle and instead used tactics developed by Bertrand du Guesclin, snatching a town here and a castle there, all the time eroding English territory. *Chevauchées* were destructive but inconclusive, and although the Peace of Paris, signed in 1396, rationalized the *status quo* it left long-term issues unresolved.

The political balance had changed when fighting resumed in 1415. The Black Prince had died before ascending the throne and his son, Richard II, was deposed by Henry Bolingbroke, grandson of Edward III, who ruled as Henry IV. The first years of Henry's reign were not easy, with trouble from Scots, Welsh and English rebels, and when the twenty-five-year-old Henry V came to the throne in 1413 his hold on power was far from secure. However, he displayed what his biographer Desmond Seward calls 'extraordinary self-confidence in governing', based on his experience as Commander-in-Chief against the Welsh leader Owain Glyn Dŵr and sharpened by uncompromising piety. When he was Prince of Wales he supervised the burning of a Lollard, John Badby. As Badby began to scream, Henry had him taken from the barrel in which he was being burnt and offered him a pension if he would recant. Badby refused, and Henry sent him back to his barrel.

Henry's belief in the justice of his claim to the throne of France, his intention of uniting France and England under a single crown, and his long-term hope of freeing Jerusalem from the infidel, helped to move him inexorably along the road to war. The condition of France can only have encouraged him. There was civil war between the Armagnacs, who supported Charles VI's younger brother the Duke of Orleans, and the Burgundians, adherents of John, Duke of Burgundy. In addition, Charles swung between sanity and madness. Henry's emissaries negotiated for territory, for the hand of Charles's daughter Catherine, and for a substantial dowry, although it was unlikely that Henry was serious in his quest for a negotiated peace. He had been steadily preparing for war, maximizing royal revenue and borrowing money from Englishmen and foreigners alike. In July 1415 he formally declared war on France and began a campaign he had been preparing for over two years.

Campaign and Battle

Henry assembled 2500 men-at-arms and 8000 archers at Southampton. All were recruited by indenture, their captains contracted to produce men at set rates of pay. Retinues varied in size. The king's brother Humphrey, Duke of Gloucester, agreed to supply 200 lances and 600 mounted archers. The duke reported with two men-at-arms short: his brother punished him by giving him no pay for a year, so he had to find the money for his retinue himself. At the other end of the scale, Lewis Robbesard Esquire turned out with three foot archers. Some of Henry's followers had fought against him in the past. Amongst the substantial Welsh contingent was Davy Gam Daffyd ap Llywellyn, once a follower of Owain Glyn Dŵr.

The word 'lance' included not only the warrior himself, but also his servants and a number of horses which reflected his rank. Dukes provided fifty horses and drew 13s 4d a day, knights served with six horses and received 2s a day, while archers, about half of them mounted, drew 6d a day. Given that a well-to-do knight would expect to live on £208 a year, a minor gentleman or merchant from £15 to £19 and a ploughman £4, this was good pay, and there was every expectation of ransom or plunder as a bonus.

There were farriers to tend to the 10 000 horses, miners and a mass of siege equipment, four Dutch master-gunners and sixty-five gunners manning 'The King's Daughter', 'London', 'Messenger' and other firearms from Bristol and the Tower of London. There was also a small army of armourers, bowyers, fletchers, masons, shoemakers, carters, cooks and chaplains. The host embarked on 1500 vessels: Henry aboard the *Trinity Royal*, at 500 tons (508 tonnes) the largest ship in the armada.

The Siege of Harfleur

The fleet set sail on 11 August, and two days later it anchored in the Seine estuary, 3 miles (5 km) from Harfleur. On the following day the army landed, toiling ashore across mud flats under a blazing sun to besiege Harfleur, an excellent base from which to overrun Normandy or

AGINCOURT
The Agincourt Campaign
October 1415

──────▶ Route of English Army

──────▶ Route of French
Main Army

•••••••▶ Route of French
Advance Guard

—·—·—·— Frontier

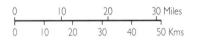

0		10		20		30 Miles
0	10	20	30	40		50 Kms

ENGLAND

Hythe•

Romney•

•Rye

Winchelsea•

•Hastings

English Channel

Dieppe•

Arque

11 Oc

Fécamp
9 Oct •

Harfleur•
8 Oct

Honfleur•

Caudebec•
8 Oct

R. Seine

Rouen•

•Lisieux

Evreux

N
W E
S

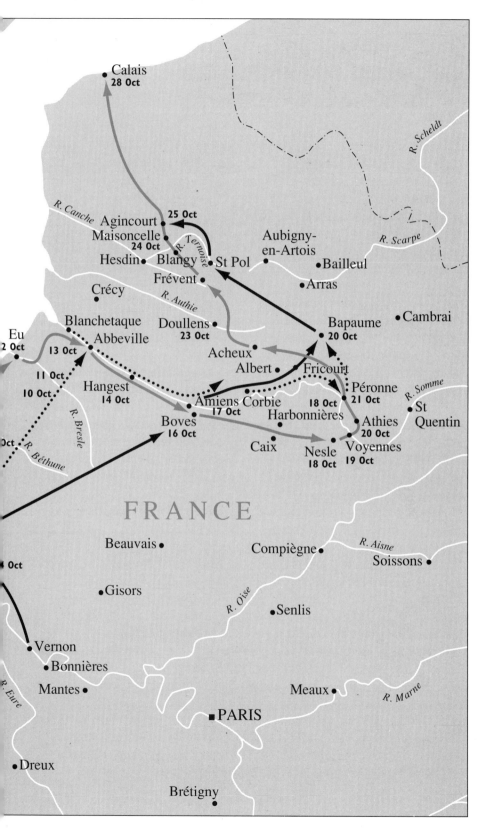

Calais
28 Oct

R. Scheldt

R. Canche
Agincourt
25 Oct
Maisoncelle
24 Oct
Hesdin
Blangy
St Pol
R. Ternoise
Frévent
Crécy
R. Authie

Aubigny-
en-Artois
Bailleul
Arras

R. Scarpe

Cambrai

Blanchetaque
Abbeville
Doullens
23 Oct
Bapaume
20 Oct

Eu
2 Oct
13 Oct
Acheux
Albert
Fricourt

11 Oct
Hangest
14 Oct
Amiens
Corbie
Péronne
21 Oct
R. Somme

10 Oct

R. Bresle
Harbonnières
18 Oct
Athies
20 Oct
St
Quentin

Boves
16 Oct
Caix
Nesle
18 Oct
Voyennes
19 Oct

Oct
R. Béthune

FRANCE

Beauvais

Compiègne
R. Aisne
Soissons

4 Oct

Gisors
R. Oise
Senlis

Vernon
Bonnières
Mantes
Meaux
R. Marne

R. Eure
PARIS

Dreux

Brétigny

threaten Paris. Its strong walls were surmounted by twenty-six towers, and barbicans of earth and timber reinforced its three gates. The defenders, 100 men-at-arms under John d'Estuteville, were well supported by the inhabitants, and had opened the sluices so as to allow the rivers Eure and Lezade to flood all but the eastern front of the town.

Henry set up his camp before the Leure Gate on the town's southwestern edge, while his brother Thomas, Duke of Clarence, established himself on Mont Cabert opposite the north-eastern walls. It took two days to finish unloading, and meanwhile Henry showed that he was bent on recovering lands that were rightfully his by announcing that looting churches and arson were forbidden. Women and priests were not to be molested, harlots were not allowed in camp, and all his men were to identify themselves by wearing the red cross of St George. Those who broke these rules were to be hanged.

The English had surrounded Harfleur with a stockade by 19 August, but before the ring was closed a local nobleman, Raoul de Gaucourt, slipped in with 300 men-at-arms. The siege went slowly. It was impossible to undermine the walls because the defenders dug counter-mines, trenches were easily flooded, and French crossbowmen and gunners kept up a destructive fire. Eventually Henry's twelve heavy guns were lugged into position and opened fire from behind wooden screens. Their 'gunstones' wrecked buildings, but the defenders repaired breaches in the walls with stakes and baskets of earth. Henry supervised the bombardment in person, and on 3 September felt confident enough to suggest that it would only take another week to reduce the place.

He was seriously wrong. Although the French made no real attempt to relieve the town, dysentery, brought on by local shellfish, foul water and contaminated food, broke out in the besiegers' cramped and filthy lines. The Duke of Clarence and the Earls of March and Nottingham were amongst the noblemen invalided home, and the Earls of Arundel and Suffolk, and Thomas Courtenay, Bishop of Norwich and one of the king's most trusted advisers, died. Perhaps 2000 Englishmen perished, and as many again were so ill that they had to be shipped home.

The fighting at the south-western gate proved decisive. On 15 September a French sortie burnt the siege tower facing the gate, but the next day Sir John Holland – son of the Earl of Huntingdon who had been killed in a rebellion against Henry IV in 1400 – led an assault which captured the gate's main bastion, already badly damaged by cannon fire. Garrison and townsmen alike knew that if the town was taken by storm, carnage would inevitably ensue. De Gaucourt offered to surrender if no help came by midday on Sunday 22 September and Henry agreed.

The inhabitants of Harfleur escaped with their lives but little else. The gentlemen amongst the garrison were freed on parole, with orders to present themselves in November at Calais. The richer townsmen were sent to England at once, and would remain there until ransoms were paid. The poorer citizens were expelled, although Henry gave them a little money to make the process marginally less unpleasant. They were replaced by Englishmen. Proclamations were made in the cities of England offering cash subsidies to artisans and merchants who would settle in Harfleur: about 10 000 took advantage of the offer.

Henry first planned to develop his campaign either by marching on Paris or by mounting a *chevauchée* south of Bordeaux. However, losses at Harfleur and the need to garrison the town (with 500 men-at-arms and 1000 archers under the Earl of Dorset) left him so badly depleted that neither option was now feasible. In the meantime, Henry sent a message challenging the dauphin to single combat for the throne of France. The plump and lethargic Louis predictably declined. Henry waited a week for the answer, and then embarked on a scheme which dismayed his council of war and was destined to bring his army to the verge of destruction. He would march straight to Calais.

It is impossible to explain this decision from a twentieth-century standpoint. The French were gathering in unknown strength. The River Somme and a dozen lesser watercourses flowed between Henry and his objective. He would have to move so fast that there would be little opportunity for plunder; even if he reached Calais he would have gained nothing that he did not already have at Harfleur; and many of his men had not recovered from dysentery contracted during the siege. But when Henry told his council that he did not intend to allow the French 'to rejoice in misdeeds, nor, unjustly against God, to possess my goods,' he meant exactly that. He would march on Calais in the hope that God would demonstrate the justice of his claim to the crown of France.

Henry set out on 8 October with about 900 men-at-arms and 5000 archers marching parallel with the coast in the customary three 'battles'. Sir Gilbert Umfraville and Sir John Cornwall, Henry's uncle by marriage and a soldier of twenty-five years' experience, led the advance guard; the king, the Duke of Gloucester and Sir John Holland rode with the main battle; while the king's uncle, the Duke of York, commanded the rearguard with the Earl of Oxford. There were no cannon or wagons, and provisions for eight days were carried on pack-horses. Henry made for the Somme, intending to march eastwards along it to the ford at Blanchetaque, and had already sent orders for the Calais garrison to dispatch a force to secure the northern bank.

The French Host

Amongst the French, military discord mirrored political friction. Charles VI hoped to lead his army in person but was in his usual delicate state of health, and the ancient Duke of Berry, leader of the Armagnacs and a veteran of Poitiers, was unwilling to risk his death or capture. 'It is better to lose a battle,' he remarked knowingly, 'than a king and a battle.' The dauphin, as unfit for high command as he was for single combat with Henry V, could not be denied the opportunity to tinker with part of the French host. That seasoned campaigner John the Fearless, Duke of Burgundy, was an obvious candidate for command but was unacceptable to the Armagnacs and, denied high command, chose not to serve.

It was decided that three royal dukes – Charles of Orleans, John of Bourbon and John of Alençon – would command, in co-operation with the senior military officials of the royal household, the constable, John d'Albret, and the marshal, John le Maingre, known as Boucicault. Amongst the dukes only Bourbon had any military success to his credit: he had beaten an Anglo-Gascon force at Soubise in 1413. The two professionals, in contrast, were accomplished soldiers, and Boucicault's fighting reputation made him, as Matthew Bennett observes, 'a legend in his own lifetime'.

Cautious deployment matched divided command. The more experienced French leaders wished to contain the English rather than fight them, and mid-September saw the dauphin with the main force at Vernon, on the northern border of Normandy, keeping track of events at Harfleur but doing little to prevent their progress. What was to become the French advanced guard was in two parts, with Boucicault at Caudebec, on the Seine north-west of Harfleur, and d'Albret at Honfleur, across the Seine estuary from the beleaguered town. As the English moved off, Boucicault followed them, and then joined d'Albret who marched up through Rouen to hold the crossings of the Somme.

Henry's March to Calais

The English advanced in the harsh style of the *chevauchée*. French chroniclers maintain that Fécamp abbey was burned and women who had taken refuge there were raped. The castellan of Arques, on the River Béthune, tried to deny the English supplies but gave way when Henry threatened to burn the town, and the same happened at Eu on the River Bresle. When Henry approached Blanchetaque on 13 October, his scouts took a prisoner who admitted that d'Albret was at Abbeville with 6000 men and Guichard Dauphin, Lord of Jaligny, had blocked the ford with stakes and held it in strength. The Calais garrison had sent a force to Blanchetaque but it had been intercepted and driven off.

The English had no choice but to march eastwards in the hope of discovering an unguarded crossing or, as gloomier souls prophesied, of reaching the river's headwaters where they could cross easily. Finding the bridge at Pont Remy held against him, Henry passed the night of the 13th at Bailleul. The following day was spent in a further fruitless search for crossings, and the army halted in and around Hangest. On the 15th Henry approached Amiens – he could not take it without artillery – and spent the night at Pont de Metz.

The next day's march took him on to Boves, whose garrison supplied bread and wine knowing that the town would be burned otherwise. When the soldiers asked to be allowed to fill their bottles with the wine Henry declared that they would 'make bottles of their bellies' and get out of hand. He was right to be on his guard against drunkenness, for soldiers across the centuries have found alcohol a relief from the shock of battle and the rigours of campaigning. German troops attacking only a few miles to the north in the March offensive of 1918 drank their way through gallons of captured alcohol: one officer complained that his men were held up not by a lack of German fighting spirit but by an abundance of Scottish drinking spirit.

There seems to have been no desertion from Henry's host, probably because fugitives would have received short shrift from the peasantry. Some inhabitants unwisely showed their sympathies for the French by hanging red clothes or blankets from their windows to symbolize the Oriflamme, the sacred red banner which signified war to the death and was kept in the royal abbey of St Denis and taken into the field at the beginning of the campaign. Henry had their houses burned, and his army left a wake of scorched timbers and empty storehouses behind it. The king showed determination to keep a firm grip on discipline by hanging a man caught stealing from a church. However, there was little cause for satisfaction, and a chaplain whose *Gesta Henrici Quinti* is one of our best sources for the campaign, summed up the army's opinion: 'We then expected nothing else, but that after having finished our week's provisions and consumed our food, the enemy by craftily hastening on ahead and laying waste the country before us, would weaken us by famine … and overthrow us who were so very few, and wearied with much fatigue, and weak with lack of food.'

On 17 October Henry swung northwards and threatened Corbie on the Somme, giving its garrison a bloody nose when it sallied out to meet him. He may have been trying to force a crossing, to raise his men's morale by letting them fight, or to persuade the French that he intended to follow the course of the river as it curls up towards Péronne. In fact he

French prisoners, wearing armour and with the visors of their helmets still lowered, are led off after surrender. Henry's decision to kill his prisoners during Agincourt was based on the fact that these men had only to pick up discarded weapons to become dangerous once again.

marched straight across the open end of the loop, and 18 October found him at Nesle, only a couple of miles from the Somme. His scouts reported that there were passable fords ahead at Voyennes and Bethencourt, and on the 19th the army splashed across two narrow causeways, both damaged by the French and patched up with bundles of sticks, straw and timber torn from nearby houses. The army marched on to Athies and, as the chaplain recorded, 'spent a joyful night in the nearby hamlets'.

The Progress of the French

Although we cannot be sure of French movements, Matthew Bennett's judicious reconstruction offers the best explanation. The French advance guard, perhaps equal in numbers to the English and under the command of d'Albret and Boucicault, mirrored Henry's movements on the north bank of the Somme. It lost time by marching on the outer edge of the river's loop while the English cut straight across, and was at Péronne when Henry crossed, too far away to oppose him in strength. Once Henry was safely across the weakness of this force, the caution of its commanders and the imminent arrival of the French main body encouraged avoidance of battle until the host was united.

The French main body, which may have numbered 50 000 men including all its camp followers, did not reach Amiens until 17 October.

Bennett points out that the riverside route taken by the advance guard was unsuitable for a force this size, especially in a rainy October, and that the French probably marched to Bapaume, on the uplands north of the river. Here they were well placed to block Henry's advance on Calais, for the French had little doubt where he was bound. On 20 October three French heralds visited him to declare that 'many of our lords are assembled to defend their rights, and they inform you by us that before you come to Calais they will meet with you and fight with you and be revenged of your conduct.' When asked what road he would take, Henry replied:

Straight to Calais, and if our enemies try to disturb us in our journey, it will not be without the utmost peril. We do not intend to seek them out, but neither shall we go in fear of them either more slowly or more quickly than we wish to do. We advise them again not to interrupt our journey, nor to seek what would in consequence be a great shedding of Christian blood.

Preparing for Battle
The English marched northwards on the 21st, leaving Péronne on their left, and crossing the tracks of what the chaplain termed 'an unimaginable host'. That night was passed at Mametz and Fricourt, on ground that was to be bitterly contested in July 1916 during the battle of the Somme, and on the 22nd Henry marched on through Albert to Acheux and Forceville. The French were moving on a parallel route, and on the 24th the English crossed the little Ternoise river at Blangy to find 'hateful swarms of Frenchmen' drawn up for battle just to the north. The French edged away to Azincourt and Ruisseauville, and took up a position blocking the Calais road where it ran between two woods. Henry halted for the night at Maisoncelle, barely 1 mile (1.6 km) to the south-east.

It was, by all accounts, a ghastly night. The English had covered about 300 miles (480 km) in sixteen days, the last of them in the teeth of rain blowing in from the west. There had been little to eat, although many could not stomach food and the army's path was smeared with the bloody flux of dysentery. The king and some nobles found shelter in the hovels of Maisoncelle, with men-at-arms and archers huddled up under hedges or in orchards. As the rain sluiced down even Henry wavered. He released his prisoners and sent a message to the French offering to return Harfleur and pay compensation in return for safe passage to Calais. Yet when Sir Walter Hungerford suggested that another 10 000 archers would help, the king rounded on him and declared that all they had were God's people. A French esquire wrote that the English played music to revive their spirits, but this is at best uncertain. We know that Henry ordered the army to keep silent: noisy gentlemen would lose horse and armour, while ranks below yeoman would forfeit their right ear. What sound there was in the English camp was chiefly the low murmur of men making their peace with God – if the queues for priests were too long, soldiers confessed to their comrades – and the furtive scraping of stone on steel as edges were put on swords and daggers.

The French camp, in contrast, was lit by fires and filled with the noise of grooms and servants preparing for the morrow. Some of the more extreme chroniclers' suggestions – that the French had a painted cart ready for the captive Henry and that their lords diced for the Englishmen they expected to capture (an archer was the worthless blank face of a dice) – owe more to subsequent propaganda than four-in-the-morning reality. An English army, even in this desperate state, was still deadly and few French knights would have wished to go into battle sleepless and hungover.

Agincourt has myth wrapped around myth like the layers of an onion. Shakespeare's 'little touch of Harry in the night' had little to do with warnings about the loss of ears, and Laurence Olivier's film compounded the felony by depicting a French mounted charge as the battle's climax. In his masterly work *The Face of Battle*, John Keegan caught the battle's bloody glint, telling us that it is:

... a school outing to the Old Vic, Shakespeare is fun, *son et lumière*, blank verse, Laurence Olivier in battle armour; it is an episode to quicken the interest of any schoolboy ever bored by a history lesson, a set-piece demonstration of English moral superiority and a cherished ingredient of a fading national myth. It is also a story of slaughter-yard behaviour and of outright atrocity.

This warning is especially apposite in a book of this sort. It is easy to cast all the English archers as hardy yeoman led by brave and generous gentlemen, forerunners of the men who stood in square at Waterloo and those footsore warriors whose rifle-fire at Mons was the twentieth-century's answer to the arrow-storm. The truth is a good deal less romantic.

As Henry's host prepared for battle at dawn on 25 October 1415 it was full of inconsistencies which still perplex us and which, in their way, are the real thread linking the men of Agincourt with later generations. There was a courage born of desperation, stiffened by tension between social classes and within small groups, as men strove to secure the respect of others – comrades, leaders or subordinates – whose judgement they valued. There was a powerful sense of national identity and a general belief in the rightness of the king's cause, although few would have been able to evaluate the merits of his claim to the throne of France.

Few men felt deep hatred for their enemy – although archers might experience a frisson of pleasure when killing social superiors – but most displayed callous disregard for an opponent who was simply different. They came from an environment where Lollards were roasted to death before large crowds, and traitors were partly strangled before being castrated and disembowelled. The profit motive was never far away, and if an enemy did not give up his purse a knife in the belly would stop his bleatings. Heroic leadership helped to keep men to their task, and there was a whiff of the main chance even in this: John Holland was fighting to redeem the family honour – and the family earldom. And in the last analysis there was simply nowhere else to go: time had run out.

Henry heard Mass and took Communion before arming for battle. Like his men-at-arms he wore full armour, its articulated plates covering his whole body, although instead of donning the visored basinet popular on both sides he opted for the heavier great helm with a crown around it. Over his armour went a silken surcoat decorated with his arms, leopards quartered with lilies. Since men-at-arms dressed alike the surcoat was a useful aid to identification, although we may doubt just how many combatants were able to tell friend from foe by heraldry alone. War-cries were more helpful: the English yelled 'St George!' and the French '*Mont-joie! St Denis!*' Henry carried the heavy knightly broadsword with its cruciform hilt, and on his right hip was a dagger, known as the misericord for it slipped between the plates of armour to let the life out of a wounded enemy. Some men-at-arms would have trusted to their swords, but others carried maces or the murderous pole-axe, a combined spear and axe about 5 feet (1.5 metres) long.

An archer was more lightly clad. A leather 'jack' or a brigandine interleaved with steel plates protected his body, and on his head he wore an open-faced helmet, a wicker cap reinforced with iron, or an aventail – a chain-mail hood. A leather bracer protected his left arm from the whip of the bowstring, and leather tabs shielded his shooting fingers. In addition to bow and arrows he bore a short sword and a dagger, the latter often what Victorians bowdlerized into 'ballock' dagger, although the two balls which formed its guard leave us in no doubt as to what archers called it. Some carried mallets, as useful for driving in the pointed stakes which they carried to protect themselves from cavalry as they were for braining an opponent.

For years it was believed that the men-at-arms formed up in three battles with wedges of archers between them and at the ends of the line. This interpretation stems from Froissart's use of the word *herce* to describe the English formation at Crécy and was elaborated by Alfred Burne and others into what Michael Prestwich sums up as 'a standard battle formation ... with each battalion of dismounted men-at-arms

This battle painting *(above)* is idealized, but it does show the castle of Agincourt, and British and French are identifiable by their banners. Archers, in the foreground, repel the French cavalry. The mêlée in the centre was in fact fought by dismounted men-at-arms. Part of an original muster-roll *(right)* lists detachments of archers and men-at-arms which made up the English army.

flanked by wings of archers.' More recently Jim Bradbury has argued that there is no justification for assuming that Froissart intended *herce* to mean harrow (the basis of the Burne deduction) rather than an alternative interpretation, and his painstaking examination of the sources suggests that 'the archers were placed on the wings, forward and fanning out-wards, so that when the enemy attacked against the main body in the centre, the archers were able to close in on them from the flanks.'

We are unlikely to be absolutely certain of the truth, but two points

are worth noting. The first is that the archers were mobile. Their stakes did not form a continuous palisade but rather a hedge within which the defenders, fighting in loose order several men deep, could easily move around. They could run forward to shoot, scuttle back into the stakes, and re-emerge to take on tired men-at-arms. Secondly, the question of numbers must give us pause for thought. Henry had only 900 men-at-arms and less than 5000 archers. Breaking up these men-at-arms into three distinct bodies separated by archers would have made for a very brittle formation, with the men-at-arms unable to offer mutual support to their fellows in another division.

I prefer to see the English forming up with men-at-arms in the centre and archers on the flanks before Henry rode out to address his men, reminding them of the justice of his claim, warning that the French had sworn to mutilate captured archers and affirming that he would fight to the end and not seek ransom. The king dismounted – he was wearing no spurs, which showed that he intended to fight on foot – and a long pause followed. Henry hoped that the French would attack him, but they seemed to have no intention of doing so, and eventually he ordered his banners to advance, and the line moved off towards the French, drawn up in the gap between the woods of Agincourt, on the English left, and Tramecourt, on their right. Despite the heartening sound of trumpet and tabor the English made slow progress across slippery ground, and there were several halts to ensure that all kept up.

As the English advanced the gap between the woods narrowed, and at the outermost flanks some archers found themselves amongst the trees: this was probably the origin of a claim that archers were sent into Tramecourt Wood to lie in ambush. At a long bowshot from the enemy the English halted. The archers hammered in their stakes and all eyes turned to Sir Thomas Erpingham, the fifty-eight-year-old veteran in overall command of the archers. His was the responsibility of deciding the moment of opening fire, and he was to give the signal by throwing his baton into the air.

The French Plan of Battle

Although d'Albret and Boucicault were cautious in their approach to battle, it is clear from a document in the British Library that, earlier in the campaign, they had devised a plan for launching a combined arms attack designed to neutralize the archers. They intended to station four bodies of men-at-arms side by side in the centre, with all the available archers and crossbowmen ahead of either wing. Mounted detachments would hook round into the English flanks or rear in an effort to catch the archers unawares. It was an intelligent scheme, although it had two signal failings. The ground on which the French elected to fight was so narrow that dismounted battles could not deploy side by side and flank attacks were rendered impossible by the woods. And in the French army of 1415 making a plan was one thing: persuading a rabble of gentility to carry it out was quite another.

The French drew up in a formation which bore a passing resemblance to the plan. Most of their 25 000 or so fighting men were men in three battles, one behind the other. Enguerrand de Monstrelet, who fought that day, recalled that there were 8000 men-at-arms, 4000 archers and 1500 crossbowmen in the first line under the command of the constable, accompanied by the Dukes of Orleans and Bourbon. The Count of Vendôme was meant to command 1600 mounted men on the left flank and Clignet de Brébant 800 on the right, but both had rather less. The second battle, under the Dukes of Bar and Alençon, was composed of up to 6000 men-at-arms and armed servants. It is possible that the archers and crossbowmen who should have been in the first battle had been literally elbowed into the second, for one disgusted French chronicler complained that not one of them fired a shot. The third division contained perhaps 8–10 000 mounted men-at-arms.

Battle and Massacre

When Sir Thomas Erpingham's baton spun into the air the first arrows thrummed off into the leading French battle. There were few formal commands. The captains nearest Sir Thomas would have seen the baton, and orders to draw and loose would have rippled down the line. A French chronicler tells us that his countrymen heard the command '*nestroque*': 'now stretch', perhaps, as goose feathers were drawn back to the head. It is likely that the French archers and crossbowmen shot a shaft or two and then drew back, as well they might in view of the terrifying disparity of fire effect.

The cavalry on each wing was weaker than it should have been, probably, as one French source laments, because men-at-arms had wandered off during the long wait. But those who remained, perhaps 150 on each flank, charged immediately the archers began to shoot. It was a hopeless venture. The ground was already churned into mud where French horses had been exercised the night before, and the woods meant that these were not flank attacks, merely frontal assaults at the ends of the English line. William de Saveuse, on the French right, bravely led a handful of men right in amongst the stakes. One caught his horse in the chest, and the knight was pitched over its head, to be knifed as he lay helpless on the ground. The fact that some of the stakes were not securely embedded enabled many of his followers to escape. The left wing did no better, and archers shot hard at the fleeing horsemen, panicking their steeds and sending them crashing into the leading battle, causing widening ripples of disorder in this close-packed formation.

Despite the chaos caused by the retreating cavalry, the first battle set off for the English line. The ground was heavy going for men in full armour carrying shortened lances or pole-axes. It would have been evident to the archers that this was the moment for their maximum effort, and they would have stepped up their rate of fire so that there may have been 80 000 arrows a minute hitting the advancing French. There would have been little in the way of formal orders. We should steer clear of novelists' inventions which have captains bellowing 'Shoot wholly together', but we can expect the experienced to have set a heartening example and to have offered the advice which old soldiers give, unasked, to young.

Boucicault and his comrades made for the English centre, defined by its forest of silk: Henry stood beneath his own standard and the banners of the Trinity, St George and St Edward. The enemy men-at-arms, their own social equals, were their real target. Secondly, they would instinctively have shifted away from those arrows plunging in from the flanks. Paradoxically, those in the centre would have been safest, because as the range closed the archers would have found it hard to engage knights who were at an acute angle to them, and would probably have concentrated on more obvious targets on the flanks of the great crocodile squelching onwards.

It speaks volumes for the courage of the French knightly class that any of the first battle pressed on to engage the English men-at-arms. But so slow was their pace and so painful their progress that they had little impact. The mêlée which ensued is best described as bloody murder. This was no place for elegant swordplay: men hacked at one another for the minutes that their strength lasted, trying to beat in an opponent's helmet, hew his legs from under him or shove a lance through his visor. Fatigue or a missed footing often meant death, for once a man was down he was

This impression of Agincourt, from a French manuscript, mixes truth and fiction. The archers would have been much more lightly-equipped, and it is unlikely that the French archers and crossbowmen engaged in this sort of contest. However, at the very start of the campaign Henry had indeed ordered his men to wear red crosses on white surcoats to help them distinguish friend from foe and to emphasise that his was a holy war.

easily finished off. Henry spent part of the battle standing astride the wounded Earl of Oxford and in doing so almost certainly saved his life. The Duke of York died, probably not killed, as is often suggested, by being suffocated under a pile of the dead, but by having his head smashed in. His nephew came close to sharing his fate. A group of French esquires had sworn to kill Henry and one of them, or possibly the Duke of Alençon, lopped a gold fleuret off his crown. The archers, with little to shoot at, joined the mêlée, moving more nimbly than exhausted men-at-arms and plying sword, dagger and mallet to deadly effect.

Historians are right to question whether there could have been piles of bodies as high as a man, but there were certainly heaps of dead and wounded (Boucicault was dragged from beneath one when the fighting ended) and the mêlée was more suggestive of slaughterhouse than tournament. Alençon lost his fight with the king, sank to his knees (probably with sheer exhaustion) and removed his helmet. This was an unmistakable gesture of surrender because he had made himself indefensible, but he was brained with an axe by a berserk Englishman. If it was not easy for a French knight to surrender to an English one, coming to terms with an archer presented particular problems. Few of them spoke French: many of the Welsh spoke no English. Trying to assure Owain ap Llywellyn as he bounded up in sweaty brigandine that you were a gentleman of fair estate was often a fruitless task.

This ghastly scrum eddied back into the second battle, but instead of reinforcing the survivors of the first battle this simply increased the pressure of jammed bodies: 'more were dead through press than our men might have killed,' claimed one Englishman. The struggle had now been going on for perhaps two hours, and the men-at-arms in the third battle were beginning to make off, joined by survivors of the first two battles. The English were extracting prisoners from the carnage and sending them to the rear, no doubt calculating their worth in ransom as they did so. Then two events occurred which were to turn the battle, already bloody enough, into sheer massacre.

A local lord, Isambart d'Agincourt, raided the lightly guarded English camp with a handful of men-at-arms and 600 peasants and carried off some items of value. At about the same time the Counts of Marle and Fauquembergues managed to persuade several hundred French men-at-arms to follow them in a mounted charge which foundered in a fresh storm of arrows. We cannot be sure how news of the attack on his camp was presented to Henry, who probably thought the raid indicated that a more substantial rear attack was under way, possibly in co-ordination with the charge by Marle and Fauquembergues. Victory was not fully secured, and the French prisoners, disarmed but still armoured, easily outnumbered their captors. The field was littered with discarded weapons, and if the prisoners re-armed themselves they could change the battle's outcome.

Henry ordered that the prisoners should be killed: only the most prominent, like the Dukes of Orleans and Bourbon, were to be spared. The order was doubly horrifying. It went against the laws of war to massacre, in cold blood, unarmed noblemen who had surrendered, and it represented a huge financial loss for the English who counted on ransoms to boost the profits of the campaign. Henry warned that he would hang anyone who refused to obey but, recognizing that even he might not exact compliance from his affronted nobility, gave the butcher's task to an esquire with 200 archers. One eyewitness said that the prisoners were 'cut in pieces, heads and faces' as daggers were thrust through their visors, and a French survivor saw some burnt to death when the hut they were confined in was fired.

The battle and the slaughter which followed may have cost the French as many as 10 000 dead, including the Dukes of Alençon, Bar and Brabant, 9 counts, 92 barons and at least 600 knights and many more gentlemen. The Dukes of Bourbon and Orleans, the Counts of Eu, Richemont and Vendôme and 1500 knights and gentlemen were taken prisoner, figures which suggest that the massacre was less than comprehensive, partly because the business of murder must have taken some time and the crisis would have been passed before all the prisoners were dead. These losses were politically as well as militarily damaging: a French historian has calculated that one-third of the monarch's supporters perished. The English lost the Duke of York, the young Earl of Suffolk, whose father had died at Harfleur, and a handful of men of note, including Davy Gam Esquire and his sons-in-law Walter Lloyd and Roger Vaughan. We do not know how many archers died: no knightly chronicler would be much concerned with the fate of these artisans of battle.

The English spent the rest of the day finding overlooked prisoners, collecting arms, armour and valuables, and cutting the throats of the wounded who were beyond help. The latter would have been numerous, for depressed fractures of the skull and penetrating wounds of the abdomen, injuries typical of this sort of fighting, would baffle medical science for another 500 years. The English dead were collected in a barn at Maisoncelle. The building was stuffed with faggots, fired and burnt

Overleaf: **In the foreground of this medieval siege, archers have stuck arrows in the ground to shoot more rapidly, and a crossbowman is using a small winch, a moulinet, to draw back his bowstring. On the left archers and handgunners exchange missiles with the defenders, protected by wooden screens.**

well on into the night while Henry's noblest captives served him at dinner on bended knee.

Withdrawal and Departure

The rain began again next morning, and the English army trudged to Calais, heavily laden with spoils and still short of food. It was not welcomed enthusiastically when it arrived, and soldiers found that they had to pay extortionate prices – or barter prisoners and captured armour – for food and lodging. Henry stayed in the nearby castle at Guisnes, and left for England on 16 November during a storm. It was typical of his confident piety that although two of his vessels sank Henry was unperturbed by an experience which French prisoners found worse than Agincourt.

Agincourt did not end the war, and bitter fighting followed until the Treaty of Troyes was signed in 1420. On the death of Charles VI the crowns of England and France were to be united in the person of Henry or his successor, although the French were to be allowed to retain their language and customs. Henry married the Princess Catherine shortly afterwards, and expressed the hope that 'perpetual peace' was now assured. He was wrong, for not all Frenchmen were prepared to accept the verdict of Troyes, and Henry was campaigning south of Paris when he fell ill, probably with dysentery, in August 1422. He was taken back to the castle at Vincennes where he died, at the age of thirty-five and just six weeks before Charles VI: he never became King of France.

A View of the Field

It is hard to comprehend the Hundred Years War without an idea of how the men who fought in it were armed and equipped; a visit to a museum with a good collection of arms and armour is a useful prelude to walking the field. British readers cannot do better than visit the Royal Armouries Museum in its new home in Leeds. There are arms and armour on display, and the Agincourt cinema shows a documentary-style re-enactment of the battle.

The longbow did not survive well. Once it was old or broken it was of no value save as firewood, and it was not until the raising of Henry VIII's warship *Mary Rose* that we were really able to see what bows looked like. We cannot be certain that the longbows are the same size as their medieval forbears but they are 6 feet (1.8 metres) long, carved from the heartwood and sapwood of yew. Their arrows, made from poplar, are 30 inches (75 cm) long without their heads, which have rusted away, and would have had 6 inches (15 cm) of spiral fletching. Some bows and arrows remain in the *Mary Rose* museum in Portsmouth and others are in the Royal Armouries. Amongst the skeletons found when the vessel was raised were two identified as archers. One had a thickened left forearm, and both had spinal deformities caused by constantly drawing a heavy bow while the body was twisted. The archer's craft followed him to the grave.

Henry's Route to Agincourt

The route of the Agincourt campaign covers too much ground, some of it now too built-up or scarred by autoroutes to be comfortably walkable, although it is easy to drive in a long weekend by landing at Le Havre and leaving through Calais, as Henry did after the battle was over. Le Havre, originally called Havre de Grâce, was begun on the orders of Francis 1 in 1514 to replace the silted-up town of Harfleur, which in Henry V's time was reached by a channel running through salt marshes to the Seine estuary. Although it is now effectively a suburb of the rather unprepossessing Le Havre, the centre of Harfleur is attractive, with several well-preserved old buildings. Substantial remains of the barbican which protected the Rouen Gate survive amongst blocks of flats south of the Place d'armes, which is now the town's main car-park and covers the site of the medieval harbour. St Martin's church is our first real contact with Henry V, for he walked barefoot to the badly damaged building on 23 September 1415 to give thanks for his capture of the town. A plaque on an outside wall informs us that the English were driven out in 1435: a statue to one of the heroes of the episode presides over the roundabout where the N15 enters the town. The little Musée du Prieuré, a short walk from the church, contains stone balls thrown by siege-engines, and a model of the siege, on the first floor, reminds us that the English used mangonels and trebuchets as well as primitive cannon.

Henry's march to the Seine took him to Fécamp, whose splendid Norman Gothic church was almost complete following the rebuilding rendered necessary by a fire caused by a lightning strike. The abbey was to become the home of the liqueur Bénédictine, and a museum in the more recent abbey buildings contains both works of art and information on the liqueur. What was Arques in Henry's day is now Arques-la-Bataille, named in honour of the Protestant victory over the Catholic League on 21 September 1589. This battle, with that fought at Ivry the following year, established the Protestant leader Henry of Navarre as Henry IV, first monarch of the Bourbon dynasty. The substantial remains of the castle, whose governor agreed to supply Henry V's troops with provisions, still dominates the town. It had been rebuilt by Henry I, William the Conqueror's youngest son, in 1123, although its massive earthworks were begun by the Conqueror's uncle, William d'Arques. During the 1589 battle the castle provided a firm base for Henry of Navarre's artillery, and a stone relief of Henry himself can be seen above the third of the fortified gates. The castle at Eu, Henry V's next port of call, is, alas, a more recent replacement: the fortress of his day was demolished in 1475.

The River Somme and its Surroundings

The River Somme has been much changed by canalization, a fact which affects Blanchetaque and Henry's crossing points further upstream. The Somme was fordable at Blanchetaque, where there was a layer of bedrock just below its surface. It was hard to identify even when Edward III crossed there on his way to Crécy in 1346 and he relied on a local guide to show him where it was. At the time the Somme was tidal and its valley marshy and liable to flooding: canalization of the river in the nineteenth century has changed all this. The ford was approached from the northern end of the village of Saigneville and although the ford itself has long since disappeared it is possible to reach its site: the northernmost of the three minor roads shown disappearing towards the Somme Canal on the Michelin map is the one to take, and ends at a pleasant picnic site on the bank.

Some fragments connect us with Henry V along his route south of the Somme. At Boves, where the king was concerned about the drinking habits of his men, the ruins of the twelfth-century castle give an impressive view towards Amiens. However, they are far less impressive than those at Arques and are approached, with some difficulty, via the D167. At Voyennes and Bethencourt, where the English crossed the Somme, the river now flows just east of the Somme Canal, and much of what was marshy ground in 1415 is now garrisoned by fishermen's huts and allotments and has little to tell us. Péronne, the base of the French advanced guard on the day Henry crossed, has been altered by the construction of subsequent fortifications, bombardment in 1870, and damage during the First World War. The town lay in the path of invading armies, and in 1536 an attack by the Holy Roman Emperor Charles V was beaten off when the townswoman Marie Foure animated the defence. Its castle, built in the thirteenth century, was reinforced by a seventeenth-century brick bastion, and more recently modified to accommodate the Historial de la Grande Guerre.

The next stage of Henry's march takes us across the battlefields of the Somme, and it is not until we reach the River Ternoise at Blangy that the Middle Ages again rise to meet us. We cannot be certain whether or not

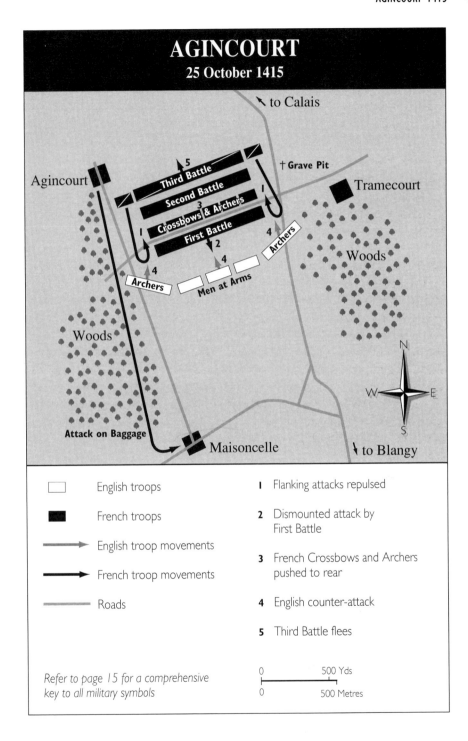

AGINCOURT
25 October 1415

↖ to Calais

† Grave Pit

Agincourt

Tramecourt

Third Battle

Second Battle

Crossbows & Archers

First Battle

Archers

Men at Arms

Archers

Woods

Woods

Attack on Baggage

N
W — E
S

Maisoncelle

↘ to Blangy

☐ English troops

■ French troops

→ English troop movements

→ French troop movements

— Roads

1 Flanking attacks repulsed

2 Dismounted attack by First Battle

3 French Crossbows and Archers pushed to rear

4 English counter-attack

5 Third Battle flees

Refer to page 15 for a comprehensive key to all military symbols

0 ———— 500 Yds

0 ———— 500 Metres

the English had to fight for the bridge at Blangy, but we do know that it was from the village that they first glimpsed the French host and recognized the full dimensions of their task.

The field of Agincourt is largely unspoiled. It lies where the D104 winds up from the Ternoise to slip through the woods between Tramecourt to the east of the road and Azincourt (as the village is now spelt) to its west. There is a small but pleasant museum in Azincourt, maintained with cordial enthusiasm by Claude and Michelle Delcusse. The castle, which could be glimpsed through the trees from the battlefield in 1415, has long since disappeared, but there are some tiles from its floor in the museum. Maisoncelle, where the English camped before and after the battle, lies south-west of Azincourt.

The Battlefield of Agincourt
It is not often that we can trace the events of a medieval battle on the ground with as much confidence as at Agincourt. It is best to approach the field, as Henry's men would have done, from the south-east. The English formed up along the little road which connects Maisoncelle with what was then the Calais road and is now the D104. There is a monument at the corner, as well as an orientation table which is less than helpful because part of the battlefield is hidden from view. It is better to stand on the high ground where the road enters Maisoncelle, and to look northwest: Azincourt church can be seen to the left, and a prominent café stands at the junction of the Calais and Azincourt–Tramecourt roads. The French drew up on the high ground on the far side of this latter road.

As one moves up this tongue of open country it is important to remember that the woods on both flanks were thicker and came closer to the road than they do now: there was little space between the Calais road and the edge of the Tramecourt wood on your right. The French position blocked the gap but gave no room to deploy, and there was no realistic possibility of flanking cavalry moving through the woods. It is a short walk, and a shorter drive, to the Azincourt–Tramecourt road. By turning left at the junction, walking about 100 yards (90 metres) towards Azincourt and then turning to face his original direction of advance, the visitor is in the epicentre of the field. The initial French cavalry charges would have come in along the wood edges to left and right – always remembering that these were closer then than they are now – and the French men-at-arms would have made their way on foot straight across the field in front to cross the road and hit the English line a little behind it. The mêlée then moved slightly towards the initial English position and then back along the French line of advance. It is easy, looking at the ground, to imagine the dreadful shambles that resulted from tens of thousands of French men-at-arms being compressed into such a tiny space, first riddled with arrows, and then compelled to fight not only men-at-arms but also far nimbler archers.

A crucifix surrounded by trees on the Calais road, to the viewer's right front, marks one of the grave-pits where the French dead were buried: the sites of the others have now been lost, but we may surmise that they are in the field between the present pit and Azincourt. Some of the dead were taken further afield. The Duke of York's body was boiled to strip the flesh from his bones, which were sent back to England. His entrails are believed to be buried in the church at Fressin, across the D928 west of Azincourt. On the edge of the D154, in the woods just south of Fressin, stand substantial remains of a castle built in the fifteenth century by Jean de Créquy, chamberlain to King Philip the Fair. Several of the French noblemen killed in the battle were buried in the abbey church of St-Georges at Auchy-les-Hesdin, on the Ternoise north-east of Hesdin itself, and some are commemorated on a plaque to the right of the door. One of them, Gallois de Fougières, Provost-Marshal to the Marshal of France and as such an ancestor of a modern gendarmerie officer, was moved to the national police cemetery earlier this century.

Calais

Henry left France from Calais, an English city from 1347 until it was retaken by Francis, Duke of Guise, in 1558: when she heard what had happened, Mary I of England lamented that the name of Calais would be found engraved on her heart. Part of the scruffy Fort Risban, which defends the western entrance to the harbour, is of English construction, and would have seen Henry's ship leave port on 16 November 1415. Rodin's statue *The Burghers of Calais*, which stands between the *hôtel de ville* and the Parc St-Pierre, celebrates Eustache de St-Pierre who led five fellow citizens to surrender the town to Edward III in 1347. They were barefoot, stripped to their shirts and had the hangman's rope about their necks. Edward, enraged by the town's long resistance, would have strung them up but his wife, Philippa of Hainault, begged him to spare them.

It is typical of the vagaries of Calais' fortune that an old German blockhouse, within sight of Rodin's statue, contains a small museum which deals with the town's occupation during the Second World War and the activities of the local Resistance. As we conclude our *chevauchée* it is chastening to remember that the Channel, now so easily crossed, has shielded Britain from things which, in their way, were as ghastly as the aftermath of Agincourt.

CHAPTER 2

Waterloo
1815

Background

The Waterloo campaign is a bloody addendum to the Napoleonic Wars. Napoleon's star began to fall with his invasion of Russia in 1812. In 1813 he was beaten at Leipzig, and although he showed flashes of his old fire the following year he could not deflect the armies that converged on Paris. The Allies were not vindictive and Napoleon was sent to rule the Mediterranean island of Elba, whence he kept a close watch on France, now governed by Louis XVIII. The trappings of the old regime were resented by men who had fought under the eagles, *émigrés* were employed while veterans were retired, and peasants feared that land confiscated after the Revolution would be redistributed. There had been widespread war-weariness during the last years of the Empire, but Napoleon's absence made French hearts grow fonder. In March 1815 he re-established himself as emperor and, against all the odds, in 100 hectic days fought a campaign which he came within an inch of winning.

The Evolution of Weaponry

It is ironic that most men who fought at Waterloo carried weapons which, in range, accuracy and rate of fire, were inferior to the longbow. There were many reasons for the bow's decline. England ran short of archers, partly because of the decline in practice, signalled by warnings that 'now the art is become totally neglected'. Complaints like this were made during as well as after the great age of archery, so we cannot assume that the rise of the 'dishonest games' signalled its end. The Wars of the Roses (1455–85) were at least as important in creating a shortage of archers. Contemporary opinions of the carnage of Towton

The Duke of Wellington was at the height of his powers in 1815. He did not spend long in bed – 'when it is time to turn over, it is time to turn out' – but his camp bed and other possessions are preserved in the regimental museum of The Duke of Wellington's Regiment in Halifax. Most of the Duke's infantry carried the flintlock musket, pictured here, known as 'Brown Bess'. Colonel George Hanger wrote: 'I do maintain and will prove ... that no man was ever killed at 200 yards, by a common musket, by the man who aimed at him.'

(1461), the bloodiest battle fought on English soil, must be treated with caution. Even so, there may have been 16 000 casualties, most of them archers or spearmen. Other factors were at work. Firearms were so noisy that they terrified men and horses. They represented fashionable modernity which made them attractive to monarchs forging nation states. It was easy to teach men to use them, and also to make them, as the hard-won skills of bowyer and fletcher were blotted out by the smoke of the Industrial Revolution.

When Michael Roberts produced his thesis on the 'military revolution' of the seventeenth century he laid emphasis on the rise in firepower produced through reforms instigated by Maurice of Nassau (1567–1625). These led to the standardization of drill and weaponry and the creation of a disciplined army, with the Swedish army of the Thirty Years War (1618–48) as its paradigm. The thesis linked changes in military organization with the shift of power within the state. New tactics demanded larger, more professional armies, which in turn aided the rise of absolutist states by taking power from subjects and concentrating it in the hands of monarchs.

Historians who develop innovative theories stride into shafts of criticism. Michael Roberts was no exception, and the military revolution thesis must now be substantially qualified. However, we must recognize that even if changes bridging the gap between Agincourt and Waterloo do not pivot on a single revolution, more a succession of key developments, with as much migration of ideas as genuine innovation, their effects on the way men fought were nothing less than revolutionary.

Armies grew bigger and were maintained in peace as well as war. In 1786, the year Frederick the Great died, Prussia had 190 000 men under arms. Although Frederick tried to reduce demands on national manpower by recruiting foreigners, a system of registration permitted swift conversion of young men into recruits. Where Prussia led others followed. First with the standing armies of the eighteenth century and then, in more dramatic guise, with the French *levée en masse* of 1793, we see the strengthening of that link between citizenship and military service which looms large in the remainder of this book. Britain was different because its navy rather than its army was the bulwark of defence. Young Britons were not conscripted into a regular army which was much smaller than those of Continental powers, but the press gang showed that Britain could be as remorseless as her neighbours when it came to securing manpower for vital functions.

Military service was not always willingly embraced, and tens of thousands of conscripts deserted. As Christopher Duffy affirms, 'desertion was the bane of the Prussian army', and during the Seven Years War (1756–63) one of its regiments lost the equivalent of its full complement through desertion. It took a unique mixture of patriotic fervour and robust discipline to bring desertion in the French army down to only 4 per cent of its strength by 1793: the number had doubled two years later.

There were sharp constraints on war-making. Successful French intervention in the American War of Independence imposed a financial burden on the country which was not least amongst the title-deeds of revolution. Even when armies took the field they were hard to feed without cumbersome baggage-trains and provision magazines located in fortresses whose attack and defence became a quintessential feature of war. Cannon brought the high stone walls of medieval castles crashing down. In their place came artillery fortification: low, geometrical works in whose development the French military engineer Sébastien le Prestre de Vauban (1633–1707) played such an important part.

In the age of the French Revolution and Napoleon, war broke free of many old bonds. Napoleon's techniques were as much a reflection of their eighteenth-century background as sparks flying from an outstanding military intellect. Napoleonic warfare rolled across Europe with unprecedented scale and rapidity. In August 1805 Napoleon led an army of over 200 000 men from Boulogne on the French coast to what is now the Czech Republic. In October, operating on a front 150 miles (240 km) wide, his army engulfed an Austrian force at Ulm, and on 5 December it trounced a superior Austro-Russian army at Austerlitz. Napoleon's ability to manoeuvre hinged on his development of *corps d'armée*, all-arms formations which marched on separate routes, making best use of roads and locally obtained provisions, but which fought united.

Napoleon sought to fight decisive battles and to win them by offensive action. At his best he moved fast so as to surprise, confuse and unbalance before striking. At his worst he relied on the power of his artillery and the morale of his soldiers to break an enemy by brute force. Napoleon recognized that much of war depended on the imponderables of the human spirit and took infinite pains, from an imperial word of approval here to an award of the Légion d'honneur there, to foster morale. Yet he had a hard edge of cynicism which saw men as a resource like any other. 'You cannot stop me,' he warned the Austrian statesman Metternich, 'I can spend thirty thousand men a month.'

Battles were linear. Formations of close-packed infantry engaged one another with the flintlock musket, whose slow rate of fire (about three rounds a minute), close range (an enemy line would receive little damage at 200 yards [180 metres]) and inherent unreliability (one shot in five

The eagles of the French 45th and 105th Regiments were captured when Ponsonby's Union Brigade charged. Sergeant Charles Ewart of the Royal Scots Greys took the former, after a desperate hand-to-hand struggle: '... the bearer thrust at my groin. I parried it off and cut him down through the head. A lancer came at me – I threw the lance off by my right side and cut him from the chin upwards, which cut went through his teeth. Next I was attacked by a foot soldier who, after firing at me, charged me with his bayonet ... I parried it, and cut him down through the head; so that finished my contest for the Eagle.'

normally misfired, and in rainy conditions it was hard to fire at all) reduced the soldier to a tiny cog in a ponderous machine. There were important exceptions. Light infantry, who fought outside the line and sometimes carried more accurate rifled weapons, were useful, especially when straight lines and massed volleys were inappropriate. The Revolutionary armies used swarms of *tirailleurs* (light infantry) who buzzed ahead of the main body, galling the enemy's line before it was ever seriously attacked.

For years writers contrasted French preference for the column with British predilection for the line. The truth is more mundane. Columns were useful for road or cross-country movement and essential for keeping men together in an assault. In about 1700 the plug bayonet, jammed inconveniently into the musket's muzzle, was replaced by the socket bayonet, which fitted round the barrel. Infantrymen were trained to push home their attack with the bayonet, but in practice large-scale clashes between bayonet-wielding infantry were rare. The steady advance of a column, well prepared by *tirailleurs* and artillery, and accompanied by whoops, patriotic songs and martial music, often proved too much for its intended recipients, who departed before the cold steel arrived.

If fire was required, then deployment in line enabled the maximum number of muskets to bear. During the Peninsular War in Spain and Portugal (1808–14), the Duke of Wellington made skilful use of the ground so that startled French columns, configured for movement, often collided with the British, deployed to fire. A variety of compromises was possible, based on versions of 'mixed order', where columns, closed up for movement or attack, were preceded by lines. If attacked by cavalry, infantry battalions formed hollow squares, with officers and colours inside and rows of uninviting bayonets outside.

As the close-range firepower of infantry grew it became harder for cavalry to break infantry by the physical impact of man and horse, even aided by the psychological blow of the charging mass. There were times when cavalry used surprise, smoke, broken ground or the fire of other arms to ride down infantry, but these were few and far between. Yet cavalry was essential for screening (preventing enemy patrols from penetrating its own outposts), reconnaissance (getting inside the enemy's cavalry screen to glean information) and pursuit (pressing a beaten foe to turn retreat into rout).

Artillery had grown markedly in power. Guns threw heavier projectiles and were increasingly grouped in massed batteries to produce concentrated fire. Field artillery enjoyed mobility that would have stunned Henry V's gunners, and horse artillery, with all its gunners mounted, could keep pace with cavalry. Field guns provided direct fire, engaging targets visible to their detachments, their usual missile an iron ball whose weight defined the piece's calibre. The 12-pdr, Napoleon's favourite, fired its ball to a maximum range of 1200 yards (1100 metres) but was really effective at perhaps half this distance.

At close range the most deadly projectile was case shot, a container filled with musket balls which split open at the muzzle to turn the piece into a gigantic shotgun. Explosive shells were fired from howitzers. Common shell was an iron sphere packed with gunpowder, and spherical case shot, sometimes called after its inventor, Henry Shrapnel of the Royal Artillery, had musket balls mixed with a bursting charge and was designed to explode in the air above its target. Inconsistencies in fuses, gunpowder and metallurgy limited the effectiveness of this sort of ammunition. Nor did they do much for the primitive rockets used by the British. When Wellington ordered a rocket battery to be equipped with more conventional weapons he was told that this would break its commander's heart. 'Damn his heart: let my orders be obeyed' was the duke's blunt response.

Campaign and Battle

On 1 March 1815 Napoleon landed at Fréjus and set off for Grenoble. Troops defected to him on the way and Grenoble opened its gates, giving him a rapturous welcome. Marshal Ney had left Paris promising to bring him back 'in an iron cage', but when they met at Auxerre on 14 March the marshal's men defected and Ney followed suit. Five days later Louis XVIII left Paris for Belgium. There could be no question of Napoleon's reassumption of power being accepted by the Allies, whose representatives were at Vienna discussing the post-war settlement. They immediately buried their differences and set about planning the invasion of France.

This was to take the form of a concentric attack involving up to one million men. The Austrians would concentrate in northern Italy and the lower Rhine; the Prussians would send an army to eastern Belgium; an Anglo-Dutch force would concentrate in western Belgium; and a Russian army would advance through Poland. Organizing operations on this scale was not the work of a moment: the Austrians would not be ready until July, and the Russians might take even longer.

Napoleon quickly set about raising troops. After only eight weeks he had nearly 300 000 men under arms, and another 150 000 would be added once the conscripts of the class of 1815 were available. He could

THE WATERLOO CAMPAIGN

Position of French and Allied Armies, and French Lines of Advance at Dawn on 15 June

	Allied troops (British/Dutch-Belgian/Prussian)
�	French troops
➤	French troop movements
	Army areas
– ×××× –	Army boundary
–·–·–	Frontier, 1815
▬▬	Roads with metalled surface, 1815
– – –	Roman roads

```
0        2        4        6 Miles
|--------|--------|--------|
0    2    4    6    8    10 Kms
```

Refer to page 15 for a comprehensive key to all military symbols

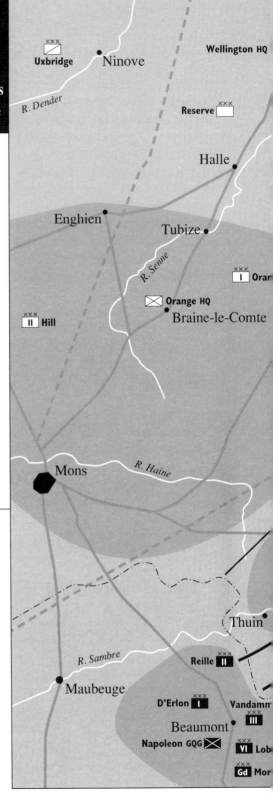

Uxbridge Ninove Wellington HQ

R. Dender Reserve

Halle

Enghien Tubize

R. Senne I Oran

Orange HQ

II Hill Braine-le-Comte

Mons R. Haine

Thuin

R. Sambre Reille II

Maubeuge

D'Erlon I Vandamm III

Beaumont

Napoleon GQG VI Lob

Gd Mor

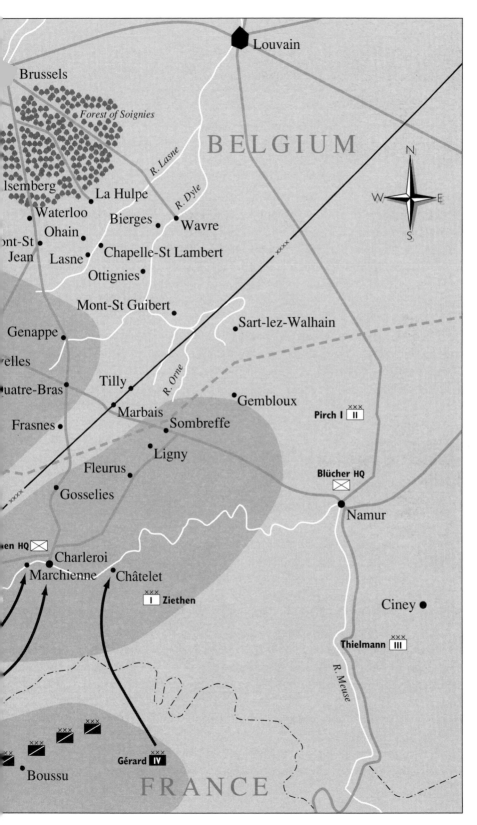

play for time, raising more troops and opposing each Allied thrust, or might repeat the pattern of 1814 and stab at invading armies in turn. He realized that his only hope lay in defeating his opponents in detail, and determined to move north as soon as possible.

Wellington's 'Infamous Army'
There were some 79 000 infantry, 14 000 cavalry and 196 guns in Wellington's Anglo-Dutch field army in Belgium. He had not used permanent corps in Spain but introduced them for the Waterloo campaign, although they had little effect on the battle when the duke commanded his army as he pleased. The Prince of Orange, twenty-three-year-old heir to the throne of the Netherlands, commanded 1st Corps (two British and two Dutch-Belgian divisions) from Braine-le-Comte. Lieutenant-General Lord Hill's 2nd Corps (two British divisions, a Dutch-Belgian division and a Dutch-Belgian brigade) was around Ath, and the Reserve Corps (two British divisions, a corps of Brunswickers under their duke, and a Nassau detachment) was under Wellington's hand around Brussels. The eleven brigades of British, Hanoverian and Dutch-Belgian cavalry were commanded by Lord Uxbridge.

The components of Wellington's force were of markedly different quality. Only six of his twenty-five British battalions had served in Spain. Others had been involved in Sir Thomas Graham's unsuccessful attack on Bergen-op-Zoom in 1814, and many had not recovered from the experience. The King's German Legion (KGL), recruited in George III's German possessions, was first-rate, encouraging Wellington to reduce its eight battalions from ten to eight companies apiece and use the spare officers and NCOs to stiffen less reliable Hanoverian units. Dutch-Belgian units were of similarly varied calibre, and Wellington observed that many of their officers 'had risen under Bonaparte and are admirers of his system and government'.

Wellington, at forty-six the same age as his opponent, had earned his first laurels in India in 1803. He defeated the French at Vimeiro in Portugal in 1808, and from 1809 he campaigned in Spain and Portugal, crossing the Pyrenees into France in 1814. Wellington had never met Napoleon in battle but had dealt with a succession of his marshals. He was more than just a canny defensive practitioner. On 22 July 1812 he caught Marshal Marmont off-balance at Salamanca with a meticulously timed attack which, it was said with little exaggeration, routed 40 000 men in 40 minutes.

Wellington's talents were not confined to the battlefield. He was a careful administrator and knew that there was an intimate connection between the maintenance of discipline and the regular arrival of rations. The duke was not helped by the fact that the commissariat, which provided the army with supplies, was administered by the Treasury and employed civilian officials who were not under military command. Soldiers were entitled to a daily ration of $1\frac{1}{2}$ lb (0.7 kg) bread or 1 lb (0.5 kg) biscuit, 1 lb (0.5 kg) beef or mutton, $\frac{1}{2}$ pint (0.5 litres) wine or $\frac{1}{3}$ pint (0.3 litres) rum, although they often found themselves on half-rations or no rations at all.

The drink ration was insufficient for many. Wellington believed that: 'Some of our men enlist from having got bastard children – some for minor offences – many more for drink; but you can hardly conceive such a set brought together, and it really is wonderful that we should have made them the fine fellows they are.' Even so, the lure of drink regularly proved too much for them. There were outbursts of collective disorder, and at the individual level many good soldiers were ruined by drink. Discipline was harsh, with flogging for minor offences. Rifleman Harris of the 95th thought it a necessary evil. 'I detest the sight of the lash,' he wrote, 'but I am convinced that the British army cannot go on without it.'

British soldiers had volunteered for service. A few joined to escape justice, and Philip Haythornthwaite is right to suggest that these formed the basis for the 50–100 incorrigibles in every regiment. Others were attracted by the enlistment bounty; found the delights of the open-air life extolled by recruiting sergeants more appealing than the drudgery of the counting house or weaving shed; were led from the militia by officers eager for the regular commission granted them for presenting forty volunteers; or simply got drunk and woke up a soldier.

Many were labourers, a description as often based on hope as on experience, and depressions in the textile trade generated waves of unemployed weavers. Recruits from the teeming industrial cities were smaller than countrymen, and most were shorter and narrower in the chest than modern recruits: in 1812 the 10th Hussars demonstrated that it was a regiment of rare distinction by announcing that it would accept no men below 5 ft 7 in (1.7 metres). Scotland and Ireland were fecund recruiting grounds, and the Irish were everywhere, manning Irish units like the inimitable 88th Connaught Rangers and leavening many an ostensibly English regiment.

The origins of officers were scarcely less diverse. Michael Glover and others have demolished the myth that the army withered 'under the cold shade of the aristocracy'. Abuses like the commissioning of children had been ended, although a young man could still buy a commission by furnishing the money for his rank. An ensigncy, the junior commissioned

The artist Denis Dighton made drawings at Waterloo after the battle. Here he shows Light Companies of the Coldstream Guards during the early stages of the fight for Hougoumont. The massive south gate can be seen centre left, and to its right some guardsmen are firing over the garden wall.

rank in the infantry, cost £400, and appointments in the Guards or cavalry were more expensive. Promotion could be purchased if an officer had sufficient service to be eligible for the next rank and could find the extra money. Many promotions went by regimental seniority: several distinguished officers, such as Harry Smith and George de Lacy Evans, rose without buying a single step. Officers of the Royal Artillery and Royal Engineers purchased neither first commissions nor subsequent promotion and, unlike their brothers of horse and foot, had to receive training at the Royal Military Academy at Woolwich before being commissioned.

This 'infamous army' had extraordinary qualities. Its soldiers were inured to hardship and had their own rough pride. In a crowded field-hospital Sergeant Michael Connolly of the 95th reprimanded a man for groaning in the presence of French wounded. 'Hold your tongue, ye blathering devil,' he barked, 'and don't be after disgracing your country in the teeth of these 'ere furriners by dying hard ... For God's sake die like a man before these 'ere Frenchers.' Ensign Leeke of the 52nd heard only one man cry out in pain at Waterloo, 'and when an officer said: "Oh man, don't make a noise," he instantly recollected himself and was quiet.' Officers tried to show gentlemanly 'bottom' at all times, and most saw death as preferable to loss of status, however recently acquired.

Wellington was chatting to the diarist Thomas Creevey in the park at Brussels when he saw a private of the line wandering about gaping at the statues. 'There,' said the duke, jabbing with a long finger. 'It all depends on that article whether we do the business or not. Give me enough of it and I am sure.' This confidence was reciprocated. Lieutenant John Kincaid of the 95th recalled that: 'We would rather see his long nose than a reinforcement of 10 000 men any day.' Private Horesfield of the 7th Fusiliers put it in blunter vernacular: 'Whore's ar Arthur? Aw wish he wor here.'

Blücher's Men

Wellington's Prussian ally, Field-Marshal Gebhard Leberecht von Blücher, had spent most of his seventy-two years fighting. His men called him 'Old Forwards', and neither considerable eccentricities nor devotion to a pungent mixture of gin, rhubarb and garlic shook their regard. Blücher lacked Wellington's grasp of detail, but his chief of staff, August Wilhelm von Gneisenau, plied pen to balance his master's sword. Blücher's 121 000 men and 300 guns formed four corps: Ziethen's I Corps around Fleurus and Charleroi; Pirch's II at Namur; Thielmann's III at Ciney; and Bülow's IV near Liège.

Blücher's lines of communication ran through Liège into Germany, while Wellington's went from Brussels to Alost and the Channel. There was a risk that, under pressure, each commander would fall back on his own lines, and when the two met on 3 May 1815 they agreed that the Anglo-Dutch would concentrate on Nivelles and the Prussians on Sombreffe if the French attacked. Liaison officers were exchanged, Colonel Hardinge joining Blücher's headquarters and Baron Müffling reporting to Wellington's.

Napoleon's Campaign

Napoleon was not at his best. David Chandler tells us that 'his mind was as alert as ever but physically he was out of condition'. Marshal Berthier, his former chief of staff, had declined to serve, and in his place Napoleon had appointed Marshal Soult, an experienced commander but not a natural staff officer. The Armée du Nord, 124 000 men and 366 guns, formed two wings and a reserve. Emmanuel de Grouchy, newly promoted marshal and a stranger to high command, led the right wing (Vandamme's III and Gérard's IV Corps with five smaller cavalry corps) south of Charleroi. Marshal Michel Ney's left wing (Drouet d'Erlon's I Corps and Reille's II) was around Maubeuge. The red-headed Ney deserved his sobriquet 'the bravest of the brave', but he had never been the same since 1812, when he was the last Frenchman out of Russia, a musket in his hand. Close to his headquarters at Beaumont Napoleon held his reserve, Marshal Mortier's Imperial Guard and Lobau's VI Corps. The army was riddled with faction, old Bonapartists mistrusting converted royalists, and not without reason, for the defection of a divisional commander was an early feature of the campaign. The French historian Henri Hossaye affirmed that: 'Napoleon had never before handled an instrument of war that was so formidable and so fragile.'

Early on 15 June the French headed for the frontier. Although bad staff work caused traffic jams, they crossed the Sambre at Charleroi despite resistance from Ziethen's Prussian I Corps. Napoleon told Ney to advance up the Brussels road while Grouchy took the Fleurus road towards Sombreffe. As for the Allies, Gneisenau ordered a concentration on Sombreffe while Wellington, who did not receive details of the attack until mid-afternoon, wrongly scented danger from the direction of Mons and decided to concentrate on Nivelles. By nightfall Napoleon had won the first round, for while Blücher was obligingly moving into his grasp, Wellington was swinging away from his ally.

Wellington attended the Duchess of Richmond's ball in Brussels that night. Absence would have heartened Napoleon's Belgian supporters, and it was useful to have senior officers to hand at the gathering. He

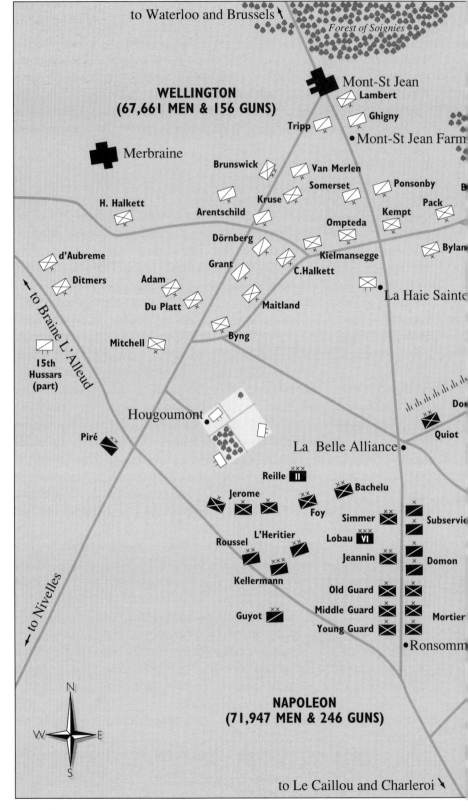

to Waterloo and Brussels

Forest of Soignies

Mont-St Jean
Lambert
Ghigny
Tripp
Mont-St Jean Farm

**WELLINGTON
(67,661 MEN & 156 GUNS)**

Merbraine

Brunswick
Van Merlen
Somerset
Ponsonby

H. Halkett
Kruse
Pack
Arentschild
Kempt
Ompteda
Dörnberg
Bylan
d'Aubreme
Kielmansegge
Grant
C.Halkett
Ditmers
Adam
Du Platt
Maitland
La Haie Sainte

to Braine L' Alleud

Mitchell
Byng

15th
Hussars
(part)

Hougoumont

Do
Piré
Quiot

La Belle Alliance

Reille **II**
Bachelu
Jerome
Foy
Simmer
Subservie
Lobau **VI**
Roussel
L'Heritier
Jeannin
Domon
Kellermann
Old Guard
Guyot
Middle Guard
Mortier
Young Guard
•Ronsomm

to Nivelles

N
W E
S

**NAPOLEON
(71,947 MEN & 246 GUNS)**

to Le Caillou and Charleroi

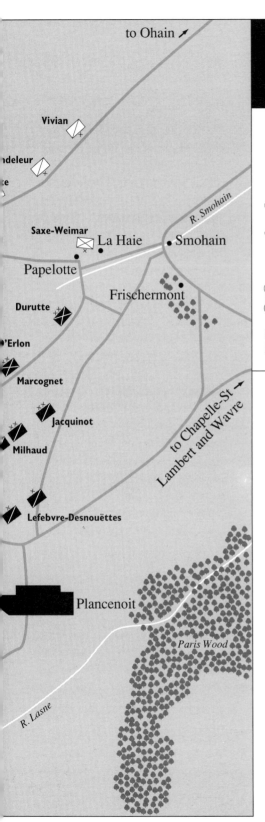

to Ohain ↗

Vivian

ndeleur

e

R. Smohain

Saxe-Weimar

La Haie   • Smohain

Papelotte

Frischermont

Durutte

'Erlon

Marcognet

Jacquinot

to Chapelle-St ↗
Lambert and Wavre

Milhaud

Lefebvre-Desnouëttes

Plancenoit

Paris Wood

R. Lasne

	Allied troops (British/ Dutch-Belgian/Prussian)
	French troops
ılı ılı ılı ılı	Napoleon's Great Battery
——	Roads with metalled surface, 1815

```
0    200   400   600   800 Yds
├──┼──┼──┼──┼──┼──┼──┼──┤
0    200   400   600   800 Metres
```

Refer to page 15 for a comprehensive key to all military symbols

heard of the Prussian move to Sombreffe before leaving for the ball, and was later told that Ney had pushed Prince Bernhardt of Saxe-Weimar's brigade of Perponcher's Dutch-Belgian division out of Frasnes on the Brussels road, but that the French had been held south of Quatre-Bras, the next major junction to the north. Wellington asked the Duke of Richmond if he had a good map, retired into the dressing room, and told his host: 'Napoleon has humbugged me, by God! He has gained twenty-four hours' march on me.' Richmond asked him what he intended to do. Wellington replied that he would concentrate at Quatre-Bras, 'but we shall not stop him there, and if so I must fight him' – his thumbnail described a line across Mont-St Jean, a little to the north – '*here.*'

Wellington rode out of Brussels at seven on the morning of 16 June. The leading division of his reserve, under Sir Thomas Picton, had already left for Quatre-Bras. The junction was only held thanks to the 'intelligent disobedience' of the Prince of Orange's chief of staff, Constant de Rebecq, who encouraged Prince Bernhardt to stand his ground and supported him with Major-General Count Bylandt's brigade of Perponcher's division.

De Rebecq's bluff worked because of misunderstandings between Napoleon and Ney. Napoleon expected the Prussians to retire out of reach and proposed to deal with Wellington first. Ney thought that because his wing was entrusted with the day's main effort he should not attack until the reserve arrived. Reille, his leading corps commander, had fought in Spain and was nervous of long crest-lines which might have nasty surprises behind them. It was not until 1 p.m. that Ney was urged to attack without delay, but by this time Napoleon had changed his plan. Blücher had not withdrawn and so while Grouchy launched a frontal assault on him, Ney was to take Quatre-Bras and move along the Nivelles–Namur road against his flank.

A Day of Battles
There were two battles on 16 June. At Ligny, on Napoleon's right, the Prussians were attacked by Vandamme and Gerard, with the Guard putting in the final assault. By nightfall the Prussians were in full retreat, having lost over 16 000 men and 21 guns and inflicted 11 500 French casualties. Blücher, leading his cavalry forward at the very end of the day, was unhorsed and ridden over before being rescued and bundled back with the fugitives.

On Napoleon's left, Ney spent the afternoon hammering the Allies at Quatre-Bras. Wellington commanded in person, his conduct of battle dictated by a bare trickle of reinforcements. Reille's French corps was checked with difficulty in the cornfields south of the junction. Sir Thomas Picton arrived in time to take the weight off Perponcher, but there was heavy fighting in which the Duke of Brunswick was killed and, by 4 p.m., with d'Erlon's corps about to engage, Wellington's plight seemed hopeless. At this juncture a staff officer from Napoleon ordered d'Erlon eastwards to take on the Prussians. He had almost reached Ligny, where the appearance of his unidentified troops stalled the French attack, when Ney, furious at his own lack of progress, ordered him back. He arrived too late to help, and in his absence the balance tilted in Wellington's favour.

Quatre-Bras was no easy battle. Very late in the afternoon French cuirassiers commanded by Kellermann, coming on very fast, caught Colin Halkett's newly arrived brigade of Alten's division in line, a formation decreed by the Prince of Orange, and cut it about badly. Ney had insufficient infantry on hand to secure the results of the charge, and the arrival of Cooke's Guards division gave Wellington the reinforcements he needed to re-establish control over the battlefield.

Blücher and Wellington had met at Bussy mill near Brye that morning, and the duke agreed to support the Prussians 'provided I am not attacked'. Gneisenau was no anglophile, and as he briefed senior officers that night he was inclined to fall back on the Prussian lines at Liège. The best route, the Nivelles–Namur road, was already lost, and it was agreed that the army would regroup at Wavre and then make for Liège. When Blücher reappeared he would not hear of it: common sense and military honour demanded that he should support Wellington.

The Eve of Waterloo

On 17 June Wellington slipped away from Quatre-Bras, his retirement covered by a spectacular rainstorm. He was too fast for Napoleon who, by nightfall, was in the farmhouse of Le Caillou, beside the Brussels road, with Wellington's army on the ridge just to his north. Napoleon received a message from Grouchy which suggested that the Prussians were falling back on Wavre, but it was not until 10 a.m. the next day that he sent Grouchy an order, and then only an imprecise one. Napoleon intended Grouchy to keep the Prussians away from Wellington, but he did not say so in as many words. When Soult suggested that the army should fight united, Napoleon turned on him: 'Because you have been beaten by Wellington you consider him a good general but I tell you that Wellington is a bad general and the English are breakfast.'

Wellington had first seen the ridge with the village of Mont-St Jean in its centre on his way to Paris in 1814. It was not an ideal position, but its slopes offered good fields of fire to their front and shelter behind. There were three robust farms on the forward slope: Hougoumont to the west, La Haie Sainte in the centre, and the Papelotte/La Haie/Smohain complex to the east. The valleys of the Dyle and Lasne rivers and Paris Wood gave some protection to the eastern flank. The western flank was open, which encouraged Wellington to post 15 500 men at Halle and Tubize, 8 miles (13 km) away.

The remainder of the duke's army, 67 661 men and 156 guns, took post along the ridge, its line running from Braine L'Alleud to Papelotte/La Haie/Smohain. Cavalry watched both flanks, but most of Wellington's horsemen were drawn up behind his centre. Almost all the cavalry and much of the infantry were behind the crest-line, and shoulder-high corn helped to screen the position. Bylandt's brigade, just east of the main road, was less lucky because a gash in the ridge meant that there was nothing Wellington could do to protect it.

The farms were held by picked troops. Battalions contained a grenadier company of tall and stalwart soldiers and a light company of lithe and nimble men, in addition to their eight 'battalion companies'. The Guards light companies garrisoned the farm of Hougoumont, with a Nassau battalion and two companies of Hanoverian riflemen supporting them. The remainder of the Guards division was not far behind, south of the crest but partly screened by the trees around Hougoumont and able to reach the farm down a sunken lane. Major Baring's 2nd Light Battalion KGL held La Haie Sainte, and the 95th a sandpit on the other side of the road. Both units carried the Baker rifle, a more accurate weapon than the Long Land Pattern musket, popularly known as Brown Bess, carried by line regiments. Saxe-Weimar's brigade of Perponcher's division garrisoned the buildings around Papelotte on the left.

The weather was worse than the night before Agincourt. Private William Wheeler of the 51st was pleased to discover that there was a good deal of drink about, so he and his comrades were 'wet and comfortable'. Comfort was strictly relative:

It would be impossible for any one to form an opinion of what we endured that night. Being close to the enemy we could not use our blankets, the ground was too wet to lie down, we sat on our knapsacks until daylight without fires, there was no shelter against the weather: the water ran in streams from the cuffs of our jackets, in short we were as wet as if we had been plunged over head in a river. We had one consolation, we knew the enemy were in the same plight.

Some officers and men huddled under the 'pitching blankets' that made improvised tents. Ensign Short of the Coldstream Guards admitted: 'I with another officer had a blanket, and with a little more gin we kept up very well.'

The Battle for Hougoumont
Soldiers set about cleaning their muskets as soon as it was light, and started by firing the charge already in the weapon. Private Matthew Clay of the 3rd Guards aimed his 'at an object, which the ball embedded in the bank where I had purposely placed it as a target.' He commented that 'the flint musket then in use was a sad bore on that occasion, from the effects of the wet, the springs of the lock became wood-bound and would not act correctly, and when in action the clumsy flints also became useless.'

The weather did little for Napoleon, who decided to delay the opening of the battle to allow the ground to dry out so that guns could move more easily. Late that morning his infantry drew up astride the Brussels road, with d'Erlon to the east, Reille to the west and most of the cavalry behind them. Lobau's corps, with the Guard to its rear, waited parallel with the road, between an inn called La Belle Alliance and the hamlet of Ronsomme. A battery of eighty-four 12-pdrs stood on a low rise just east of the Brussels road and hinted at the emperor's intention, made clear when he issued his orders at 11 a.m., to launch Ney straight against Wellington's centre. He had 72 000 men and 246 guns, and proposed to hit the Anglo-Dutch army as hard as possible in the hope of breaking it.

Reille's French corps started the battle at about 11.50 a.m. with an attack on the Hougoumont farm, intended to draw troops from Welling-ton's centre. His leading division was commanded by Prince Jerome, Napoleon's youngest brother, who sent four regiments into the wood south of the farm. Its Nassau and Hanoverian defenders fought well and fell back only slowly. When the attackers burst through a hedge at the northern end of the wood it was to find themselves facing the farm's south gate and long garden wall, pierced with loopholes by the defending guardsmen. The French did their best to break into the enclosure, grab-bing muskets protruding from loopholes and even exchanging bayonet thrusts across the top of the wall, but could make no progress and fell back into the wood.

The battle for Hougoumont was still isolated, allowing Wellington to devote his attention to it. He sent Lieutenant-Colonel Lord Saltoun with the light companies of Maitland's brigade to relieve the Nassauers, in dif-ficulties in the orchard; posted Bull's howitzer battery behind the farm with orders to shell the wood; and brought du Plat's KGL brigade of Clinton's division down to join Byng's Guards brigade just behind

Hougoumont. Scarcely less important was the contribution made by Joseph Brewster of the Royal Wagon Train, who took a tumbril of ammunition down into Hougoumont, under fire the whole way. Part of the wood was reoccupied, but when Jerome's French troops renewed their efforts about half an hour later, assisted by elements of Foy's division, they quickly regained lost ground and surged right round the buildings to attack the north gate.

Second Lieutenant Legros of the 1st Light Infantry, a giant of a man nicknamed 'the smasher', weakened the gate with an axe and led a rush which burst it open. The defenders fought back with bayonet and butt, aided by musket fire from the surrounding buildings until eventually Legros and all but one attacker were killed. The fight was still raging when a fresh wave of attackers appeared at the gate, and Lieutenant-Colonel Macdonnell, commanding the light companies of Byng's Guards brigade, collected a party of officers and men who closed the gates and jammed them shut.

Further attacks fared no better, and reinforcements were constantly slipped down the covered way. Some set about raiding the cherry trees in the orchard, oblivious of the heavy fire and the fury of Macdonnell, who roared out: 'You scoundrels! If I survive this day, I will punish you all.' At 2 p.m. the French belatedly brought up a howitzer, and followed it with others. Their shells set fire to the buildings but could not shake the defence. Matthew Clay recalled that his officer placed himself across the door of an upstairs room and would not allow the defenders to leave until just before the floor gave way, and some guardsmen perished when floors collapsed beneath them. The wounded had been carried into the great barn, and when it began to burn there were agonized cries but no one could be spared to rescue them. Corporal James Graham, one of the party which had closed the gates, asked Macdonnell for permission to save his wounded brother Joseph, then dragged him from the burning barn and returned to the fight.

The struggle at Hougoumont raged on without reference to the rest of the battle, and Ensign Wedgwood of the 3rd Guards acknowledged that he had no idea what was happening outside his own field of interest. 'I remember that I was myself completely ignorant of what was going on or what the result of the action was likely to be,' he wrote, 'until we saw parties of the French passing us in full retreat with the Brunswickers in pursuit ...'

About 10 000 men fell in and around Hougoumont. The overwhelming majority were French, for Wellington used only about 3500 men in all to hold the farm. The action exhausted the French divisions under

Although, at 46, Napoleon was the same age as Wellington in 1815, he was out of condition, and looked less trim than he did when this painting by Robert Lefevre was completed three years before. Napoleon had replaced the fleur de lys of the Old Regime with the imperial eagle, which adorned French uniforms, accoutrements and regimental colours. A gilt eagle topped the staff which bore a regiment's colours and these were defended not only by the officer who carried them but also by an escort of veteran NCOs.

Jerome and Foy and made inroads into Bachelu's men but did not succeed in inducing Wellington to weaken his centre. The duke had no doubt that Hougoumont was the pin on which the battle turned, and affirmed afterwards that victory had depended on closing its gates.

The battery opposite Wellington's centre thudded into action at about 1 p.m. Gunners tried to hit the ground just in front of the enemy so that cannon balls would ricochet through an entire formation. Not only did the French have few infantry to aim at, but the soggy ground absorbed many projectiles which might have bounced over the crest to plough into troops on the far side. Bylandt's brigade was more visible than most and suffered accordingly, but overall the bombardment was disappointing for the French.

So too was the news that troops seen on the French right, at first believed to be Grouchy's, and therefore French, were in fact Prussian. Napoleon sent two cavalry divisions and part of Lobau's corps to keep them off, and remarked that although the odds had shifted they were still in his favour. Then, at about 1.30 p.m., he ordered Ney to unleash d'Erlon's infantry. The centre pair of d'Erlon's four divisions, under Donzelot and Marcognet, advanced in thick columns. Only two cavalry brigades went forward with the corps, one on its extreme left and the other down the line of the Brussels road. The lack of a cavalry threat enabled Wellington's infantry to await the attack in line, and his gunners did frightful damage to the French columns as they moved up. The garrison of La Haie Sainte and the 95th on the other side of the road raked Quiot's division with rifle fire, although when the Prince of Orange sent a battalion down the slope to reinforce the riflemen it was destroyed by French cavalry hovering on the left flank of the attack.

Despite the ghastly effect of artillery fire – muskets, packs and limbs were thrown into the air by its impact – the French columns reached the hedge beside the Ohain road. Their evident bravery, the moral effect of their advance, the growling of their drums and yells of *'Vive l'Empereur!'* all contributed to shake the defence. Bylandt's men, sorely tried by the artillery fire, slipped back, and Sir Thomas Picton, whose division awaited the assault on the far side of the road, was shot through the head.

Lord Uxbridge chose this moment to launch two brigades of heavy cavalry, husbanded on the reverse slope for just such an eventuality. Somerset's Household Brigade charged west of the road, driving off French cavalry and cutting down many of Quiot's men. Corporal Shaw of the Life Guards may have killed as many as nine Frenchmen before he died: he had been at the gin that morning and was fighting drunk. East of the road the Union Brigade – English, Scots and Irish regiments –

smashed squarely into Donzelot and Marcognet, as Major George de Lacy Evans testified. 'By the sudden appearance and closing of our cavalry upon them (added to their previous suffering from musketry and grape),' he wrote, 'they became quite paralysed and incapable of resistance, except occasionally, individually, a little.'

The British charge broke both divisions and took two eagles, and had the horsemen rallied at once all would have been well. But although the brigade commander, Sir William Ponsonby, and most of his officers knew what would happen if the charge carried on there was no way of stopping the men. As Evans lamely explained: 'Finding that we were not successful in stopping the troops we were forced to continue on with them in order to continue our exclamations to halt.' The cavalry hurrooshed on into the great French battery, cutting down gunners and artillery drivers: an officer recalled that the latter were 'mere boys', sabred as they sat on their horses and weeping helplessly. The inevitable counter-attack by French lancers and cuirassiers herded the survivors back up the slope: of the 2500 British horsemen who had charged at least 1000 were killed or taken.

D'Erlon's counter-attack was not a total failure because his right-hand division, Durutte's, took the farm of Papelotte. The British cavalry brigades of Vivian and Vandeleur helped to extract the survivors of the charge and prevented Durutte from exploiting his success. Wellington, meanwhile, made some adjustments to his centre. He was only just in time, because Ney sent some of d'Erlon's surviving battalions against La Haie Sainte – the attack was beaten off, but the defenders' rifle ammunition was running very low – and then followed them with Milhaud's cuirassiers who spurred up the slope at about 4 p.m. in the first of the series of cavalry charges which characterized this phase of the battle.

Allied Tactics
Infantry was trained to receive cavalry in a square whose formation was a matter of a commander's judgement and his soldiers' skill. By forming too early, a battalion presented artillery with an attractive target, for a cunning cavalry leader would alternate charges with the fire of horse artillery. By forming too late it invited a mêlée in which an empty musket was rarely a match for a sabre. There were many ways of forming squares; oblongs, whose extended sides gave a better volume of fire, were widely used.

The principles were always the same. Fire was carefully controlled, with half-company volleys crashing out at targets within 50 yards (46 metres). Major Eeles of the 95th saw the effect of volleys from his company

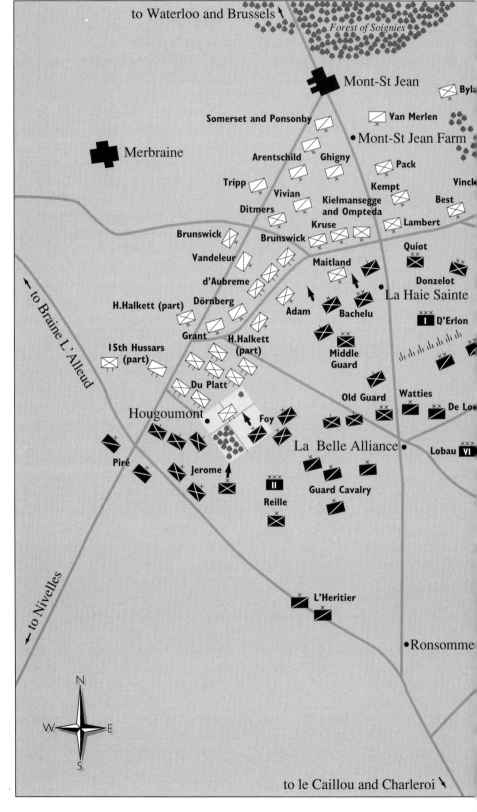

to Waterloo and Brussels

Forest of Soignies

Mont-St Jean

Byl

Merbraine

Somerset and Ponsonby

Van Merlen

Mont-St Jean Farm

Arentschild   Ghigny

Pack

Tripp

Vivian

Kempt

Vincl

Ditmers

Kielmansegge
and Ompteda

Best

Brunswick

Brunswick

Kruse

Lambert

Vandeleur

Maitland

Quiot

d'Aubreme

Donzelot

H.Halkett (part)   Dörnberg

Adam

Bachelu

La Haie Sainte

Grant   H.Halkett
(part)

Middle
Guard

D'Erlon

15th Hussars
(part)

Du Platt

Watties

Old Guard

De Lo

Hougoumont

Foy

La Belle Alliance

Lobau   VI

Piré

Jerome

II

Reille

Guard Cavalry

L'Heritier

Ronsomme

N
W   E
S

to Braine L'Alleud

to Nivelles

to le Caillou and Charleroi

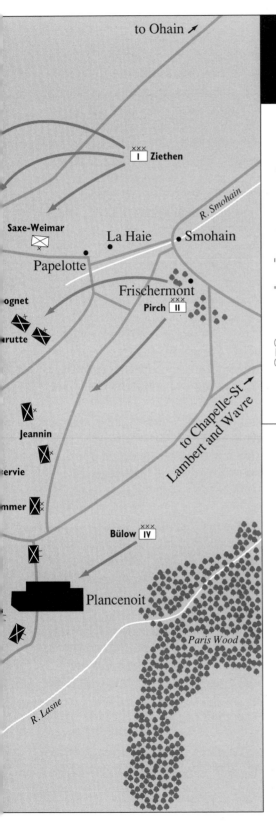

WATERLOO
18 June 1815:
Situation at 7.30 p.m.

to Ohain

Ziethen

Saxe-Weimar

La Haie

Smohain

Papelotte

R. Smohain

Frischermont

ognet

Pirch

rutte

Jeannin

ervie

mmer

Bülow

to Chapelle-St Lambert and Wavre

Plancenoit

Paris Wood

R. Lasne

Allied troops (British/
Dutch-Belgian/Prussian)

Allied troops movements

French troops

French troop movements

Napoleon's Great Battery

Roads with metalled
surface, 1815

0   200   400   600   800 Yds

0   200   400   600   800 Metres

*Refer to page 15 for a comprehensive
key to all military symbols*

and a square of the 71st on a body of French cuirassiers. 'I certainly believe that half the enemy were at the instant on the ground,' he remembered, 'some few men and horses were killed, more wounded, but by far the greater part were thrown down over the dying and wounded.' Private Wheeler thought that his comrades did rather better: they fired a volley at nearly a hundred cuirassiers and when the smoke cleared they could see only one, making off on foot.

At all costs men had to face outwards, front rank kneeling with muskets braced against the ground. Avoiding incoming roundshot, which bounded along with deceptive slowness, was discouraged. Wellington's battalions were fortunate that Ney did not combine cavalry and artillery more carefully, but standing firm in square was one of their greatest trials that day. If a square was under fire with its men already shaken, as many were, officers and sergeants had to strain every nerve to keep it together. Captain Cavalié Mercer of the Royal Horse Artillery watched the Brunswick squares near his own battery. 'The Brunswickers were falling fast,' he recorded in his journal, 'the shot every moment making great gaps in their squares, which the officers and sergeants were actively employed in filling up by pushing men together and sometimes thumping men ere they could make them move.'

When ammunition ran short, individual horsemen might approach unscathed, and many combatants remembered a very personal battle. Moustachioed cuirassiers, grimacing in impotent fury, induced one officer to get his men to scowl back. 'Now, men,' he ordered, 'make faces!' Mercer was narrowly missed by a *tirailleur* 'so I shook my finger at him, and called him *coquin* etc. The rogue grinned as he reloaded, and again took aim.' The shot missed Mercer but killed one of his drivers. It was hard not to admire French bravery. 'By God,' muttered an officer, 'those fellows deserve Bonaparte: they fight so nobly for him.' The defenders of Hougoumont respected their assailants' bravery but gave them no quarter: the only survivor of Legros' assault group was a drummer boy.

Roundshot, grape and musketry caused a variety of wounds. One of Wheeler's comrades was 'knocked to atoms' by a roundshot, and Driver Crammond of Mercer's troop lost 'the whole head except barely the visage, which still remained attached to the torn and bloody neck'. Limbs were shot off or left dangling by a thread, abdominal wounds grew progressively more painful, and head shots produced a variety of effects from sudden death through snuffling mimicry of sleep to shot-rabbit jerks. Some wounded were carried back to reeking field-hospitals behind the crest, but many had to remain in the squares: Ensign Gronow of the 1st Guards thought that the inside of his square, with its piles of wounded, was 'a perfect hospital, being full of dead, dying and mutilated soldiers'.

There was gallows humour at death's door. An ensign, bearing his colour inside a square, was splashed by the brains of a soldier and drawled 'how extremely disgusting' in his best Pall Mall voice. A doctor carrying an umbrella to ward off a sudden shower 'lounged up' to Mercer's guns during a lull in firing, and when 'the heavy answers' began to arrive made off at once. One shot passed just over his head, so he dropped to his hands and knees and, umbrella still erect, 'away he scrambled like a great baboon ... whilst our fellows made the field resound with shouts and laughter.'

The attack and defence of colours had a logic of its own. Some bore scars of previous campaigns and others, like that carried by Lieutenant Robert Belcher of the 32nd, were brand new. In either case they were natural targets. When d'Erlon's men attacked Picton's division, a French officer, who had just extricated himself from beneath his dead horse, grabbed the staff of Belcher's colour. Belcher retained the colour itself, and 'the Covering Colour Sergeant, named Switzer, thrust his pike into his breast, and right rank and file of the division, named Lacy, fired into him.' Colours were passed amongst the subalterns as their bearers were hit, sergeants carried them if all junior officers were down, and no one flinched from the deadly honour of bearing them. Lieutenant Edward Macready's 30th Regiment was so weakened that it could no longer guarantee to protect its colours, which were marched off the field. 'I know I never in my life felt such joy,' he wrote, 'or looked on danger with so light a heart, as when I saw our dear old rags in safety.'

The French Response

Ney's horsemen were still eddying around the squares when the Prussians took Plancenoit. It was retaken, lost, and retaken again as first Lobau and then the Imperial Guard tried to bolster up the sagging flank. Napoleon eventually had the situation well enough under control to pull the Guard back into reserve, but he was still dealing only with Bülow's corps. Of the other Prussian troops, Pirch was close behind, Ziethen was marching on Mont-St Jean by the Ohain road, and Thielmann was holding off Grouchy. Gneisenau knew that the fate of the Allied campaign hung in the balance, and turned down an appeal for help from Thielmann. 'It doesn't matter if he is crushed,' he snapped, 'providing that we gain the victory here.'

The Allies came close to losing when Ney threw everything into a last attack at 6 p.m. It was far better co-ordinated than his previous efforts.

La Haie Sainte was taken after its defenders ran out of ammunition: Baring and forty-two of his men escaped. The Prince of Orange ordered Baron Ompteda to counter-attack with his KGL brigade. Ompteda knew the task was impossible, but the prince pressed the point and the baron had to obey. Both Ompteda's nephews were serving with him: he asked a brother officer to try to save them, and then went for the enemy with such courage that French officers vainly tried to prevent their men from killing him. He was shot dead at close range and his brigade was cut to pieces. A French battery unlimbered nearby and subjected Major-General Sir John Lambert's brigade of the British 6th Division, east of the Brussels road, to a fire which left the 27th 'lying dead in square'. Colin Halkett warned Wellington that two-thirds of his men were down and begged for his brigade to be relieved. The duke's reply caught the dour mood of the moment: 'What he asks is impossible: he and I, and every Englishman on the field, must die on the spot which we now occupy.'

The duke knew that this was the crisis of the day. Napoleon, unable to feel the battle's pulse, did not. When Ney asked for more troops the emperor snapped: 'Some more troops! Where do you expect me to get them from? Do you want me to make them?' Ney might have pointed out that part of the Guard was still fresh, and David Chandler has argued that if they had been committed at this moment 'the battle would almost certainly have been won'.

Wellington's line held by the thinnest of margins. The Prince of Orange, his personal courage of higher order than his tactical judgement, was wounded on the spot where the Lion Monument now stands, and Sir Hussey Vivian, bringing his cavalry brigade across from the eastern flank, crossed 'ground that was actually covered with dead and dying, cannon shots and shells flying thicker than I ever heard musketry before, and our troops – some of them – giving way.' Somehow the tired Allied battalions stood their ground and as the attackers slid back gunners emerged from squares in which they had taken refuge to pound them. Müffling led up the first units of Ziethen's Prussian corps, and the worst was over.

The End of the Battle
Napoleon played his last card too late. At about 7 p.m. he led part of his Guard forward in person before handing it over to Ney. As the Guard, probably eleven battalions strong, began its advance there was an attempt to raise morale in the rest of the army by spreading the word that the troops coming up on the right were French rather than Prussian. We cannot be sure of the details of the Guard's attack, but it seems likely that

the column began its advance west of the road in a single mass perhaps 60 yards (55 metres) broad and 500 yards (457 metres) deep, grim-faced veterans stepping out under colours whose battle honours embodied a decade of imperial glory. The column detached two battalions to face Hougoumont and then inclined westwards, away from the road and up the trampled slope, splitting into three smaller columns, two of grenadiers and one of *chasseurs*, as it did so.

Two grenadier battalions, with some support from d'Erlon's men, reached Wellington's line close to the Brussels road, forcing back Halkett's exhausted brigade before being repulsed by Chassé's Dutch-Belgians. The main body of grenadiers, marching into a gale of shot, approached the Ohain road where the guardsmen of Maitland's brigade were sheltering behind the high banks. The duke was right behind them and called out 'Now, Maitland! Now is your time,' before ordering: 'Up Guards! Make ready! Fire!' Maitland's line overlapped the head of the column, and the French grenadiers could make no response to the half-company volleys that crashed out at point-blank range. It was an unequal contest, and the grenadiers were driven back down the slope. The *chasseurs* hit Adam's brigade, partly concealed by corn. Colonel John Colborne swung the 52nd, an experienced Peninsular War battalion, out at right angles to the line and fired into the *chasseurs'* left flank while the remainder of the brigade took on the head of the column. The result was the same, and the *chasseurs* too fell back.

This shocking repulse snapped French morale. There were cries of '*Trahison*' and '*Sauve qui peut*', and most of the army dissolved into rout. Several Guards battalions retained cohesion, checking the pursuit and enabling Napoleon to leave the field. Wellington doffed his hat and motioned his whole army forward, anxious that the French should not be given a chance to rally. He met Blücher at La Belle Alliance at about 9.30 p.m. They embraced on horseback and the old Prussian, who had been treating himself with gin and rhubarb, apologized: 'I stink a bit.' When he tried to describe the day, somehow only French would do: '*Quelle affaire.*'

Waterloo might not have been decisive in itself. On the French side, Napoleon lost 25 000 men in the battle and another 8000 afterwards, while Grouchy lost 2600 at Wavre. The Allies were scarcely better off: Wellington suffered 15 000 casualties and Blücher 7000 at Waterloo, and another 2500 Prussians were killed or wounded at Wavre. The Allies, with fresh armies on their way, could sustain these losses while the French could not, and defeat had broken Napoleon's spell. An armistice was signed on 3 July and the Allies entered Paris four days later. This time the quality of their mercy was decidedly strained. Napoleon was packed off to the rocky island of St Helena in the South Atlantic, and stayed there until he died six years later.

A View of the Field

The field of Waterloo remains evocative although it is often extremely crowded, and has been affected by 'commemoration' and other works. The Lion Monument, erected in 1823–6 on the spot where the Prince of Orange was wounded, consumed 42 000 cubic yards (32 000 cubic metres) of earth and altered the topography of the centre of the battle-field. An autoroute, mercifully in a cutting, separates Braine L'Alleud from the rest of the field, and the old Brussels road is so busy as to make walking along it scarcely less hazardous today than on 18 June 1815. The proprietors of cafés and souvenir shops have not missed a trick, and a visitor might be forgiven, looking at their wares, for imagining that Napoleon had been victorious.

Quatre-Bras
It is best to approach the battlefield as Napoleon did, from the south along the Brussels road, and the visitor who can afford the time should start at Quatre-Bras, now just on the Belgian side of the Franco-Belgian border. A large monument on the road's eastern edge south of the junction marks the spot where the Duke of Brunswick was killed. The French attacked from the south and took Gemioncourt Farm, a block of buildings on the modern border, early in the battle and then advanced up the slope. Their approach was obstructed by Bossu Wood, which stood well to the west of the road but has now disappeared, and by Materne Lake, east of the road, which is now somewhat larger than in 1815.

Looking east from the Brunswick monument the visitor gains a good impression of the ground held by Picton's men on the afternoon of 16 June 1815, although we must remember that there was standing corn which offered cover until it was trampled down. Halkett's brigade went into action on the other side of the road, and was mauled by Keller-mann's cuirassiers charging straight up its axis. The 69th Regiment was caught in line and broken perhaps 150 yards (137 metres) north-west of the monument.

Genappe
The Brussels road, now the N5, bypasses Genappe but in 1815 it ran right through the little town. Napoleon, hotly pursued after Waterloo,

abandoned his coach in the Place de l'Empereur. The old inn, Au Roi d'Espagne, is now a house bearing the number 58. On 16 June Wellington lunched there, probably lightly because he was an abstemious man. The French commanders Reille and Jerome dined at the inn the following day, and late on the 18th it became Blücher's headquarters. General Duhesme, mortally wounded while commanding the Young Guard at Waterloo, died there and is buried in the nearby churchyard of St Martin des Ways.

Museums and Monuments
The farmhouse of Le Caillou, where Napoleon spent the night before the battle, is further towards Brussels. It is now a museum of Napoleonic memorabilia, and a museum of the Dutch-Belgian contribution to the battle stands nearby. Still further north is the Wounded Eagle monument, which marks the spot where the last squares of the Old Guard held the Allies so the emperor could get away. On the other side of the road, a column commemorates the French writer, Victor Hugo. Hugo grew up when France was trying to put the Napoleonic experience into context, and described the emperor as the 'mighty somnambulist of a vanished dream'. Although Hugo did not always write accurately of Waterloo, his own thoughts, and those of so many Frenchmen of his generation, were haunted by the place.

Plancenoit, Papelotte and La Haie Sainte
La Belle Alliance, where Wellington and Blücher met after the battle, is now a restaurant. A short way down the Plancenoit road, which breaks eastwards off the N5, is a spot marked as L'Observatoire de Napoleon. The emperor and his staff used this as a forward command post at various stages of the battle and it still offers an admirable view of Wellington's left centre and left. The Lion Monument is clearly visible and to its right, by a cluster of trees, the Ohain road crosses the Brussels road. The Ohain road runs along the ridge in the middle distance – traffic usually obligingly materializes to mark its route. Well over to the right is the big farm of Papelotte which was taken by the French under Durutte. La Haie is on its right and Smohain even further to the right.

Plancenoit is a short walk away. It was viciously disputed between French and Prussians and badly damaged in the process. A Gothic monument in the village marks the spot where a battery of Bülow's corps fought, and commemorates the Prussian dead. The Prussians called the battle La Belle Alliance, which is scarcely surprising as they went nowhere near Waterloo itself, which is well behind the battlefield. Mont-St

Jean might have been a better name for the battle, but perhaps Wellington feared that his countrymen would never get their tongues round it, and so Waterloo it was.

The farm of La Haie Sainte, which was held by Major Baring's 2nd Light Battalion KGL until the French took it, stands beside the Brussels road just short of the Ohain crossroads. Visitors must bear in mind that it is a working farm and also beware of the juggernauts barrelling along to Brussels. It is not now entered by the gates on the main road, but by a track leading down the hill from opposite the 1815 Hotel, west of the crossroads. It is easy to see why the spot was so important, standing in front of Wellington's main line like a ravelin on a Vauban fortress. Turning along the Ohain road towards the Lion Monument we pass across the front held by Ompteda's and Kielmansegge's brigades of Charles Alten's 3rd British Division. The road was sunken in 1815 and is scarcely so today (the Lion Monument has seen to that) but we should be cautious in believing Victor Hugo's description of a chasm which swallowed up charging French cuirassiers: Maitland's men, a little ahead of us, were able to use the banks as cover.

The Visitor's Centre below the mound has excellent electronic maps and a film show, although I find the older-style Waterloo Panorama, with its circular painting of the battle at the time of the French cavalry charges, almost as telling. Directly opposite, on the ground floor of the Hôtel du Musée, built by Sergeant-Major Edward Cotton in 1818, is the Waxworks Museum, with life-sized models of the leading participants in the battle.

Studying the Field
Much as I abuse the Lion, his mound, ascended by 226 steps, offers an unrivalled view of the field. Looking east, the Ohain road runs off to Papelotte. Due south the straight line of the Brussels road disappears behind the roofs of La Haie Sainte and goes on to La Belle Alliance over a gentle swell which marks the site of the grand battery. With the ground so wet, gunners would not have wished to haul 12-pdrs or ammunition wagons far from a cobbled surface, and we would have expected to see some guns on both sides of the main road.

Opposite the Waxworks Museum a tiny road leads to the area where Maitland's guardsmen repulsed the French grenadiers and Mercer's troop of horse artillery took on the French cavalry. Mercer did not fire until the head of the column, led on at a steady and deliberate trot by a heavily decorated officer, was 50–60 yards (46–55 metres) away, and his guns were loaded with both roundshot and case. When they fired: 'The effect was terrible. Nearly the whole leading rank fell at once, and the round-shot, penetrating the column, carried confusion throughout its extent.' There is a monument to Mercer himself and another to Lieutenant Augustin Demulder of the 5th Cuirassiers, perhaps one of the victims of that dreadful fire. By turning eastwards just beyond the Mercer monument, the visitor can take a track which runs all the way to La Belle Alliance and the Brussels road.

The Farm of Hougoumont

Hougoumont, now known as Goumont, is best approached along the Ohain and Brussels–Nivelles road. A long metalled track leads to the farm, which is a working concern like La Haie Sainte. It was badly damaged in the fighting and has been altered since, but it is hard to grasp its importance without a visit. In 1815 its buildings formed a rectangular enclosure pierced by several entrances, with a great barn on the western side, other domestic and farm buildings and a chapel. A formal walled garden stood at its eastern end, with an orchard beyond that. A track bordered by a stout hedge ran parallel with the southern edge of the garden wall, and a substantial wood stretched off to the south.

The northern section of Hougoumont has been substantially altered, but the southern gate and the garden wall defended by the Guards light companies look the same today as in contemporary illustrations, and many loopholes are intact. The Guards had improvised a firestep which enabled them to fire over the top of the wall as well as through it, and we can sense the fury of Jerome's men when faced with what was, to unsupported infantry, an impenetrable obstacle. The tiny chapel can usually be visited, and there are several memorials on and around it. The graves of Captain John Lucie Blackman of the Coldstream, killed in battle, and Sergeant-Major Edward Cotton, who wrote *A Voice from Waterloo*, made a good living as a guide to the battlefield, and died in 1849, are on the southern edge of the old orchard.

Wellington's Positions

To reach Wellington's left centre we retrace our steps, taking the Ohain road to its junction with the Brussels road where there are monuments to the young Colonel Sir Alexander Gordon of Wellington's staff and the Dutch-Belgian dead. Wellington spent much of the battle here, near an elm tree on the south-western edge of the junction. The original tree has long since disappeared but it has a more recent replacement. A tramway built along the eastern edge of the main road altered the area's complexion and filled the sandpit held by the 95th: the base of

Gordon's monument shows where the ground level used to be.

Bylandt's brigade stood immediately east of the crossroads within view of the grand battery, and Lambert's men, slightly further back, were hard hit once Ney had remembered to bring guns up. The Ohain road was sunken here as it was on the other side of the junction, and was bordered by hedges so stout that British gunners had hacked holes in them. The gallant Sir Thomas Picton had warned the duke that his nerves were not up to the strain of another campaign. 'I must give up,' he begged. 'I am grown so nervous that when there is any service to be done it works upon my mind so that it is impossible for me to sleep at nights.' But he turned

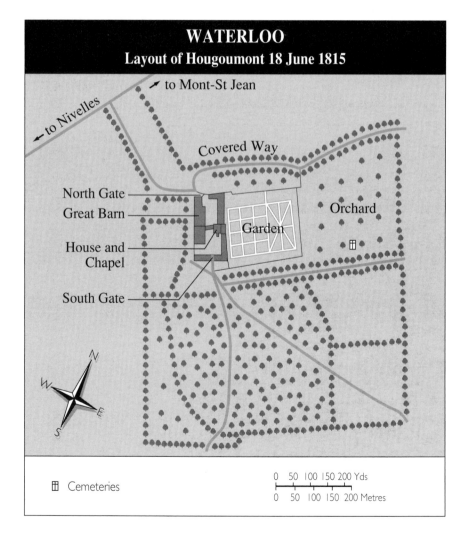

WATERLOO
Layout of Hougoumont 18 June 1815

to Mont-St Jean

to Nivelles

Covered Way

North Gate

Great Barn

House and Chapel

South Gate

Garden

Orchard

Cemeteries

0 50 100 150 200 Yds

0 50 100 150 200 Metres

out to command his division as ordered, and a memorial marks the spot where he fell, in civilian frock coat and top hat. Another monument stands where the dead of the 27th marked the position of its square.

The Town of Waterloo

Waterloo itself is well off the battlefield, further along the N5. The former Hôtel Boderglieu, just across the main road from St Joseph's church, is now the Wellington Museum, containing helpful maps of the battle and an interesting assortment of memorabilia including the wooden leg worn by the Marquess of Anglesey, as Lord Uxbridge became. Wellington ate supper at the hotel after the battle, looking sadly at the door to see if any of his young sparks would come in to fill those empty places at the table. Some historians suggest that Colonel Gordon died in the duke's bed while Wellington slept on a pallet on the floor, although the museum has beds for both officers. When woken and told that Gordon had died, this iron man wept, tears furrowing the grime on his cheeks. 'Well, thank God, I don't know what it is to lose a battle,' he said in a broken voice, 'but certainly nothing can be more painful than to win one with the loss of so many of one's friends.'

CHAPTER 3

Mons and Le Cateau
1914

Background

On 23 August 1914 fighting spread westwards along the Mons–Condé Canal like flame through brushwood. German columns, flowing down through Belgium towards France in a grey torrent, found the British Expeditionary Force directly in their path. The battle of Mons, the first major engagement of the First World War, was a day of shock and confusion, characterized by the unequal contest between Germans and British, the former advancing in formations which might not have astonished Wellington, the latter delivering firepower which the deftest archer would have envied. Corporal John Lucy of the Royal Irish Rifles told how, when the Germans appeared:

A great roar of musketry rent the air … The satisfactory sharp blasts of the directing whistles showed that our machinery of defence was working like the drill-book, and that the recent shelling had caused no disorganization … For us the battle took the form of well-ordered rapid rifle-fire at close range as the field-grey human targets appeared, or were struck down … after the first shock of seeing men slowly and helplessly falling down as they were hit [it] gave us a great sense of power and pleasure. It was all so easy.

Waterloo ushered in a long peace in Europe. In France, neither the Bourbons nor the July monarchy which replaced them in 1830 could compete with Bonapartist mythology or do much for the thousands who flooded into the towns from

Harry Easton joined the 21st Lancers in 1906, but transferred to the 9th to go to South Africa, where this picture was taken, the following year. He went onto the reserve after spending seven years with the colours, and was a Berkshire policeman when mobilized in August 1914. Captured during the charge near Audregnies on 24 August, Easton (seated) spent part of his captivity working on a farm in Germany. British cavalry carried the same rifle as the infantry, this Short Magazine Lee Enfield. Adopted in 1902, it weighed just over 8lb (18kg) and one expert called it 'one of the most efficient rifles ever to be put into the hands of a fighting soldier.'

a saturated countryside, providing Victor Hugo with raw material for *Les Misérables*. After a foray into republicanism, France found herself an empire once more with Napoleon III, the great man's nephew, on her throne. Although he claimed that 'the empire is peace', Napoleon pursued foreign policy intended to give his countrymen a taste of the glory that had faded with their defeat at Waterloo. The French army played a major role in the Crimean War in 1854–6, invaded Austrian-occupied northern Italy in 1859, and even sent an expedition to Mexico in 1862–6. Those who knew it well realized that its victories owed much to a tactical style which would have suited an old bruiser like Marshal Ney, and that the reform needed to fit it for European war would take more courage than the government possessed.

The Franco-Prussian War
At the beginning of the nineteenth century, Germany was divided into a score of states linked largely by language. Even those who sought a united Germany were divided between the big solution, with Austria in, or the small, with Austria out. Otto von Bismarck, Minister-President of Prussia, the dominant north German state, had to cope with Liberal opposition in parliament and, at the same time, advance towards his goal of German unification. He grabbed Schleswig and Holstein from the Danes in 1864–5, isolated Austria, enabling the reformed Prussian army to show its mettle and eliminating Austria from German affairs (1866), and then deluded the government of Napoleon III into declaring war in the summer of 1870.

The Franco-Prussian conflict of 1870–1 is the military watershed between 1815 and 1914. It was the first war in which the infantry on both sides carried breech-loading rifles, their deadliness awesomely demonstrated when the Prussian Guard lost over 8000 men while attacking St-Privat on 18 August 1870. Gunners still used direct fire, but shells had replaced roundshot and the Germans had excellent breech-loading Krupp guns. The French even had a machine-gun, the Mitrailleuse, but this had been kept a secret from friends as well as enemies and was largely ineffective. Cavalry had a dangerous and disappointing time. For every successful charge like von Bredow's death-ride (16 August 1870), there were a dozen others which ended in heaps of dead men and kicking horses.

Some of the most important developments were less spectacular. The telegraph enabled Helmuth von Moltke, the German commander-in-chief, to maintain contact with his armies as they sprawled across France. Contemporaries focused on the first phase of the war, marked by the destruction of the imperial armies in August–October 1870, to produce the paradigm of lightning war. Yet it was not lightning war at all. With her regulars dead or captured and her capital besieged, France fought on, conjuring up the Armies of National Defence to wage a war marked by deepening bitterness.

The war laid the foundations of future conflict. For France, the loss of the provinces of Alsace and Lorraine was a profound national humiliation, while Germany found in victory and the proclamation of William I of Prussia as German emperor the impulsion towards militarism. For the next forty years European diplomacy was played out with an arms race as its backcloth. The great powers fine-tuned arrangements for mobilization, bought modern arms and equipment and encouraged young men to anticipate a struggle of national survival from which only the worthless would hang back.

French Planning

The first French plans were defensive, and fortifications marked the new Franco-German border. Although the alliance between army and nation which had followed the Franco-Prussian War faltered with the Dreyfus affair, planners grew confident enough to adopt bolder schemes. In 1913 Plan XVII decreed: 'Whatever the circumstances, it is the Commander-in-Chief's intention to advance with all forces united to attack the German armies.' The edge of the sword was tempered by doctrine which knew no law save that of the offensive, and was applied by determined soldiers in long blue overcoats and red trousers. Fire support came from the legendary *soixante-quinze*, the 75mm quick-firing gun which was 'Father, Son and Holy Ghost' to French tacticians. One realist remarked that it would have been nice to have seen it surrounded by a few saints of heavier metal.

The Schlieffen Plan

The Germans could not afford to be so single-minded, for they had dangerous neighbours to east and west. In 1894 France and Russia concluded an entente, convincing Count Alfred von Schlieffen, German chief of the general staff from 1891–1906, that Germany would fight her next war on two fronts. He believed that he could win only 'ordinary victories' over the Russians, who would retreat into the fastnesses of their empire, and that the highest expression of military art was a battle of encirclement, like that won by Hannibal against the Romans at Cannae in 216 BC. Logic urged him to deal with France first, but he could not do so by direct attack because of those fortresses along the frontier.

Schlieffen's solution was the plan which bears his name, although its final version owed much to his successor, the younger Moltke, nephew of the architect of victory in 1870–1. Three armies, 1st, 2nd and 3rd, would sweep into northern France, passing through Belgian territory to do so. The 4th Army would turn in north of Sedan, while the 5th, 6th and 7th would defend Alsace-Lorraine. Schlieffen emphasized that the 1st Army must swing wide, passing west of Paris before jabbing in to fight a battle of encirclement in Champagne. Schlieffen always had reservations about the scheme, doubting whether even the German armies were strong enough for it. Moltke had abandoned Schlieffen's notion of violating Dutch as well as Belgian neutrality, so the armies of his right wing would have to pass through the corridor between the 'Maastricht appendix' of Dutch territory and the hilly Ardennes, dealing with the mighty fortress of Liège.

Britain's Position

Britain, concerned with the preservation of her empire and the maintenance of maritime power, was a latecomer to the Continental ball. In 1870 her sympathies had largely been with the Prussians, but as the war went on they swung towards the French. Nevertheless, old habits and colonial rivalries contributed to Anglo-French coolness, while there were sympathetic ties with Germany. William II was Queen Victoria's grandson and a field marshal in the British army, and many British regiments had fraternal relations with their German counterparts.

These British regiments had been having a frustrating time. In the South African War of 1899–1902 they had found it hard to defeat the tiny armies of the Boer republics and the mobile commandos which waged a long guerrilla struggle. The war showed that military reform was indispensable, and the most important work was carried out under the aegis of R.B. Haldane, secretary of state for war in the Liberal government which took office in late 1905. It was becoming clear that Britain's main rival was not France but Germany, and that Britain was more likely to become involved in a European war than to fight Russia on the north-west frontier of India. In 1904 Britain and France concluded the Entente Cordiale and in 1906 Haldane authorized the newly created general staff to open 'conversations' with the French on the understanding that they were not politically binding.

If the army was to operate on the Continent alongside a major ally it would be more than 'a bullet fired by the navy' and in so doing would alter the balance of British defence policy. Major-General Henry Wilson, who became director of military operations in 1910, was an ardent francophile, committed to the recovery of France's lost provinces. When discussing the size of the British contingent he asked General Ferdinand Foch what the smallest useful force would be. 'One single private soldier,' replied Foch, 'and we would take good care that he was killed.'

Haldane's reforms produced a regular expeditionary force of one cavalry and six infantry divisions, brought up to strength on mobilization by ex-regulars and members of the part-time Special Reserve. Most non-regular forces were combined into the Territorial Force of fourteen infantry divisions and fourteen brigades of yeomanry cavalry. It was intended to defend Britain while the expeditionary force departed overseas, but on outbreak of war many Territorials volunteered for foreign service and the first Territorial battalion was in action in October 1914.

Some saw the Territorial Force as little more than a device for avoiding conscription. The National Service League argued that Britain could not fight a great power while retaining a system of recruitment which Wellington would have recognized. The army's structure had certainly changed. The Cardwell reforms of the early 1880s had combined pairs of numbered regiments into the 'linked battalion' system of county regiments. John Colborne's 52nd, for instance, joined the 43rd, its Peninsular War comrade-in-arms, to form the Oxfordshire and Buckinghamshire Light Infantry. By 1914 this had two regular battalions, a Special Reserve Battalion and two Territorial battalions. In the pages that follow I adopt the practice of the British official history of the First World War by styling 1st Battalion The Oxfordshire and Buckinghamshire Light Infantry as 1/Oxfordshire and Buckinghamshire, and do the same for other regiments.

Most recruits were unemployed, and only half even claimed to have a trade. There were more 'town casuals' than countrymen, and areas such as Ireland, Scotland, London and Birmingham supplied soldiers to many regiments which claimed English county connections. One man spoke for many when he said that 'unemployment and the need for food' had driven him to enlist. There were scores of other reasons. Fred Milton left his farm to see the bright lights of Newton Abbot and finished up in the Devons. William Nicholson was attracted by family tradition – a grandfather had charged at Balaclava – and the glamour of full dress. R.G. Garrod, a young clerk, saw 'a gorgeous figure in blue with yellow braid and clinking spurs and said to myself "That's for me" ...' John Lucy and his brother went 'a bit wild' when their mother died. Bored with small-town life they joined the Royal Irish Rifles.

Although officers no longer bought commissions, it was hard to survive without a private income. Most went from public school to Sandhurst for the infantry and cavalry, or to Woolwich for gunners and

94

MONS AND LE CATEAU

The Battlefields and the British Expeditionary Force Troop Movements
August 1914

1 Battle of Mons

2 Battle of Le Cateau

3 Battle of the Marne

→ British troop movements

BEF's Concentration Area

- - - ► French 5th Army movements

→ German troop movements

| 0 | 10 | 20 | 30 Miles |
| 0 | 10 20 | 30 40 | 50 Kms |

Refer to page 15 for a comprehensive key to all military symbols

Cala

Boulogne •

R. So

Main British port of entry

Le Havre

Rouen **By rail**

R. Seine

FRANCE

N
W E
S

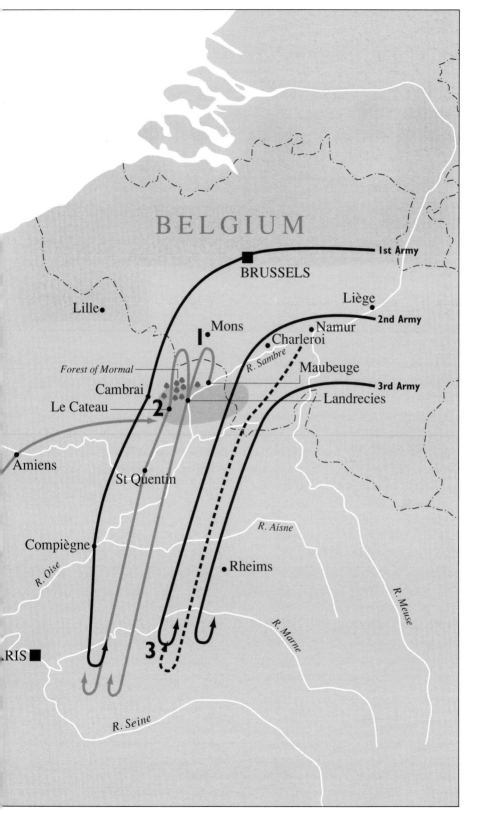

BELGIUM

1st Army

BRUSSELS

Liège

2nd Army

Lille

Mons

Namur

Charleroi

R. Sambre

Forest of Mormal

Maubeuge

Cambrai

3rd Army

Landrecies

Le Cateau

2

Amiens

St Quentin

Compiègne

R. Aisne

R. Oise

Rheims

R. Meuse

R. Marne

PARIS

3

R. Seine

Field Marshal Sir John French, seen disembarking from HMS
Sentinel at Boulogne on 14 August 1914 *(above)* had a history of poor
relations with General Sir Horace Smith-Dorrien *(right)*. Smith-
Dorrien's decision to fight at Le Cateau on 26 August proved crucial.

sappers. Promotion was slow, and although efforts to improve training
lengthened the working day there was plenty of time for sport. Relations
between officers and men were formal and sometimes remote, but there
were often bonds of mutual regard linking them. Company Sergeant-
Major Ernest Shephard described his company commander as 'a real
sample of the Regular "Officer and Gentleman" … Absolutely fearless
and first and last thought for his men.'

It was the assassination in Sarajevo, on 28 June 1914, of the Arch-
duke Franz Ferdinand, heir to the throne of Austria-Hungary, that struck
the spark which blew the old world apart. The Austrians blamed the
Serbs for the outrage and demanded humiliating concessions. The Serbs
appealed to their Slav brothers in Russia, and on 1 August Russian mobilization provoked a German declaration of war. France would not guarantee to remain neutral, and reports of fictitious French border violations
were used to justify the German declaration of war on France on 3
August. Britain might have held aloof, but on 4 August the Cabinet was
told that the Germans had violated the Belgian neutrality guaranteed by
Britain, and duly declared war on Germany.

Campaign and Battles

A Council of War met at 10 Downing Street on 5 August and agreed to
implement the existing plan for concentration around Le Cateau and

Maubeuge on the left of the French 5th Army. Only the cavalry division and four infantry divisions would be sent out at first, under the command of Field Marshal Sir John French, a cavalry officer who had made his reputation in South Africa. They would form two corps: 1 Corps (1st and 2nd Divisions) under Sir Douglas Haig, a quiet Lowland Scot who had once served as French's brigade-major; and 2 Corps (3rd and 5th Divisions) under Sir James Grierson, a more affable character who quipped that the medals on his well-filled chest commemorated many a battle with knife and fork.

French was given his orders by the newly-appointed secretary of state for war, Field Marshal Lord Kitchener. They did not get on: French was a mercurial man with an eye for the ladies, while Kitchener was dour and monkish. French was told to 'coincide most sympathetically with the plans and wishes of our ally' but was warned not to expose his force unduly and reminded that 'you will in no sense come under the orders of any Allied general'. Sir John visited Paris on 15 August and went on to see the French commander-in-chief, General Joseph Joffre, the following day. Joffre assured him that all was going well, and that the British Expeditionary Force (BEF) would at the worst be facing two German corps and a cavalry division.

The Arrival of the BEF

Most of the BEF landed at Le Havre, Rouen and Boulogne between 12 and 17 August and went on to its concentration area by train. British soldiers were surprised by the warmth of the French welcome. A guardsman did his best for Anglo-French relations by yelling '*Vive l'Empereur*', and Sergeant William Edgington of the Royal Horse Artillery (RHA) recorded 'enthusiastic reception by French population who shower us with flowers (and kisses) …' Private Frank Richards of the Royal Welch Fusiliers, like many of his comrades a recalled reservist, was pleased to discover that many girls proved themselves 'true daughters of France'. His mates left cap-badges as souvenirs, along with other mementoes which would not make their presence felt for a few months. One soldier, wandering around Amiens cathedral, told Richards that it would be a fine place to loot.

Sir James Grierson got no further than Amiens. He died of a heart attack on the train and was replaced by Sir Horace Smith-Dorrien, an experienced but irascible infantry officer who had been one of the few survivors of the Zulu victory at Isandalwana. Smith-Dorrien was not French's first choice, and their relationship was not improved when Sir Horace announced that King George V had asked him to keep him informed of the doings of 2 Corps. By this time French's confidence had been jolted by a frosty interview with General Lanrezac, commander of the 5th Army, and by 'silly reports of French reverses'.

On 19 August the Royal Flying Corps mounted its first-ever operational sortie. It saw no Germans, but the next day sighted a huge column moving through Louvain. Liège had held up the Germans, but its forts were smashed by heavy howitzers and the Belgian field army fell back on Antwerp, enabling the Germans to occupy Brussels on 20 August. Even Joffre could not ignore this news. He shifted the weight of his attack to the north and sent one of his cavalry corps on a circuitous march behind the BEF to come up on its left flank.

By the time the BEF set out towards the Belgian mining town of Mons on 21 August the Allied plan had gone badly wrong: the French attack, pressed home with all the dash demanded by theorists, ran bloodily into German machine-guns and howitzers. British soldiers on the long and baking road had no inkling that their allies were being so roughly handled in the opening of what became known as 'the Battle of the Frontiers'. Lieutenant James Pennycuik of the Royal Engineers, riding up from Landrecies, remembered: 'I got quite good at cracking an egg on my saddle and swallowing it raw,' although his fellow sapper, Second Lieutenant Kenneth Godsell, witnessed an unforeseen result of gifts of fruit and wine when 'falling out among the troops became very frequent and men were seen rolling in agony by the roadside'.

Not all the agony was gastronomic. Cobbled roads made for difficult marching, especially for reservists with new boots. Each man's kit, consisting of a loaded pack, webbing equipment, an entrenching tool, ammunition, rifle and bayonet, weighed about 80 lb (36 kg) and bore down on his back. Private Harry Beaumont of the Royal West Kent wrote: 'We all began to feel the effects of the intense heat. Some were more or less in a state of collapse, and had to be supported by their comrades, while others carried their rifles.'

The Battle of Mons

The first British shot of the war was fired on the morning of 22 August when C Squadron 4th Dragoon Guards clashed with German cavalry at Casteau, on the Mons–Brussels road. That day saw the BEF move up with 1 Corps, on its right, north-east of Maubeuge, and 2 Corps, on its left, reaching the line of the Mons–Condé Canal. Sir John French still believed that he was participating in a general advance, but Lieutenant Edward Spears, liaison officer with the 5th Army, knew that Lanrezac's men had been fought to a standstill around Charleroi, and on the night of the 22nd he visited French at Le Cateau and warned him that Lanrezac was not attacking. When, shortly afterwards, French was asked to fall on the right flank of Germans facing Lanrezac he declined to do so but agreed to hold his ground for twenty-four hours. The scene was set for the battle of Mons.

Sir John French saw his corps commanders early on 23 August at Smith-Dorrien's headquarters at Sars la Bruyère. It seems likely that the commander-in-chief passed on some of his doubts and warned corps commanders to be prepared to advance or retreat. Smith-Dorrien was worried that his corps, 3rd Division to the right and 5th to the left, was stretched across 20 miles (32 km) of difficult country. He was already preparing the canal bridges for demolition and reconnoitring a line south of Mons on to which he could withdraw his right-hand formation, 8th Infantry Brigade, exposed in the Nimy–Obourg bend of the canal. French's main headquarters was in Le Cateau with an advanced element at Bavay, but he planned to be up and about. He had been told that 4th Division was being sent to join him, and converted the infantry assigned to the lines of communication into 19th Infantry Brigade, which he was to visit that day.

The 'close, blind country' around Mons was a mining area, with pit-heads, slag-heaps, rows of miners' cottages fronting on to narrow cob-bled streets, and 'mineral railways' taking coal to the main line. Corporal W.H.L. Watson, an Oxford undergraduate who had volunteered to serve as a motor-cycle dispatch rider, had a frustrating time. 'The roads wandered round great slag-heaps,' he wrote, 'lost themselves in little valleys, ran into pits and groups of buildings … Without a map to get from Elouges to Frameries was like asking an American to make his way from Richmond Park to Denmark Hill.'

The canal had been dug when Napoleon was emperor. It was an average of 64 feet (19 metres) wide and 7 feet (2 metres) deep, and was crossed by eighteen road and railway bridges in addition to lock gates which infantry could use. Smith-Dorrien had too few engineers, too little explosive and too little time to destroy them all, but his sappers did what they could, and Kenneth Godsell received an insouciant wave from the driver of a shunting engine which puffed across the bridge at St Ghislain as his men were laying demolition charges.

The troops holding the canal had arrived on the 22nd, too late to do more than scratch 'lying trenches' on and around the towpath, and use furniture to barricade the village streets behind. There was a cement factory at Obourg, and the soldiers of 4/Middlesex, holding the station, improvised defences from sacks of cement. The British had fought in

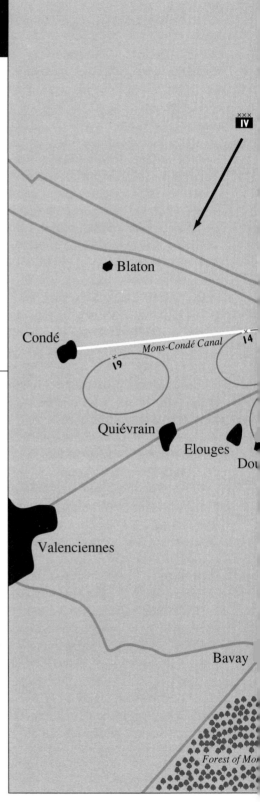

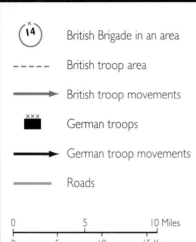

MONS
Situation on 23 August 1914

(×/14)	British Brigade in an area
- - - - -	British troop area
→	British troop movements
▪ (×××)	German troops
➡	German troop movements
▬	Roads

```
0          5          10 Miles
├─────────┼─────────┤
0    5        10    15 Kms
```

Refer to page 15 for a comprehensive key to all military symbols

Blaton

Condé

Mons-Condé Canal

×/19

Quiévrain

Elouges

Dou

Valenciennes

Bavay

Forest of Mo

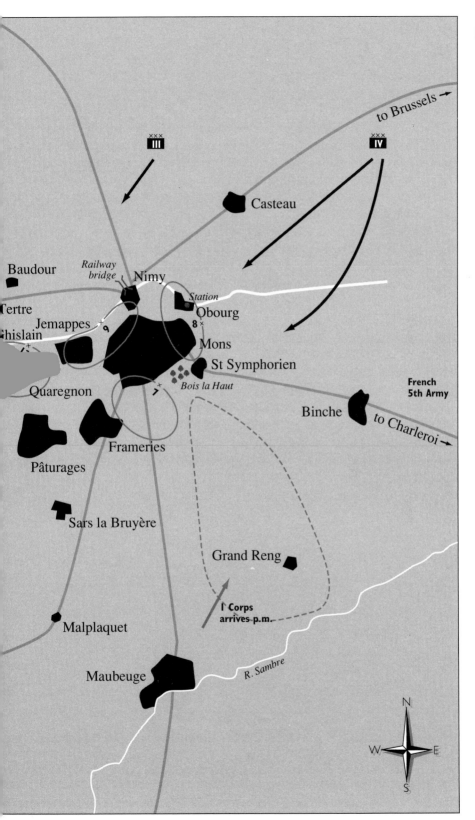

XXX
III

XXX
IV

to Brussels →

Casteau

Baudour

Railway bridge

Nimy

Station

Obourg

Tertre

Jemappes

+ 9

8 ×

Ghislain

Mons

St Symphorien

Bois la Haut

French 5th Army

Quaregnon

+ 7

Binche

to Charleroi →

Frameries

Pâturages

Sars la Bruyère

Grand Reng

I Corps arrives p.m.

Malplaquet

Maubeuge

R. Sambre

N
W E
S

khaki since the 1880s, and the South African War had reminded them of the importance of fieldcraft and marksmanship. The .303 Lee-Enfield rifle carried by infantry and cavalry alike was sighted up to 2000 yards (1830 metres) and men shot regularly at targets 600 yards (550 metres) away. They were expected to put fifteen shots a minute into the 2-foot (60-cm) circle of a target 300 yards (225 metres) away, and many could do better. Marksmen received proficiency pay which added to the pleasures a man might find foaming in the wet canteen or loitering outside the barrack gate.

Like his Continental counterpart, the British soldier was taught that wars were not won by defence, and Infantry Regulations enjoined him to use his skill in musketry to get to close quarters and take the bayonet to the king's enemies. At the moment of the assault 'the men will cheer, bugles will be sounded and pipes played'. Belief in the offensive had a rationale of its own. Nobody could ignore the advances in killing-power that had come with smokeless powder, the magazine rifle and the machine-gun: there were two belt-fed Vickers-Maxim machine guns in every British battalion. But without 'unconquerable and determined offensive spirit' men would go to ground and firepower would impose a paralysis that would lead to long and exhausting wars.

There was offensive spirit aplenty that Sunday morning of the 23rd. The German soldiers of Colonel-General Alexander von Kluck's 1st Army, marching south-west, had no idea of what lay before them. Kluck

Field-grey replaced the blue uniforms of German infantry for manoeuvres and war, and their spiked helmets had a cloth cover with the regiment's number stencilled on it.

knew that the British were in France, because one of their aircraft had been brought down by ground-fire and news of the cavalry action at Casteau had reached him. However, he thought that the BEF had landed at Ostend, Boulogne and Calais, had detrained at Lille and so were probably at Tournai. Mist kept his aircraft on the ground until midday, and the action at Casteau helped to give British cavalry an edge over his own. At the back of Kluck's mind was the principle which had stood the Germans in good stead in 1870–1. Attacking infantry did well if they pinned an enemy to his position and prevented him from manoeuvring. While they fixed, others could strike, seeking flanks and rear so that the defender's success in holding ground, and thus making it easier for his attacker to get in behind him, only made his eventual destruction more certain.

At 6 a.m. German horsemen approached the canal. They had been on the move since crossing the frontier over two weeks before, and their first contact with British infantry was a shock. The Middlesex at Obourg shot the first horsemen who appeared, and when a patrol galloped down the road towards the swing bridge at Nimy, 4/Royal Fusiliers killed four men and wounded the officer, Lieutenant von Arnim, whose father was commanding the German IV Corps a few miles away. The infantry came later, trudging down the road in column. 'They were only about 1000 yards [900 metres] distant,' records the Fusiliers' regimental history, 'and the rapid fire, aided by the machine-guns, in a few minutes destroyed the leading section of fours.' The Middlesex also had the best of the early

Men of 4/Royal Fusiliers in the square at Mons on 22 August 1914. This battalion, consisting largely of reservists, held the Nimy sector of the Mons–Condé canal the next day.

action: a battery unlimbered in the open 1500 yards (1370 metres) from the canal and was driven off by their machine-guns.

Then the tone of battle changed. German guns deluged the canal line with a fire to which the British made no response. This was because the bulk of 2 Corps' artillery, of limited use around Mons, was away to the west, with most of the cavalry, helping to cover the open flank. Guns could now engage a target invisible from the gun-line, but communication between observer and battery was by semaphore or telephone. The Germans moved with artillery well up the line of march and soon had telephone lines laid and guns in action.

After the shelling came German infantry, advancing shoulder to shoulder in the face of fire which cut them down like corn before the scythe. The Middlesex regimental history acknowledges that 'they were brave fellows, those Germans ...' On the north-eastern edge of the Nimy–Obourg salient, Germans began to cross the canal to the east, using unguarded bridges, and to work their way through the broken ground behind the station. As the battle gained momentum 2/Royal Irish, in reserve on the edge of Mons, was ordered forward to support the Middlesex, but by early afternoon it was clear that both battalions would have to fall back.

The Royal Fusiliers at Nimy were also under pressure. Shelling caused casualties amongst soldiers on the canal bank, and the machine-gun section, under Lieutenant Maurice Dease, was cruelly exposed up on the abutment of the railway bridge. Dease was hit twice and then mortally wounded as he went back and forth keeping his guns in action. Eventually, with the gunners all dead or wounded, Private Sid Godley climbed up on to the bridge, hauled the bodies out from behind a gun, and kept firing until he ran out of ammunition. He beat the gun against a bridge stanchion and staggered off into Nimy, where he collapsed from loss of blood. Lieutenant Dease and Private Godley were both awarded the Victoria Cross, the first of the war. By this time the Fusiliers had been ordered to withdraw to the new line south of Mons. One brave German, Private Niemayer of the 84th Regiment, swam the canal and clambered up to operate the bridge mechanism and swing the bridge back across the canal. He was killed, but as the Fusiliers withdrew through Nimy the Germans were close behind them, with local inhabitants – fugitives or hostages – between the combatants.

Things were more difficult for the Middlesex and Royal Irish. Smith-Dorrien's right flank, running back from Obourg on to the wooded eminence of Bois la Haut, was vulnerable because 1 Corps did not arrive to extend the line to the south-east until early afternoon. There were also problems of co-ordination which left the Bascule crossroads, directly behind the Middlesex, unguarded. Regimental Quartermaster Sergeant Fitzpatrick of the Royal Irish was in the Segard Brewery, where the road from Bascule enters Mons, sending beer forward to the firing-line. He looked up towards the junction, saw soldiers of his battalion falling back across the road, and at once collected about forty cooks, grooms and storemen and took them to the crossroads.

Fitzpatrick was just in time to take on the leading elements of the German 35th and 85th Infantry Regiments, moving straight up the road. An officer of the Gordon Highlanders, the next battalion to the south-east, arrived but was hit almost immediately, and more volunteers came up with a machine-gun. The little band held on until well past midnight, when the Royal Irish and Middlesex had been gone for hours, and withdrew after burying their fifteen dead and smashing the machine-gun. Fitzpatrick was awarded the Distinguished Conduct Medal and a commission for the day's work: he was a Lieutenant-Colonel by the end of the war.

Fighting spread along the canal, and the action at St Ghislain is typical of a dozen other clashes. A Company 1/Royal West Kent was north of the canal, between Tertre and Baudour, covering 5th Division's cavalry squadron, which was to retire as the Germans approached. The battalion's other three companies were on the south bank, and to the left 2/King's Own Scottish Borderers covered the St Ghislain bridge: four field guns had been manhandled on to the towpath.

Captain Walter Bloem, a forty-six-year-old German reserve officer snatched from a comfortable literary existence to command a company of 12th Brandenburg Grenadiers, approached Tertre after a sweaty morning's march. His men had been joking about the British in their funny scarlet tunics, and Hussar patrols announced that the country was clear for 50 miles (80 km) ahead. The mobile cookers had just been brought up with lunch when two wounded Hussars galloped up with the news that the British were on the canal. A third limped past carrying his bloodstained saddle: they were in Tertre too.

The Brandenburgers went forward at once. A battalion attacked Tertre, and Bloem's men made for the wood south-west of the village. As he passed farm buildings Bloem saw a group of horses, and a British cavalryman was shot dead as he ran for cover. There was no sign of the British on the water meadows, but fire from invisible marksmen left German dead and wounded to mark the ground gained. Cows in fields ahead bellowed and collapsed, and men followed suit. Bloem described the scene:

'I'm hit, sir! O God! Oh, mother! I'm done for!'

'I'm dying, sir!' said another one near me. 'I can't help you, my young man – come, give me your hand.' …

Behind us the whole meadow was dotted with little grey heaps. The hundred and sixty men that had left the wood with me had shrunk to less than a hundred.

About 500 yards (460 metres) from the canal Bloem stopped to let his men catch their breath. The fire ceased when they lay down, because the embankment on the German side created a wafer of dead ground invisible to the defenders. A raffish corporal produced a bottle of champagne. Bloem shared it with Lieutenant Gräser, the corporal and an orderly, and ordered his men on again.

The enemy must have been waiting for this moment to get us all together at close range, for immediately the line rose it was as if the hounds of hell had been loosed at us, yelling, barking, hammering as a mass of lead swept in amongst us … 'Gräser!' I called out. 'Where is Lieutenant Gräser?' And then from the cries and groans all around came a low-voiced reply: 'Lieutenant Gräser is dead, sir, just this moment. Shot through the head and heart as he fell. He's here.'

They were little further forward by nightfall, and when Bloem met his battalion commander he found that he was the only captain left. 'Our grand regiment, with all its pride and splendid discipline, its attack full of dash and courage, and now only a few fragments left,' mused Bloem. It had lost 25 officers and more than 500 men. The survivors would not have enjoyed hearing Harry Beaumont of the Royal West Kent call them 'easy targets'.

Smith-Dorrien pulled back that night, sappers blowing up as many bridges as they could: Captain Theodore Wright and Lance-Corporal Charles Jarvis were both awarded the VC for their part in the work. The British had lost 1642 men, most of them from the Royal Fusiliers, Middlesex and Royal Irish. German losses cannot have been less than 5000 and may easily have been much more.

The Retreat from Mons

The British corps chiefs of staff were given orders for withdrawal to a line running east-west though Bavay at 1 a.m. on 24 August, and told to agree details between themselves. It was fairly easy for 1 Corps to break clear but 2 Corps had a testing time. Smith-Dorrien decided to get 3rd Division away first. By mid-morning 5th Division's commander, Major-General Sir Charles Fergusson, learned that the cavalry had already gone, exposing his left flank, and a German corps was making for it. He sent Lieutenant-Colonel Ballard with 1/Norfolk, 1/Cheshire and 119th

Battery Royal Field Artillery (RFA) to attack the Germans, but this order was soon modified. Ballard was to hold the ridge between Audregnies and Elouges and buy time, and Fergusson asked Major-General Edmund Allenby of the cavalry division to support him.

Ballard's detachment formed a line on the ridge. The Cheshires, on the left, had a company in Audregnies itself, and the Norfolks, on the right, continued the line north-east towards Elouges, with 119th Battery towards the middle. L Battery Royal Horse Artillery joined in from the high ground on the eastern edge of Audregnies. Two German divisions, each of four three-battalion infantry regiments, swept down towards Ballard's force, supported by nine batteries firing from the Quiévrain–Mons road.

Captain Wilfrid Dugmore of the Cheshires lay in the open while shrapnel hit the ground around him. 'The situation seemed pretty miserable,' he told his wife, 'the fire was so heavy as to defy description … I was dead-beat not having touched a mouthful of food for over twenty-four hours, nor had a drink, less than two hours sleep, we had been marching in a sort of trance, receiving orders which were promptly counter-ordered … I think I would have welcomed a bullet through a vital spot.'

His opponents were also taking punishment. Major Tom Bridges of the 4th Dragoon Guards saw the gunners of L Battery at their work 'as steadily as if they had been on the ranges at Okehampton,' and Major 'Sally' Home of Allenby's staff watched the German infantry debouch from Quiévrain into their fire: 'Every shell burst low over them: they stood it for five minutes and then bolted.'

Dismounted cavalry had already joined the firefight when Allenby rode up and ordered Brigadier-General de Lisle of 2nd Cavalry Brigade to charge the guns. De Lisle shouted to Lieutenant-Colonel David Campbell of the 9th Lancers: 'I'm going to charge the enemy. The 4th Dragoon Guards will attack on your left. As soon as you see them deploy, attack on their right with at least two squadrons.' Corporal Harry Easton was doing so well against easy targets that he missed the order to cease fire, and got back to his troop just in time to hear Captain Francis Grenfell say: 'Get mounted, lads, we're going to charge the guns.' Private Wells scrawled snatches of those last few seconds: 'Move off at trot and ride knee to knee. "Carry Lances." See figures running about in distance. "Lance Engage." Gallop …'

In a flash of clarity, Easton looked to his left and saw his boyhood friend Jackie Patterson riding with the Dragoon Guards. Then it was chaos, as Second Lieutenant Roger Chance of the Dragoon Guards recalled:

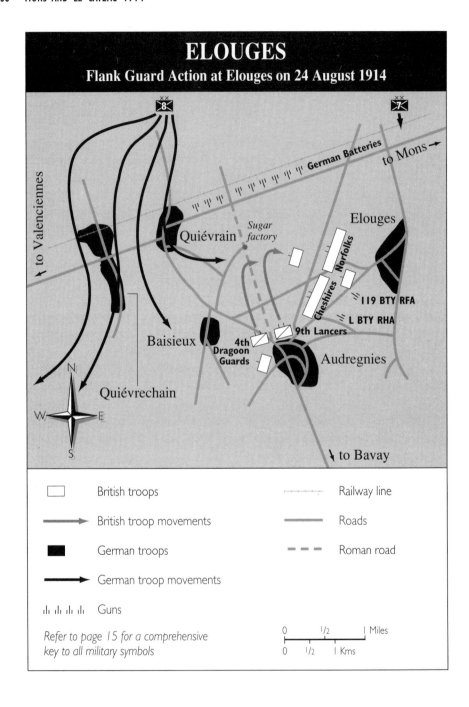

ELOUGES
Flank Guard Action at Elouges on 24 August 1914

to Valenciennes

to Mons →

German Batteries

Quiévrain

Sugar
factory

Elouges

Norfolks

Cheshires

119 BTY RFA

L BTY RHA

9th Lancers

Baisieux

4th
Dragoon
Guards

Audregnies

Quiévrechain

N

W   E

S

to Bavay

	British troops		Railway line
→	British troop movements	—	Roads
■	German troops	- - -	Roman road
→	German troop movements		
ılı ılı ılı ılı	Guns		

*Refer to page 15 for a comprehensive
key to all military symbols*

0   1/2   1 Miles
0   1/2   1 Kms

A cloud of dust has risen ahead, pierced with the flash of shell bursts. If there is a hail of bullets I am not aware of it, as with [Sergeant] Talbot glimpsed alongside, the men thundering after us, I endeavour one-handed to control my almost runaway steed ... He has gone – Talbot has gone down in a crashing somersault, to be ridden over dead or alive, and no sooner is he lost to us than I am among the ranks of those who, halted by wire, were right in disorder like a flock of sheep.

The wire fence ran in front of a sugar-beet factory on a Roman road leading from Audregnies towards the guns. Easton came down just short of it, and staggered to his feet, lance gone, rifle still with his horse and the Cheshires' fire cracking overhead: he was captured moments later. Tom Bridges, unhorsed and stunned, was helped on to a loose horse and galloped back up the Roman road. He lost that horse too, and was wafted off to safety by the brigade signals officer in a blue and silver Rolls-Royce. Despite Ballard's best efforts, the Cheshires never received the order to withdraw and fought on until the survivors surrendered at 6.30 p.m. The battalion had gone into action nearly one thousand strong: two officers and two hundred men answered their names at roll-call that evening.

The first day of the retreat, 24 August, cost the BEF almost 2600 men. The next was quieter, although the forest of Mormal which lay behind the BEF split its retreat as the cutwater of a bridge divides the torrent; 1 Corps marched to its east and 2 Corps to its west, competing for road space with refugees whose plight many soldiers found more depressing than their own. Men were already very tired: John Lucy thought that he

British horsemen during the retreat from Mons. They carried a sword, hung from the saddle on the horse's left, and a rifle, in a leather bucket on its right.

had covered '75 miles [120 km] in five days and a battle into the bargain'. Refugees, hovering German cavalry, heat and lack of food bore down on the retreating columns, and on the evening of the 24th a spectacular summer thunderstorm left them soaked as well.

The Battle of Le Cateau
GHQ moved back from Le Cateau to St Quentin on the 24th and ordered both corps to spend the night on a line running east-west through Le Cateau, and to move off again the following morning. It was a bad night. The Germans clashed with 1 Corps at Landrecies, and the normally stolid Haig, tired and inconvenienced by a radical cure for constipation, sent worrying messages back to GHQ. Smith-Dorrien, in the village of Bertry, south-west of Le Cateau, learned at midnight that the cavalry had relinquished the ridge covering his bivouacs and that his rearguards were still coming in, dead-beat. Unless he was clear by first light the Germans would be on him. He decided to fight in the hope of striking 'a stopping blow'. Both Allenby and Major-General Snow of the newly arrived but incomplete 4th Division agreed to fight under his orders. GHQ was less than convinced, and eventually approved his decision in a telegram replete with double negatives: 'Although you are given a free hand as to method this telegram is not intended to convey the impression that I am not anxious for you to carry out the retirement and you must make every endeavour to do so.'

2 Corps fought on the ground it occupied. There were a few troops in Le Cateau itself: most got clear before the Germans entered at 6.30 a.m. on the 26th, the day of the battle. Smith-Dorrien's own divisions, 5th on the right and 3rd on the left, took up post south of the ruler-straight road from Le Cateau to Caudry, whence 4th Division took the line on towards Esnes to the south-west. As the day wore on Sordet's cavalry corps at last reached the British left, and the rapid fire of its 75mm guns helped to hearten the defence.

On the British right, the artillery commanders of 3rd and 5th Divisions agreed to push batteries forward to hearten the infantry, and some were tucked into folds of ground between the main road and a sunken track which runs parallel to it to the south. A prominent knoll on 5th Division's right, held by 2/Suffolk, had three batteries, eighteen guns in all, right up on it. There would be occasions in future when British gunners would engage targets with direct fire, but Le Cateau was the last battle when it would be done deliberately on this scale. As the attack gained momentum, with columns rolling down from the north, gunners fought like their ancestors at Waterloo. Officers took over as men fell.

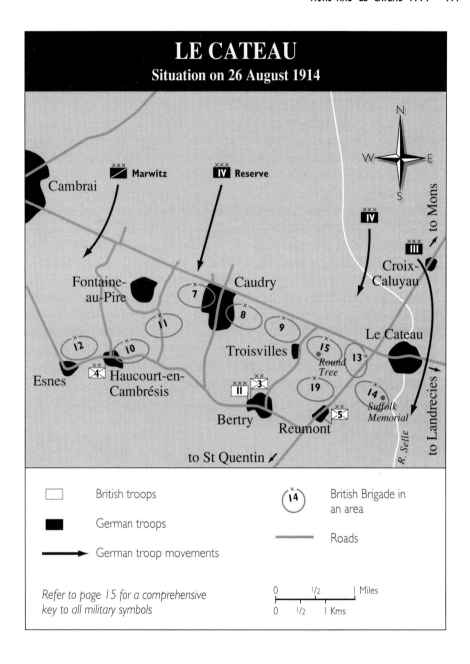

LE CATEAU
Situation on 26 August 1914

Cambrai

×××
Marwitz

×××
IV Reserve

×××
IV

×××
III

Croix-
Caluyau

Fontaine-
au-Pire

Caudry

×
7

×
8

×
11

×
9

Le Cateau

×
12

×
10

××
4 Haucourt-en-
Cambrésis

Esnes

Troisvilles

×
15
Round
Tree

13 ×

×××
II

××
3

×
19

×
14
Suffolk
Memorial

Bertry

Reumont

××
5

to Mons

to Landrecies

R. Selle

to St Quentin

Key:

British troops

German troops

German troop movements

×
14 British Brigade in
an area

Roads

*Refer to page 15 for a comprehensive
key to all military symbols*

0   ½   1 Miles

0   ½   1 Kms

Lieutenant Tom Butt of the King's Own Yorkshire Light Infantry, in the angle between the main road and the Bavay–St Quentin road, saw the gun behind him manned by the battery commander and his sergeant-major, and Lieutenant Rory Macleod, up with the Suffolks, remembered the rattle of rifle-fire against the shield of the gun he served.

Not all the gunnery was old-fashioned. In addition to its fifty-four 18-pdr guns and eighteen 4.5-inch howitzers, each division had a four-gun battery of 60-pdr heavy guns manned by the Royal Garrison Artillery. The RGA was heir to a more scientific tradition than its more swash-buckling brothers of the RFA and RHA. The heavy battery of 5th Division, tucked into a re-entrant north-east of Reumont, spotted flashes from German guns around Croix-Caluyau on the Bavay road and brought a destructive fire to bear on them. Later, when the Suffolks had been engulfed, the battery burst shells right on the knoll. The big 60-pdrs and their sturdy Clydesdales became something of a totem, and exhausted infantrymen patted the guns as they staggered past.

The Germans made little progress against the front of Smith-Dorrien's position but pushed back his left flank and, more threateningly, lapped entirely right round his right. Although the Suffolks were supported by elements of 2/Manchester and 2/Argyll and Sutherland Highlanders,

An 18-pounder near Ypres in October 1914. At Le Cateau there was no time to construct posi-tions like this: guns were fought in the open, using whatever natural cover was available.

their position was untenable. The Germans dragged machine-guns up from the main road to rake the knoll, two field howitzers shelled it over open sights and infantry lurked in gullies behind. The Suffolks' commanding officer was killed early on, and the second-in-command was wounded taking ammunition to the machine-guns. By midday Fergusson, who could see the battle from a rooftop in Reumont, knew that his right was near collapse, asked Smith-Dorrien for permission to withdraw, and decided to get his guns away.

Field guns and howitzers were attached to a limber drawn by six horses. After the guns had been brought into action the teams were led off, to be brought back when the guns were to be moved. Rory Macleod was serving one of his battery's two surviving guns when he looked back to see the teams hurtling up. 'Shells were bursting all round them,' he recalled. 'It was a magnificent sight. Now and then a man or a horse or a whole team would go down. It was like Balaclava all over again!' Three VCs were won for saving one of 37th (Howitzer) Battery's pieces, and so stirring was the sight of teams at the gallop that the Royal West Kent rose and cheered as they tore through its line south of the sunken road.

On the edge of the sunken road, 122nd Battery RFA had been hard hit by the time its teams arrived. Second Lieutenant 'Clarrie' Hodgson watched the Germans redouble their fire as they reached the position: 'Men and horses were just blown to pieces.' The gun-line was a shambles, and he was relieved when a shout went up: 'Every man for himself. Destroy the guns.' Lieutenant Lionel Lutyens saw one of his two guns away safely, but as the other team reached the sunken road the horses jibbed, and fire felled horses and drivers. Lutyens looked behind and saw that his groom was still there with his charger, Bronco. He found it hard to mount, but eventually got up. He:

... let him go down the road as fast as he could gallop ... it was an extraordinary sight, a wild scene of galloping horses, and then everyone gone, dead horses and dead men everywhere, four guns left solitary on the position, a few wagon limbers lying about and one standing on the skyline with its pole straight up in the air. *Voilà tout.*

At 1.40 p.m., Fergusson was given permission to withdraw. Once 5th Division was on the move, 3rd would follow suit, with 4th Division moving last of all. The retirement went better than might have been expected, and Smith-Dorrien thought the retreating men resembled a crowd coming away from a race meeting. The Suffolks were swamped at about 2.45 p.m., and 1/Gordon Highlanders, over at Audencourt, never received an order to withdraw, remained on the position until nightfall, and were forced to surrender as they stumbled into superior German forces in the dark. Although 2 Corps lost 7812 men and 38 guns, Smith-Dorrien had succeeded in his aim: the pursuit was never as pressing again. French paid him a handsome tribute in his dispatch, but he was never comfortable with the decision to stand and fight, and Smith-Dorrien's dismissal in 1915 has an echo of Le Cateau to it.

The Continuing Retreat
The retreat from Mons went on until 5 September, taking the BEF beyond the River Marne, where it contributed to the counter-attack which halted the German advance and then turned it into a retreat. As they reached the River Aisne the Germans dug in, and the war of movement began to freeze into immobility. Sir John French had had a trying campaign, and his suggestion that the BEF should withdraw from the line to refit had earned him a difficult interview with Lord Kitchener. But he caught the new tone of the war very quickly, telling the king: 'I think the battle of the Aisne is very typical of what battles in the future are most likely to resemble. Siege operations will enter largely into the tactical problems – the *spade* will be as great a necessity as the rifle, and the heaviest calibres of artillery will be brought up in support on either side.' It is as well that soldiers cannot see too far into the future. On their retreat, some of Smith-Dorrien's men crossed a little river at Voyennes, which Henry V's men had passed on their way to Agincourt. It was, of course, the Somme.

A View of the Field

The town of Mons was fought over in August 1914, and again when the Canadians liberated it in November 1918, but it sustained little damage. Its ring road and one-way system are unforgiving, but the town centre is unquestionably worth a visit. The Grande Place, at its centre, is largely unspoilt, and there is a museum in the Jardin du Mayeur behind the town hall, reached through an archway off the square. Its ground floor is devoted to the First World War and contains a good selection of Allied and German uniforms, weapons and equipment. The machine-gun in the entrance hall was used by the Cheshires at Audregnies and buried to avoid capture, and there is a photograph of Regimental Quartermaster Sergeant Fitzpatrick nearby. One of the upstairs floors contains a collection of ceramics, and the other is a sombre record of Mons under occupation.

Casteau

The British army's first and last shots of the war were fired on opposite sides of the N6 Brussels road in Casteau, across the canal from Mons. Just beyond Supreme Headquarters Allied Powers Europe, a monument north of the road commemorates the action of the 4th Dragoon Guards on 22 August 1914. Tom Bridges, the squadron leader, had prepared an ambush on the road with a mounted troop under Captain Charles Hornby ready to exploit it. An oncoming German cavalry patrol smelt a rat and fled, but Hornby pursued and there was a brief mounted clash before the Germans met the rest of their leading troop east of Casteau. Both sides dismounted, and Corporal Edward Thomas fired the first shot at a German officer who fell to the ground. The 4th Dragoon Guards then galloped on to Soignies where there was a more serious mounted action in the village street. 'Captain Hornby ran his sword through one Jerry,' remembered Private Ted Worrell, 'and Sergeant-Major Sharpe got another. I got a poke at a man but I don't know what happened to him.' Further down the road more German cavalry and lorried *jäger* appeared and the pursuit was called off. Across the road from the 1914 memorial, a plaque on a wall recalls the fact that Canadian infantry fired the last shots of the war nearby on 11 November 1918.

Nimy and Obourg

In the inter-war years the Mons–Condé Canal was re-routed to become part of the Canal du Centre, and now runs north-westwards towards Blaton from a new large pool at Nimy. A sadly diminished version of the old canal follows more or less its original path in a grubby concrete channel, but the old bridges have disappeared. Between Nimy and Obourg the canal follows its old route and, although wider and deeper, looks much the same as it did in 1914. Both Nimy Bridge and Obourg station are worth a visit. The former can be approached by parking in the little square at Nimy, just south of the modern span which replaces the old swing bridge, or driving on to the towpath. The current railway bridge is a girder construction much like its predecessor. Dease's guns were up on the abutments, and it is easy to see why the Fusiliers manning them fell like flies. A plaque beneath the bridge pays tribute to Dease, an Irishman from Meath, and Godley, a solidly built Londoner who sported the bushy moustache so characteristic of the Old Bills of 1914.

Obourg station is also on the south bank of the canal, east of the belching chimneys of Obourg cement works, the major local employer now that the mines have closed. When the old station building was demolished, a small section of wall was left to commemorate the stand made by 4/Middlesex and, in particular, one unknown hero. As the company at the station withdrew a soldier climbed on to the roof to cover his comrades' retreat, and continued to fire until the burning roof fell in. The nearby Middlesex Farm, defended by A Company 4/Middlesex, was, and still is, owned by the Abell family. A was Able Company in the phonetic alphabet of the day, and its commander, killed in action, was coincidentally called Major Abell.

The Bascule crossroads, where the N90 to Binche and Charleroi meets the N40 to Beaumont, is very busy, but there is a lay-by on the N90 and parking near an electrical showroom with the inspired name of So Watt. The Obourg chimneys help to establish the position of the canal, and the Middlesex and Royal Irish had a difficult time pulling back south-westwards, from right to left as we face the chimneys, through the tangle of houses, gardens and little woods, not to mention convent and town cemetery, between the canal and Mons itself.

The Château Gendebien lies amongst trees where the Bois la Haut begins to rise west of the crossroads. It was used as a field hospital in 1914 and was badly damaged by fire started by shells aimed at Fitzpatrick's men. It now houses NATO's Supreme Allied Commander Europe and is not open to the public. On one side of the Binche road a large monument, once in the centre of Mons, marks the town's significance for the British army of the First World War. On the other stands a Celtic cross, unveiled by Sir John French, a memorial to the Royal Irish Regiment whose forebears had fought for Marlborough nearby at Malplaquet.

War Graves

It was not until the First World War that British soldiers killed in action received individual burial as a matter of course. Most dead of battles such as Waterloo were stripped of anything of value by comrades, enemies or the looters who flocked to battlefields like vultures round a carcass, and were then tumbled, half-naked, into communal grave-pits. Officers might be interred in individual graves or repatriated in one grisly guise or another. In 1914 it soon became clear to Fabian Ware, then a Red Cross volunteer, that the nation would demand some account of its dead, and he was appointed to head the Graves Registration Commission which grew in 1917 into the Imperial (now Commonwealth) War Graves Commission.

Trips around battlefields often degenerate into cemetery crawls. It is easy to see why, for there is something unutterably poignant about these silent cities. They offer so much. Family inscriptions on headstones range from heart-rending through mawkish to triumphal. There are stark reminders of the age of the dead, from fourteen (Private John Condon of

British officers at the memorial commemorating the battle of Malplaquet (1709). The cobbled road is now busy tarmac: Mons lies a few miles beyond the crest.

the Royal Irish, killed in May 1915) to sixty-eight (Lieutenant Henry Webber of the South Lancashires, died of wounds in July 1916). Then there is military demography by microcosm, with old reservists with Boer War medals, youthful colonels with Distinguished Service Orders and Military Crosses and, most tragically, boys consumed by an omnivorous army as Britain ran out of men. 'School, War, Death' reads a family's bitter inscription on a headstone near Cambrai. Finally, there is pure military history, with those cap-badges of yesteryear, shining pride turned to stone.

If you only visit one war cemetery then St Symphorien, on a gently wooded hillock just down the Binche road, should be it. It was started by the Germans for their own and the British dead of Mons, although many others lie elsewhere. Heavy German headstones of regimental pattern bear a man's name, rank, unit and home town, and officers are buried separately. The first British were interred on the same basis, and there is a short 'officers' row' at the back of the cemetery. Many of the defenders of Obourg were buried in a mass grave, above which the Germans raised a column to the *Royal* Middlesex Regiment, taking the view that a unit which fought so hard must have been royal. A circle of British headstones around it names the men who are known to rest beneath.

Lieutenant Dease lies in the first group of British graves across from the left-hand entrance gate, with Private Price, the last Canadian killed, behind him. Where the path begins to wind around towards the rear of the cemetery lies Private Parr of the Middlesex, killed on reconnaissance, as the amended date on his headstone tells us, on 21 August 1914. On the other side of the path is Private Ellison of the 5th Lancers (private soldiers in line cavalry regiments were not called troopers until 1922) killed on 11 November 1918 and the last British fatality of the war. Futility, courage and irony are all there, and in the War Graves Commission's tending of this peaceful spot we are reminded that even in war, when human life may count for little, the human spirit is all.

Elouges
The scene of the flank-guard action near Elouges can be reached via the N30, which grinds its way out of Mons through forlorn suburbs. It is easier to take the autoroute, turning off at the Ville Pommeroeul exit and then heading south. The Roman road, down whose axis the 4th Dragoon Guards and 9th Lancers charged, runs from the northern end of Audregnies, past the sugar factory, to the N30, then the German gun-line. Tom Bridges and Roger Chance were on the road itself, and David Campbell's lancers charged through the field to their east. The road is barely passable to cars, but there is a good walk from Audregnies towards the sugar factory, and by turning right in a sharp cutting and then right again at l'Avaleresse (a colliery works in 1914) one can follow a narrow metalled road back to Audregnies on precisely the line held by the Norfolks and the Cheshires.

The Forest of Mormal
The direct route to the forest of Mormal crosses the border into France just south of Audregnies. A diversion takes the visitor through Hergies, Hon-Hergies and Taisnières-sur-Hon to the sprawling village of Malplaquet. Beyond its northern edge, close to the border, is an obelisk in the centre of the position defended, on 11 September 1709, by a French army under Marshal Villars. Although the Allies emerged as masters of the field it cost them 25 000 men and was Marlborough's bloodiest victory.

The forest of Mormal still divides major roads, but there are pleasant drives through it and a number of sylvan *auberges* at their quiet junctions. It was not impassable in August 1914, although poor maps and fear of ambush deterred most British units from using it.

Le Cateau
Le Cateau lies south of the forest in the valley of the little River Selle. It was the birthplace of Napoleon's Marshal Mortier, whose statue presides over the long and narrow square. In 1914 GHQ was in the attractive neoclassical school at the lower end of the square. The building now houses

the Matisse Museum, for the painter is another of Le Cateau's sons.

The sunken road runs south of the N43 Le Cateau–Cambrai road. It is crueller to cars than the Roman road at Audregnies, but a walk down it from Troisvilles towards Le Cateau puts Smith-Dorrien's right flank into perspective. Half-way along stands a prominent tree – l'Arbre Rond on the IGN map. This replaces a tree which stood there in 1914, on part of the road held by Ballard's Norfolks. The battalion stood in the second line that day with 1/Bedford towards the main road on its left front and 2/King's Own Scottish Borderers to its right. The tree was an obvious aiming mark for German gunners, and Ballard ordered his pioneers to fell it. The tree was almost down when the wind changed and threatened to blow it into the lane, blocking this valuable covered route. It had to be guyed up with ropes and was eventually pulled down into the field behind.

On the track's northern edge, just before its junction with the D932 St Quentin road, was 122nd Battery RFA. Lionel Lutyens and his fellow section commanders stood on the track, their six guns – a pair for each of the battery's three subalterns – in the field, sheltered from frontal fire by a smudge of rising ground. The gun-line soon became very unsafe, and we can see why. The spire of St Martin's church in Le Cateau, into which the Germans had inserted machine-guns, peeps up over the crest-line, and there were more machine-guns on the near lip of the cutting carrying the Cambrai road through a spur: a water tower stands helpfully above it.

To the right of the church, as Lutyens would have seen it, a handsome cenotaph in a square of trees shows where the Suffolks stood. The tracks on the far side of the St Quentin road are not helpful to the walker, and the Suffolk memorial is best reached by driving into Le Cateau, swinging south at the first set of lights and parking near the Collège J. Rostand before walking up on to the knoll. It is easy to see why the Suffolks and their supporting gunners were so vulnerable to fire from front and right flank and to attack by infantry seeping up the re-entrant behind the ceno-taph. Reumont, whence Sir Charles Fergusson commanded his division, is visible on a rise on the D932. There was once a plaque on the house itself, the second on the left when entering the village: its screw-holes still remain. A water tower in the centre of the western horizon marks the position of Bertry, Smith-Dorrien's headquarters, central in his corps' position. It is a tiny battlefield, and Wellington would have understood so much about it. Lines of infantry, kept steady by discipline, the bonds of mateship, a touch of sheer nastiness – Frank Richards hoped for 'a bang at the bastards' – brave leaders and the remembrance of things past. Gun-ners who would abandon neither the pieces they served nor the infantry they supported. Le Cateau was the last battle of the old war.

CHAPTER 4

The Somme
1916

Background

At 7.30 a.m. on 1 July 1916, 60 000 British soldiers scrambled out of their trenches on the uplands north of the Somme to begin the 'Big Push'. By noon almost 100 000 had been committed to battle, and by nightfall 57 470 were dead, wounded or missing. The British army lost more soldiers than it had fielded at Waterloo, Mons or Le Cateau, and probably more than fought on either side at Agincourt. It was the first day of a battle that ground on until November, and by its close there were 418 000 British casualties. These were the best of the nation's volunteer manhood, and the merest glance at its casualty roll shows what the Somme did to the old world of brass bands and cricket fields, pit-head cottages and broad acres.

It levelled the exalted. The prime minister's son, Lieutenant Herbert Asquith, and Lieutenant the Hon. Edward Tennant were part of that fusion of Leicestershire hunting world and London society known as the Souls: they lie in the same cemetery at Guillemont. Nearby, Second Lieutenant George Marsden-Smedley, not long out of Harrow, where he had captained both the cricket and football teams, died in his first action. It mauled the artistic. H.H. Munro, who wrote short stories as Saki, was killed while serving as a Lance-Sergeant in the Royal Fusiliers. Lieutenant William Noel Hodgson MC, poet and Cambridge contemporary of Rupert Brooke, had begged for strength to face the death he found on 1 July.

> By all the delights that I shall miss,
> Help me to die, O Lord.

George Butterworth, the composer, whose music for *A Shropshire Lad* breathes the scent of peacetime's last summers, died as a captain in the

To My Truest of Pals.

"MY MOTHER."

May the LORD watch for ever between me and thee
When we are absent one from the other ;
Are the words that I send with heart full of love.
To the best of dear pals, MY MOTHER.

For King, Queen and Country we're fighting,
"Honour and Right " is our watchword true ;
Tho' " Might " at first seemed to hold the sway,
Naught shall conquer the Red, White and Blue.

'Twas some time since that I left my loved home,
To answer old England's cry ;
The parting was hard, and tho' she tried to be brave,
There was a tear in my dear mother's eye.

" God bless you " said she, " God bless her," say I,
For of mothers, no man had a better ;
And while I'm at FOVANT or when I go to the Front
She knows I shall never forget her.

So, cheer up, Dear Mother, my Truest of Pals,
Tho' at parting your heart may feel sore,
We will all look forward with hearts full of hope
To true happiness when peace comes once more.

From _____ " FIT AND READY."

The first day of the Somme saw terrible losses amongst the Pals' battalions of wartime volunteers. H.D. Riley *(above, centre)* founded the Burnley Lads' Club in 1905, and in 1914 commanded the Burnley company of the Accrington Pals *(below)*. He died, with many of his men, on 1 July 1916. The words of this postcard reflect the fact that many of the Pals were very young.

Durham Light Infantry, and like so many of his comrades has no known grave.

It blighted families. Sergeant George Lee and his son Corporal Robert Frederick Lee died on 5 September. Lieutenant Arthur Tregaskis lies beside his brother Leonard in Flat Iron Copse Cemetery with two other pairs of brothers, Corporal T. and Lance-Corporal H. Hardwidge, and Privates Ernest and Herbert Philby. It decimated communities. Three battalions of Lancashire Fusiliers, recruited from 'the docklands, engineering workshops, mines and mills of Salford', lost 41 officers and 942 men on 1 July.

It savaged the new world as it rallied to the old. The Newfoundland Battalion lost 715 officers and men on 1 July, the heaviest casualty rate of any battalion that day. Later, the South Africans suffered in Delville Wood and the Canadians at Courcelette. The Australians lost an appalling 23 000 men at Pozières. It is difficult to be objective about the Australian experience, shot through with myth and counter-myth. Even at the baldest level there was something remarkable about those rangy characters in slouch hats, summoned to a distant fight that brought disillusionment or death. Lieutenant Bert Crowe scribbled his last lines home:

The pain is getting worse and worse. I am very sorry dear, but still you will be well provided for and I am easy on that score. So cheer up dear I could write on a lot but am nearly unconscious. Give my love to Dear Bill and yourself, do take care of yourself and him. Your loving husband Bert.

They expected no privileges: W.J. Johnson, a member of the Australian parliament, fell as a private in the infantry. And above all they tried to die game. Lieutenant Archie Dean appeared at a dressing station with a verse from a popular song – 'Here we are! Here we are! Here we are again!' – and the top blown off his skull. 'He was as game as any man could be,' wrote his platoon sergeant, 'and refused attendance until the wounds of the others were dressed.' He died nearly five months later.

The Progress of the War

The Somme was the misshapen child of 1915. By Christmas 1914 the British Expeditionary Force (BEF) had lost 90 000 men: in those thousand-strong battalions which had marched up to Mons in August there remained on average one officer and thirty men. France's losses were even more catastrophic, approaching a million men and nearly half her regular officers. The Western Front was locked in stalemate, and in 1915 the Allies hoped to break the deadlock either, as the 'Westerners' argued, by beating the Germans in France or, as the 'Easterners' hoped, by finding another, more promising, theatre.

They failed. Attempts to break the German line by assault – the British attacked at Neuve Chapelle, Festubert and Aubers Ridge in the spring and at Loos in September 1915 – made little progress. Sir John French blamed early defeats on lack of ammunition, and the ensuing 'shells scandal' helped to replace the Liberal government with a coalition. Although the one major German offensive in the west, at Ypres in May, was repulsed, it claimed many men and much ground. A bid to knock Germany's ally Turkey out of the war failed when an Anglo-French force was unable to secure the Gallipoli peninsula.

In December 1915 Allied representatives met at Chantilly to determine strategy for the coming year. They concluded that a decision could only be achieved on those fronts where the enemy was massed: France, Italy and Russia. Offensives were to be co-ordinated so that German reserves could not be moved from one front to another. Local attacks to wear out the Germans could be launched 'by those powers which still have abundant reserves of men'. With ninety-five divisions on the Western Front, France was beginning to reach the end of her available manpower. Britain had thirty-eight divisions in France and fifty-one in training or in other theatres, and her human resources had never been better. It was evident that whatever form the war took in 1916, Britain's share of the burden could only increase.

Sir John French was one of the casualties of Loos: on 18 December 1915 he was replaced by Sir Douglas Haig, who had commanded 1 Corps at Mons. Scarcely had Haig assumed command than the French announced that they were only strong enough for one major attack that year, which they proposed to co-ordinate with a Russian effort in July. They hoped that the British would undertake 'wearing-out fights' to whittle down German resources. Haig argued that these would 'entail considerable loss on us with little to show for it'. On 14 February 1916 he persuaded the French commander-in-chief, General Joseph Joffre, to abandon them, and in return agreed that 'the main French and British attacks are to be "jointives", that is, side by side' where the Allied armies met on the Somme. In fact, Haig was not convinced. There were compelling arguments for an offensive at Ypres, where a short advance might put the key rail junction at Roulers within reach. Nor were his political masters any clearer, and it was not until April that they formally agreed to support a joint offensive in the west.

By this time circumstances had changed. General Erich von Falkenhayn had replaced the worn-out Moltke as *de facto* commander-in-chief of the German army in autumn 1914. In December 1915 he concluded that Germany's most obdurate foe was England, and that his best chance of victory was to knock 'England's best sword', the French army, from her hand. This could be achieved by attacking an objective 'for the retention of which the French General Staff will be compelled to throw in every man they have. If they do so the forces of France will bleed to death ...' The chosen target was Verdun, and the attack began in February 1916, supported by the heaviest artillery concentration the world had seen. It soon bogged down, and if the French were being bled white the Germans were also haemorrhaging. Verdun not only demanded a speedy opening of the Allied offensive but also reduced the number of French troops available for it.

We cannot be sure of Haig's real hopes for the Somme. The evidence suggests that he hoped to break through the German lines although he was unwilling to tell the cautious government so. The British military theorist Basil Liddell Hart maintained it was only when it was evident that there would be no quick victory that 'the story was spread by officially inspired apologists that Haig was throughout aiming at a campaign of attrition and had not dreamt of a "breakthrough".' General Sir Henry Rawlinson, whose 4th Army was to launch the attack, thought that the commander-in-chief hoped for a breakthrough. He himself had more restrained expectations, and favoured 'bite and hold' operations, with artillery rendering the German front line untenable so that it could be occupied with little cost. Haig felt that Rawlinson's proposals did not go far enough, and urged him to consider 'the possibility of pushing our first advance further than is contemplated in your plan'. Rawlinson did so, although he confided to his diary: 'I feel pretty confident of success, though only after heavy fighting. That the Boche will break and a debacle will supervene I do not believe.'

As the British army expanded it took over the front from the French, and by July 1916 its line ran from Ypres to Maricourt, above the Somme. The Ypres area was held by 2nd Army, 1st Army covered the low-lying ground around Loos and La Bassée, 3rd Army was responsible for Vimy Ridge and Arras, handing over to Rawlinson's 4th Army south of Gommecourt. A new Reserve Army, intended to capitalize on 4th Army's breakthrough, had just been formed under Lieutenant-General Sir Hubert Gough, and during the Somme fighting it became 5th Army.

Kitchener's 'New Armies'
This astonishing growth in the size of the British army owed much to Lord Kitchener. Whatever his failings, the secretary of state for war was

amongst the minority who believed that the war would not be over by Christmas 1914. No sooner was he in office than he took steps to increase the army and called for 100 000 volunteers. He had a mistakenly low regard for the Territorial Force and, instead of recruiting through its County Associations, he raised the 'New Armies' through the Adjutant-General's Department at the War Office. Further appeals produced sufficient volunteers to send thirty New Army divisions abroad by 1 July 1916. Such was the scale of this achievement that, as Peter Simkins points out, 'more men joined the Army voluntarily between August 1914 and December 1915 than were conscripted in 1916 and 1917 combined.'

Patriotism, duty, boredom, pressure from friends or employers, the lure of adventure or momentary whim all encouraged men to enlist. Mining and industrial areas were well represented: Lancashire, Yorkshire and Scotland between them provided more than one-third of the overall total of 250 New Army battalions. Many of 'Kitchener's men' came from backgrounds which had not usually furnished soldiers. Lieutenant-Colonel C.H. Cobb, commanding 5/Oxfordshire and Buckinghamshire Light Infantry, recalled:

There were a great many from the most respectable homes and businesses. Some gentlemen, many indoor servants, grooms, gardeners, gamekeepers, well-to-do tradesmen, hotel-keepers, clerks, etc., etc., to say nothing of the engineers, fitters and hands from the great works in Birmingham and Coventry. All these men had left good, comfortable homes, with good wages, and had come voluntarily out of a sheer sense of duty.

Lieutenant Charles Douie of 7/Dorsets agreed. His comrades 'took soldiering seriously, as a means to an end, in their hope of a rapid end. The war was not a crusade in their eyes; it was a disagreeable job which had to be seen through, however long it took and whatever sacrifice it entailed ...'

Most volunteers joined 'Service' battalions of county regiments, numbered consecutively after Regular, Special Reserve and Territorial battalions. Many were raised locally, with eager support from civic authorities, and rejoiced in names which never appeared on the Army List but summed up identity better than a formal title ever could. Glasgow's three new units were battalions of the Highland Light Infantry. The 15th, recruited from employees of the City Tramways, was the Tramways Battalion; old members of the Boys' Brigade joined the 16th, the Boys' Brigade Battalion; while the 17th, raised by the Chamber of Commerce, answered to the name of the Glasgow Commercials.

Let one of these Pals' battalions speak for so many others. Councillor

THE BATTLEFIELD OF THE SOMME
July-November 1916

—xxxx—	Army boundary 1 July
—xxx—	Corps boundary 1 July
—xx—	Division boundary 1 July
••••••	British Gains 1 July
•	Place of Interest
——	Roads

```
0        1        2        3 Miles
├────────┼────────┼────────┤
0    1    2    3    4    5 Kms
```

Refer to page 15 for a comprehensive key to all military symbols

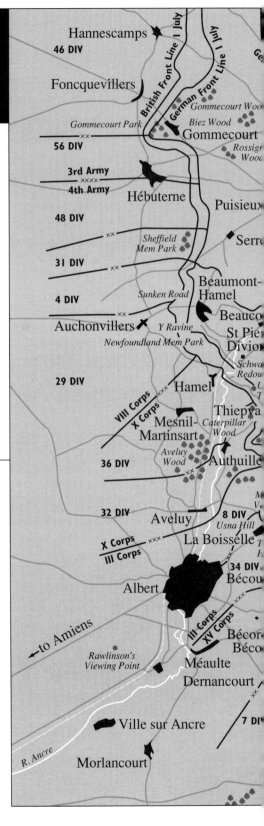

British Front Line 1 July
German Front Line 1 July

Hannescamps
46 DIV
Foncquevillers
Gommecourt Woo
Biez Wood
Gommecourt Park
Gommecourt
56 DIV
Rossign
Woo
3rd Army
4th Army
Hébuterne
Puisieux
48 DIV
Sheffield Mem Park
Serre
31 DIV
Beaumont-Hamel
4 DIV
Sunken Road
Beauco
St Pier
Auchonvillers
Y Ravine
Divion
Newfoundland Mem Park
Schwa
Redou
29 DIV
Hamel
Thiepva
VIII Corps
X Corps
Mesnil-Martinsart
Caterpillar Wood
36 DIV
Aveluy Wood
Authuille
32 DIV
Aveluy
8 DIV
Usna Hill
X Corps
III Corps
La Boisselle
34 DIV
Bécou
Albert
III Corps
XV Corps
Bécor
Bécor
to Amiens
Rawlinson's Viewing Point
Méaulte
Dernancourt
7 DIV
Ville sur Ancre
R. Ancre
Morlancourt

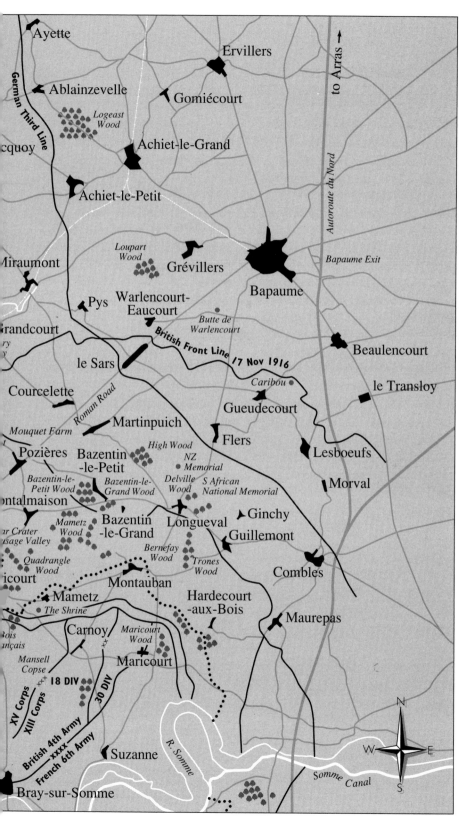

Ayette

Ervillers

to Arras →

German Third Line

Ablainzevelle

Gomiécourt

Logeast Wood

Achiet-le-Grand

Autoroute du Nord

cquoy

Achiet-le-Petit

Miraumont

Loupart Wood

Grévillers

Bapaume

Bapaume Exit

Pys

Warlencourt-Eaucourt

randcourt
ry
y

Butte de Warlencourt

British Front Line 17 Nov 1916

Beaulencourt

le Sars

Caribou

le Transloy

Courcelette

Gueudecourt

Roman Road

Martinpuich

Flers

Lesboeufs

Mouquet Farm

Pozières

High Wood
NZ
Memorial

Bazentin
-le-Petit

Morval

Bazentin-le-Petit Wood

Bazentin-le-Grand Wood

Delville Wood

S African National Memorial

ntalmaison

Mametz Wood

Bazentin
-le-Grand

Longueval

Ginchy

r Crater
sage Valley

Guillemont

Quadrangle Wood

Bernefay Wood

Trones Wood

icourt

Combles

Mametz

Montauban

Hardecourt
-aux-Bois

The Shrine

Maurepas

Carnoy

Maricourt Wood

Bois
nçais

Mansell Copse

18 DIV

Maricourt

XV Corps

XIII Corps

30 DIV

British 4th Army

French 6th Army

Suzanne

R. Somme

Somme Canal

Bray-sur-Somme

N
W · E
S

John Harwood JP, Lord Mayor of Accrington, offered to raise a battalion. The War Office accepted his proposal, and he began recruiting in and around Accrington on 7 September 1914. In 10 days 36 officers and 1076 men joined what was officially the 11th (Service) Battalion The East Lancashire Regiment, but which has left its mark on history as the Accrington Pals. Loyalties within the battalion mirrored peacetime associations. H.D. Riley, prominent local employer and Justice of the Peace, was a leading supporter of the Burnley Lads' Club. In September 1914 Riley volunteered for D (Burnley) Company of the Pals, and seventy Lads' Club members enlisted with him. Councillor Harwood selected his own officers, and it was natural that Riley should command D Company.

The case of the Accringtons highlights the problem of providing officers and NCOs. Martin Middlebrook, whose book *The First Day of the Somme* broke new ground in the historiography of the war, examined the 21st Division and found that every battalion commander had been a retired officer on the outbreak of war. Of the other officers, only fourteen had any military experience. The remainder, over 400, were newly commissioned. Some had been on a War Office list of 2000 'young gentlemen' who had just left public school or university, and others were professional men. Yet not all professional men wanted to be officers. The 1st Sportsmen's Battalion (23/Royal Fusiliers) included in its ranks two England cricketers, the country's lightweight boxing champion and the former lord mayor of Exeter. 8/East Surreys found itself with one sergeant-major as its only NCO. A dozen old reservists were made lance-corporals, 'much to their horror and indignation,' and anybody 'who had been in charge of anyone else or who wanted to be' also found himself a lance-corporal. The adjutant acknowledged that it was 'a rough and ready system, but it worked out well and nearly all of them made good'.

It was less easy to improvise weapons and equipment, and some battalions spent their first weeks in tented camps with no uniforms. Blue serge uniforms, unpopular because they resembled those worn by postmen, were eventually replaced by khaki. Rifles were slow in coming: the 12/York and Lancaster, the Sheffield City Battalion, received its full complement in November 1915. Machine-guns were as hard to acquire, and much early training was carried out to the accompaniment of policemen's rattles. Gunners were even worse off: 34th Division's artillery had only three days' practice on real weapons before embarkation.

Lack of experienced officers and NCOs combined with the shortage of modern weapons to restrict training, and not all divisional commanders were as imaginative as Major-General Maxse of 18th Division, who placed special emphasis on the thorough training of platoons by the young officers in command of them. In any event it was not clear what training should consist of. As Paddy Griffith has demonstrated in *Battle Tactics of the Western Front*, the British army had begun to develop doctrine for trench warfare. Nevertheless, it was poor at distillation of best practice, and Griffith is right to maintain that in July 1916 the 'machine looked magnificent on the drawing board, but … in reality was unready in almost all of its parts'. The Somme turned a largely inexperienced mass army into a largely experienced one. But the men who were to attack on 1 July had not come to the Somme to learn: they had come to win the war.

The Battle

There was no particular merit to attacking on the Somme: it was simply where the Allied armies met. The Roman road from Albert to Bapaume slashes the battlefield. When Henry V passed on his way to Agincourt, Albert was known as Ancre from the river of that name which winds southwards to join the Somme at Corbie. It had been a pilgrimage centre, although the number of pilgrims had never come up to expectations and the basilica of Notre-Dame-des-Brebières, topped by a gilded statue of the Virgin, seemed large for a town of 9000 souls. It is a big, confident landscape, downland sprinkled with woods, large hedgeless fields growing wheat and sugar-beet, farms four-square like fortresses, and villages of close-ranked redbrick houses.

The sector had been quiet since the front solidified in 1914, and German positions took advantage of the fields of fire offered by open countryside and the protection afforded by villages. As it ran down from the north, the German front line looped in front of Gommecourt Wood and crossed the fields between Hébuterne and Serre, the latter, like other front-line villages, a self-contained strongpoint. After dipping across the Serre–Mailly-Maillet road the line clung to the crest of what the British called Redan Ridge, then slid into a re-entrant on the western edge of Beaumont-Hamel to ascend Hawthorn Ridge, where a redoubt dominated the approaches from Auchonvillers.

Just beyond Hawthorn Ridge Redoubt the line jinked south-eastwards through the gash of Y Ravine and then fell gently into the marshy valley of the Ancre, rising again to curl with the contours in front of Thiepval and Ovillers. It followed the Roman road on the northern edge of La Boisselle, crossing south-west of the village to stretch out over the ridge to the western edge of Fricourt. From Fricourt the line turned to run almost due west to the Maricourt–Longueval road, where British and French forces met. Although the Germans looked down from the long ridge from Mametz to Montauban, the ground favoured them less in this sector than on those spurs further north, each dominated by its fellows to left and right so that local successes would be cancelled out by flanking failures.

In the Trenches

The trenches of 1916 bore as much relation to the scratchings of British defenders of Mons as a jumbo jet does to a paper dart. The Germans had originally believed in having 'one good line and that a strong one', but experience of 1915, where the British had broken through the front line to be stopped further back, had shown the value of depth, and by 1916 the Germans thought in terms of forward, reserve and support positions. Each position comprised several parallel trenches, connected to one another and to positions further back by communication trenches. Second and third positions on the Somme were incomplete, but the ridges lent themselves to defence in depth and the Germans had done much work on a second position running across the crest behind Pozières and had begun a third through Le Sars.

The construction of front-line trenches varied, but most were about 8 feet (2.5 metres) deep, with a parapet of earth and sandbags facing the enemy and a lower parados at the rear. Sides were revetted with planks, wattle or corrugated iron, and a firestep enabled occupants to step up from the comparative safety of the duckboards to peer out across the parapet. Narrow trenches known as saps, with listening posts at their ends, poked out towards the enemy. Trenches followed the crenellated line of a Greek frieze so that the effect of shellbursts would be minimized and enemy intrusions contained. A belt of barbed wire, often 20–30 yards (18–27 metres) deep, ran on the enemy side of the trench. There was a strip of no man's land, whose width varied from a few yards to several hundred, then the enemy's wire and finally his own trench systems.

Although most infantrymen carried a rifle, this was of limited use in trench warfare. When field guns were not busy on other tasks they were laid on what the British termed 'SOS lines' in front of trenches, their fire called down by field telephone or signalling pistol. Trench-mortars lobbed 'toffee apples' or 'flying pigs' to blow in sections of trench; snipers picked off individuals; and machine-guns, sited to fire obliquely along the wire, dealt with larger targets. Both armies still manned medium machine-guns on tripods or sledges, but had developed lighter versions, the Lewis for the British and the 08/15 Spandau for the Germans.

Men of 1/Lancashire Fusiliers (29th Division)
fixing bayonets before attacking Beaumont-
Hamel, by way of the sunken road, on 1 July
1916. The officer in the centre is wearing a private soldier's tunic to appear less conspicuous.
Company Sergeant-Major Ernest Shephard was
in 1/Dorset, part of 32nd Division, which
attacked Thiepval. His beautifully-kept diary
describes receiving 'heavy shell and shrapnel'
in the concentration area, and then a day of
'miraculous escapes' which cost his company
over 100 men. Commissioned in December
1916, Shephard was killed near Beaumont-
Hamel the following month and is buried in
the AIF Military Cemetery, Flers.

Once attackers entered a trench they relied heavily on hand grenades, the British Mills bomb and the German stick grenade, and would try to bomb their way from traverse to traverse, bayonet men dashing in as grenades exploded.

Units rotated between tours of duty in front-line trenches, support systems and rest or training: a German battalion might spend four days in the front line, two in support and four at rest. Soldiers lived in dug-outs, entered by steps leading down from the trenches. Somme chalk lent itself to dug-out construction and the Germans, with no advance in mind, had built some splendid specimens, 30–40 feet (9–12 metres) deep, many with electric light and wood-panelled walls. These were impenetrable by all but the heaviest guns, although a direct hit could blow in a dug-out's entrance and entomb the occupants.

The Plan of Campaign
We have seen that Haig and Rawlinson had different expectations. Haig directed Rawlinson to advance $1\frac{1}{2}$ miles (2.4 km) on a front of 14 miles (23 km) on the first day of the Somme, enabling Gough's Reserve Army to push through the gap and seize Bapaume before swinging north towards Arras. Although Rawlinson doubted if things would be this simple, he was confident that the German first position would be taken, and the process could be repeated as 4th Army chewed its way to Bapaume bite by bite. Brigadier-General Gordon of 8th Infantry Brigade was expounding orthodoxy when he told men that they could 'slope arms, light up your pipes and cigarettes, and march all the way to Pozières before meeting any live Germans'.

This assurance stemmed from the fact that 1 500 000 shells were to be fired in the week before the attack, 18-pdrs working on wire and trenches, and heavier pieces concentrating on strongpoints and batteries. Once the battle began, a 'creeping barrage', a novelty for its day, would move ahead of the infantry. The artillery preparation proved inadequate and, on 1 July, men discovered to their cost that many Germans had survived in their dug-outs. There were proportionately fewer guns than had been available at Neuve Chapelle: the French to the south had twice as many heavy guns per yard of front line. A combination of faulty fuses and shot-out barrels meant that as many as one in three shells failed to explode. It was difficult to cut wire with shrapnel, and a high-explosive round with a 'graze' fuse was not readily available. There was no universal answer to the problem of dug-outs. However, the most menacing German positions would be dealt with by eight large and eleven small mines. Tunnels were dug forward from the

British lines to create explosive-packed chambers beneath features like the Hawthorn Ridge Redoubt. Most of these were to be blown at 7.28 a.m., two minutes before the assault began.

The bombardment began on 24 June. 'My Lord the gun has come into his own,' wrote one artillery officer, 'and his kingdom today is large: it is the world.' Another, standing on a gun-pit in the dark, felt 'the thousands of tons of metal rushing away from one'. A major in the Grimsby Chums reflected on the beauty of the German trenches under fire, 'our shells bursting over them in yellow, black or white puffs, many of the trenches covered by a bright yellow weed; while between the heavy white lines of chalk marking the principal trenches, there are frequently large fields of brilliant scarlet poppies.'

Above the battlefield, reconnaissance aircraft took photographs and spotted for the guns. Lieutenant C.S. Lewis found it hard to hold his plane steady in the torrent of shells. 'At two thousand feet [610 metres] we were in the path of the gun trajectories,' he wrote, 'and as the shells passed, above or below us, the wind eddies made by their motion flung the machine up and down as if in a gale. Each bump meant that a passing shell had missed the machine by four or five feet [1.2–1.5 metres] …' The attack had been intended to start on 29 June, but heavy summer storms restricted visibility, vital for accurate observation of artillery fire, and persuaded Rawlinson to delay it until 1 July.

Postponement tweaked pre-battle nerves. Patrols brought in news that the wire was uncut, and a gunner officer in 29th Division told his head-quarters that the barrage would move faster than the infantry could follow. The plan was too complex to be altered by mere fact. Rawlinson had long since closed the debate, warning that 'All criticism by subordinates … of orders received from superior authority will, in the end, recoil on the critics.'

As battalions packed the crowded trenches on the night of 30 June, men asked themselves how they would cope with the challenge that approached with every tick of the watch. Many realized that they had no time to say all they needed to, and did their best in last letters. Second Lieutenant J.S. Engell told his parents:

The day has almost dawned when I shall really do my little bit in the cause of civilization … Should it be God's holy will to call me away, I am quite prepared to go … I could not wish for a finer death, and you, dear Mother and Dad, will know that I died doing my duty to my God, my country and my King.

Another officer gazed at the stars, and mused: 'What an insignificant thing the loss of say 40 years of life is to them …Well, Goodbye, you darlings.'

The Start of the Battle

At 7.20 a.m. on 1 July, as the bombardment reached its crescendo, the Hawthorn Ridge mine was blown, and the others exploded eight minutes later in what was then the loudest ever man-made sound. At 7.30 a.m. officers blew whistles and led their men across the parapet, through pre-cut gaps in the British wire and out into no man's land to form up for the assault. Most battalions were expecting to move forward at a walk, occupying defences levelled by artillery, not conducting a fighting advance against determined opposition, and men were heavily laden. General Sir Anthony Farrar-Hockley declared that 'no man carried less than 65 lb [29 kg]. Often additional grenades, bombs, small arms ammunition or perhaps a prepared charge against obstacles increased the load to 85 or 90 lb [38 or 41 kg].'

The difficulties of forming up a battalion of 600–800 men on ground hacked by shell-holes and trenches and strewn with wire merit consideration. What were to look like lines of advancing infantry were a series of columns moving side by side, with battalions moving on a front of one or two companies, and most covering perhaps 400 yards (365 metres) of frontage and a depth of 900 yards (823 metres). Control was by voice and whistle, although some officers tied pennons or handkerchiefs to walking sticks to help men to find them, and at least one wore his sword. Coloured triangles fixed to packs distinguished officers and NCOs, and tin reflectors worn on the back helped low-flying 'contact patrols' of the Royal Flying Corps to identify British troops.

What happened after 7.30 a.m. followed no consistent pattern, although there were grim similarities. In the north, at Gommecourt, two Territorial Divisions of 3rd Army mounted a two-pronged attack designed to draw in German reserves. The elaborate digging of trenches for waiting troops had left the Germans in no doubt of what was to come, and attackers in the northern division, 46th North Midland, were hewn down by machine-gun fire as they bunched in front of the few gaps in the German wire. The southern division, 56th London, fought its way into Gommecourt Wood. Some brave souls almost reached the point at which they were to have met the Midlanders, but were swamped by the inevitable counter-attack. One defender felt 'it wasn't fair to send these young soldiers against us. Some of them were only students and we felt very sorry for them.'

The story was the same opposite Serre, where the 31st Division left its strength on the German wire. Across the Serre road, elements of 4th Division took the Heidenkopf strongpoint on Redan Ridge and briefly got some little way beyond it. Further south, opposite Beaumont-Hamel, the attackers came from the last of the old regular divisions, a veteran of Gallipoli. It is no reflection on the quality or courage of what was widely known as the 'incomparable' 29th Division that it made no progress whatsoever.

Things were different south of the Ancre. The Schwaben Redoubt, dominating the high ground between the river and Thiepval, was attacked by the 36th Ulster Division. This had largely been recruited from members of the pre-war Ulster Volunteer Force, sworn to resist the imposition of Home Rule. It is as difficult to be objective about the Ulster Division as it is about the Australians. In fact, it contained soldiers from both sides of Ireland's cultural divide, although the majority were indeed Protestant. Some wore their Orangemen's sashes over their equipment, and there was a mood of exultation that would not brook waiting about in no man's land.

The Ulstermen were fortunate in that their assembly area in Thiepval Wood was close to the German front line and in dead ground, and at 7.30 a.m. they were into the German position before survivors had a chance to emerge from their dug-outs. The official history speaks of 'a steady pace with the precision of a parade movement', but one of the reasons for the division's success was its dash and momentum. The Schwaben was captured after the sort of hand-to-hand fighting that a veteran of Agincourt might have identified with. Men killed one another with bayonet and butt, shovel and explosive. Attackers dropped bags of grenades and trench-mortar bombs into dug-outs: one remembered that 'the yells and screams of those boys down there were wicked'.

A follow-up brigade tried to push through into the German second position, but machine-guns in Thiepval laced the flanks of the advance and artillery drew a curtain of fire across no man's land. When his West Belfast Company wavered, Major George Gaffikin took off his orange sash and waved it, bellowing 'Come on, boys! No surrender.' A few of the Ulstermen got into the second line but, unsupported, could not remain there. Nevertheless, although the Germans regained the Schwaben late in the afternoon, when 36th Division was relieved that night it handed over 800 yards (730 metres) of German front-line trench.

The Thiepval spur was the key to the whole front between the River Ancre and the Roman road. Thiepval's houses had been demolished by shellfire, but their debris covered deep cellars and defenders had tunnelled between them to create a position of enormous strength. On the

Overleaf: Artist André Devambez has caught French troops at the moment of assault on the Somme. Belts of French and German wire are clearly visible. Attacking troops are climbing ladders out of the front-line trench, into no-man's land, while others pack the communication trenches behind them.

southern face of the spur, grinning out south and west, stood the Leipzig Redoubt. When 32nd Division attacked Thiepval its only success came at the Leipzig. Brigadier-General Jardine had been attached to the Japanese army during the Russo-Japanese War (1904–5), and had noticed that successful Japanese infantry assaults went in over very short distances. Accordingly, at 7.23 p.m. the leading companies of Glasgow Commercials crept close to the German line and rushed it when the barrage lifted. They were in the Leipzig before its defenders surfaced.

Between Thiepval and the Roman road, 8th Division attacked Ovillers, its right flank pushing up Mash Valley, a long re-entrant with the La Boisselle spur to its south. The feature was twinned with Sausage Valley, named after the German observation balloons which had flown above it, on the other side of the spur. That day it was mash valley indeed, and 2/Middlesex, whose commanding officer had been concerned about the problem of flanking fire, lost 623 of its soldiers.

The fate of 34th Division, on the other side of the spur, was even crueller. Only two of its brigades could start from the British front line at the foot of the slope, and the third, 103rd (Tyneside Irish) Brigade, had to begin its advance from the far side of a low ridge, its twin peaks known as Tara and Usna hills, moving almost 1 mile (1.6 km) across open country to the front line. The explosion of the huge Lochnagar mine and a cluster of smaller mines further north enabled assaulting battalions to penetrate the German front line, and isolated parties got as far as Contalmaison, deep in the second position. But the flanks of the penetration were not secured, and as Tyneside Irish marched forward, keeping step to the beat of a single bass drum in the centre of the brigade, they were subjected to unceasing and accurate machine-gun fire. The division lost 6380 men that day, including a brigadier and seven out of twelve battalion commanders.

At Fricourt, further south, 21st Division made poor progress, but on its right 7th Division took and held Mametz. Major-General Maxse's 18th Division pushed on to seize Montauban Alley, the trench system on the far side of the Mametz–Montauban road. As for 30th Division, it did even better. It profited from the fact that the French, on its immediate right, were well provided with heavy guns and the bombardment was unusually effective. However, a single German machine-gun, firing with cool deliberation from 18th Division's sector into the flank of the advance, hit every company commander in the leading waves and remained in action until knocked out by a Lewis gun team of 2/Manchester Pals.

The performance of German machine-gunners attracted the admiration of many British soldiers. One officer called them: 'Topping fellows.

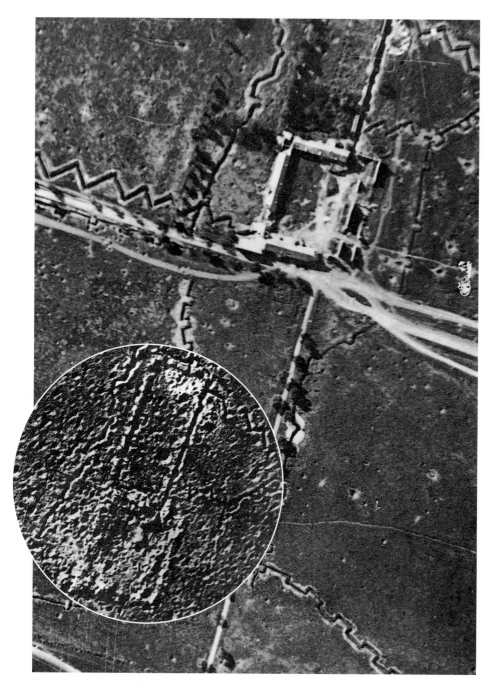

This aerial view of Mouquet Farm, strongpoint in the German second position, was taken in July and shows the outline of trenches and the fact that little damage had been done to defences this far back. The inset was taken in September, revealing how incessant bombardment transformed the area.

Fight until they are killed. They gave us hell.' Another saw a grey-haired German machine-gunner slumped behind his gun surrounded by a pile of empty cases almost as high as the gun. When an advancing section passed a dead machine-gunner, one of its members heard 'a murmur of approbation' from his mates.

Despite the efforts of the unknown machine-gunner, 30th Division took Montauban and the nearby brickworks. North of the Somme, General Balfourier's 'Iron' Corps had made good progress, while south of the river, where the French achieved surprise by attacking at 9.30 a.m., results were even more impressive. They had heavier guns than the British: eighty-five heavy batteries had engaged 7983 yards (7300 metres) of trench for nearly eight days. Their tactics were more flexible, attackers shoving on in small groups, ducking and weaving their way forward and supporting one another by fire.

This had little to do with abstract thought and much to do with experience. The first day of the Somme was the 132nd day of Verdun, and the French had been learning. The British, too, were to learn fast, although we must doubt whether 57 470 men were a fair price for the teaching. The Germans, for their part, lost 2200 prisoners, and casualties for the bombardment and the first day of the battle may have totalled 8000.

The Battle Goes On

Over the next few days Haig shifted his balance, giving Gough command north of the Roman road, where the German first position was largely intact, while south of the road Rawlinson took on the second position. This ran along Longueval Ridge, with two prominent woods, Delville Wood and High Wood (Bois des Fourcaux) astride it. Its fall would expose Pozières and in turn isolate Thiepval, undermining the German position south of the Ancre. Before Rawlinson's men could get to grips with the position they had to deal with Mametz Wood, 'that menacing wall of gloom', which stood like a bastion in front of it. Most of its trees – oak, beech and birch – were still standing, and those that had been blown down by shellfire thickened the tangled undergrowth. Second Lieutenant Siegfried Sassoon's 2/Royal Welch Fusiliers had approached it on 3 July, passing British dead 'their fingers mingled in bloodstained bunches, as though they were acknowledging the companionship of death,' to discover that even if the wood had been empty two days before it was now 'full of Germans'.

On 7 July, Mametz Wood was attacked by the New Army's 38th (Welsh) Division, whose composition owed much to the political influence of David Lloyd George. It had not fought a major action before, and

Sassoon found his trench filled by 'a jostling company of exclamatory Welshmen ... I understood the doomed condition of these half trained civilians who had been sent up to attack the Wood.' An initial attack failed, and on 10 July the division mounted a more forceful effort under a new commander, crashing into the wood from the south.

The attackers tried to clear the wood in sections, ride by ride, but it was impossible to keep direction in the tangle. Shelling only worsened matters. Lieutenant Wyn Griffith saw 'limbs and mutilated trunks, here and there a detached head, forming splashes of red against the green leaves ... one tree held in its branches a leg, with its torn flesh hanging down over a spray of leaf.' Captain Robert Graves crept into the wood at night in search of German overcoats to use as blankets, and found it 'full of dead Prussian Guards Reserve, big men, and dead Royal Welch and South Wales Borderers of the New Army battalions, little men.' By the time it was relieved by 7th and 21st Divisions on 12 July, when the wood was at last cleared, 38th Division had lost 4000 men, including seven battalion commanders.

The attack on Longueval Ridge was altogether more successful. On the night of 13/14 July Rawlinson launched 22 000 men against it after only a short bombardment. By mid-morning the second position was breached all along the ridge, and for a few heady moments there was a possibility of exploitation as cavalry moved up to High Wood. But the opportunity slipped away, and for most of that unseasonably wet summer 4th Army was stalled in front of High Wood and Delville Wood. Shelling reduced both to what Lieutenant Max Plowman called 'a collection of stakes stuck upright in the ground like the broken teeth of some vicious beast.' The Germans were able to relieve their garrisons by trickling troops up from the dead ground behind the woods while attackers had to cross the shell-scoured slopes to their front.

There had been gradual progress on the Roman road. La Boisselle fell on 7 July and Ovillers on the 16th but Pozières remained obdurate. In pitch darkness on 23 July the Australians were launched against the village, keeping close to the barrage to take their first objective in the almost unrecognizable heap of ruins. The Germans always riposted sharply – Falkenhayn ordained that 'the first principle of position warfare must be to yield not one foot of ground; if it be lost, to retake it immediately by counter-attack ...' – and an immediate counter-attack was driven off with heavy loss. As John Terraine has observed, the texture of the Somme was 'attack, counter-attack; attack again; counter-attack again' and when attackers knew their business these counter-attacks were very roughly handled.

On 7 August, after bludgeoning through Pozières yard by filthy yard, the Australians shrugged off the last counter-attack to remain masters of the village. They then edged north to attack Mouquet ('Mucky') Farm whose capture was expected to unlock Thiepval, still standing secure on its bluff. On 5 September they were relieved by the Canadians and left the sector with deepening contempt for 'the British Staff, British methods and British bungling'. As Peter Charlton tells us in his fine book *Australians on the Somme: Pozières 1916*: 'If Australians wish to trace their modern suspicion and resentment of Britain to a date and a place, then July–August 1916 and the ruined village of Pozières are useful points of departure. Australia was never the same again.'

The First Tanks in Action

Even before Pozières fell, Haig was warned by Robertson that there was widespread disquiet over huge losses for small gains. Haig replied that he proposed to maintain steady pressure to wear down the Germans and would snatch any chance of a break-out. Another major effort would be made in mid-September, and as part of it he intended to use what he termed 'a rather desperate innovation'. There was nothing new in the notion of what H.G. Wells had called 'The Land Ironclads', but stalemate had encouraged the British to experiment with an armoured, trench-crossing machine whose box-like structure inspired the dissembling name of tank. The crews, provided by the Heavy Section Machine-Gun Corps, were subjected to deafening noise from the engine and guns, thrown about by the monster's lumbering gait and nauseated by its exhaust fumes. The tanks arrived at Abbeville in early September, were moved up to a railhead at Bray-sur-Somme, and thirty-two of them were available on 15 September when the battle of Flers-Courcelette, the last major offensive on the Somme, began.

The distinction of being the first tank in action went to 'D1', which cleared an isolated pocket of resistance on the eastern edge of Delville Wood shortly before the main attack began at 6.20 a.m. on the 15th. In the north, Gough allocated all his tanks to 2nd Canadian Division, which intended to use them in its drive on the sugar factory at Courcelette. This was taken without the aid of the tanks, which broke down or failed to keep up with the infantry. On the Canadian right, 15th Scottish Division took Martinpuich with the help of four tanks. Another four were assigned to assist 47th London Division in its attack on High Wood – 'Ghastly by day, ghostly by night, the rottenest place on the Somme.' Tank officers had warned that their machines were likely to belly on tree-stumps. Three eventually ditched, and the fourth reached the

German support line where it was destroyed by a shell. The Londoners took the wood after a trench-mortar battery put 750 bombs into it in seven minutes, at last knocking the fight out of the Bavarian defenders.

It is an indication of the massive concentrations now applied to small objectives that XV Corps had three divisions available for its attack on Flers across the strip of blighted landscape between High Wood and Delville Wood. Fourteen of the eighteen tanks allocated had reached their points of departure, and when the battle opened they jarred and rumbled their way forward. There was little the German infantry could do: it took a direct hit from a field gun or, more commonly, an obstacle or a mechanical breakdown, to stop them. 'The monsters approached slowly,' wrote one German, 'hobbling, rolling and rocking but they approached. Nothing impeded them: a supernatural force seemed to impel them on. Someone in the trenches said, "The Devil is coming" ...' A British pilot reported 'A tank is walking up the High Street of Flers with the British Army cheering behind it,' but the truth was more familiar: the gap was sealed before advantage could be taken of it.

The End of the Battle

Although there were further successes – Morval and Lesboeufs fell on 25 September and Thiepval, at long last, on the 26th – the fighting petered out in a sea of mud on what was barely recognizable as the German third position. Lieutenant E.G. Bates of the Northumberland Fusiliers described: 'Ponds of standing water; what looks like a fairly safe crossing, in reality a 10-foot [3-metre] shell-hole; trenches falling in and impossible to repair; men done up before they ever get under fire.' Max Plowman saw how: 'Corpses lie along the parados, rotting in the wet; every now and then a booted foot appears jutting over the trench. The mud makes it all but impassable.' The battle struck its dying fall with the capture of Beaumont-Hamel – a 1 July objective – on 13 November.

Even now we cannot be certain how many men died or were wounded on the Somme. Allied casualties totalled about 600 000, two-thirds of them British. Differences in casualty reporting procedure mean that the official German figures are certainly too low, although many have accused Brigadier-General Sir James Edmonds, the British official historian, of over-optimism in inflating them to 660–680 000. It is safer to suggest that the Germans lost 600 000 men, many in counter-attacks and more to artillery. Erich von Ludendorff, deputy to Field-Marshal von Hindenburg, who had replaced the discredited Falkenhayn in August 1916, admitted that the Germans were 'completely exhausted', and a survivor wrote:

'The Somme was the muddy grave of the German field army.'

That the Somme had worn down the German army and contributed to the tactical skill of the British cannot be denied. But much else had been worn down, and the New Armies had lost their innocence. On 1 July a soldier of 12/London Regiment emerged from Gommecourt Wood with a smashed arm and a gashed head, asking where the dressing station was. A signaller told him to wait while he found a stretcher-bearer. 'I don't want him for *me*,' said the young man tersely, wiping blood out of his eyes. 'I want someone to come back with me to get my mate. *He's hurt*!'

A View of the Field

If any battlefield can be described as a congenial spot for a long walk then the Somme is it. We might do best to drive on to it, passing through Querrieu on the Amiens–Albert road, which Sassoon remembered as 'a big village cosily over-populated by 4th Army Staff'. Rawlinson's headquarters were in the château where the road from Amiens swings right on entering the village. Its owners, the Count and Countess d'Alcantara, are generally prepared to receive visitors who phone in advance – the number is (22) 4011409 – and have converted their stables into pleasant bed and breakfast apartments which can be booked on the same number.

Rawlinson did not spend all his time at Querrieu. Sassoon got 'a glimpse of his geniality' as he 'squelched among the brown tents in his boots and spurs'. He observed the opening of the battle from 'the Grandstand' near Dernancourt, and the military historian Martin Middlebrook, whose knowledge of the battle is encyclopaedic, has found it. A minor road connects the Amiens–Albert highway with Dernancourt, in the Ancre valley south of Albert. A metalled farm track strikes off north-eastwards 150 yards (137 metres) north of a copse equidistant between Dernancourt and the main road, and from the end of the track the entire southern portion of the battlefield can be seen. Ulster Tower, close to the site of the Schwaben Redoubt, cuts the skyline to the north-north-east, with the Thiepval Memorial to its right. Further right, past Ovillers and Pozières, both Mametz Wood and Delville Wood are smudges on the horizon.

Albert

Albert is a bustling town, overlooked by the rebuilt basilica and its golden Virgin. The tower was hit by shellfire in January 1915 and the statue began to list dangerously, but French engineers secured it with steel cable and it remained 'the hanging Virgin' for most of the war.

Some said that the war would end when the statue fell, and others unkindly maintained that it was the only virgin to be found in Albert. The town was taken by the Germans in their spring offensive in 1918, and on 16 April British guns levelled the tower to prevent artillery observers from using it. After the First World War the presence of an aircraft factory south of the town led the citizens to fear air raids in future conflicts, and shelters in the square beneath the basilica now house a rather jumbled war museum.

Following the Front Line
The 1 July front line can be followed for almost all its length. Gommecourt Wood New Cemetery, on the D6 linking Gommecourt to Foncquevillers, provides a clear view of the ground over which 46th Division attacked. Looking north, a small copse in the valley bottom marks a bulge in the German line called Schwalben Nest by the men who held it and The Z by the British. The German front trench ran along the edge of Sartel Wood, on the right, and there were further trenches in the wood behind it. A battalion of 91st Reserve Regiment held the sector attacked by the twelve battalions of 46th Division, a similar ratio of defence to attack on many other parts of the front that day.

The two forward brigades of 46th Division – 137th on the right and 139th on the left – formed up in no man's land east of Foncquevillers, but when they advanced most were stopped by wire, machine-gun and artillery fire although a few got into the wood. The follow-up brigade, 138th, with four battalions of Sherwood Foresters, did somewhat better, and a few attackers crossed the first German trench. Five battalion commanders were killed and one, Lieutenant-Colonel C.E. Boote of 1/6th North Staffordshire, a Boer War veteran, is buried in the cemetery.

Captain J.L. Green, medical officer of 1/6th Sherwood Foresters, was hit while treating the wounded in no man's land, and was eventually killed as he dragged a wounded officer back towards British lines. He won one of the nine VCs awarded that day, and lies in Foncquevillers Military Cemetery. Captain Green's death points up one of the sad truths of the first day. The proportion of killed to wounded (21 000 to 36 000) was unusually high because many who could have recovered with prompt attention perished as they lay in no man's land. Initially the Germans took few chances, and men who moved between the lines were sniped or machine-gunned. Later, especially in areas where the attack had palpably failed, they sometimes allowed the wounded to be recovered. Often men took huge risks to drag in survivors or search for friends, and many remembered the

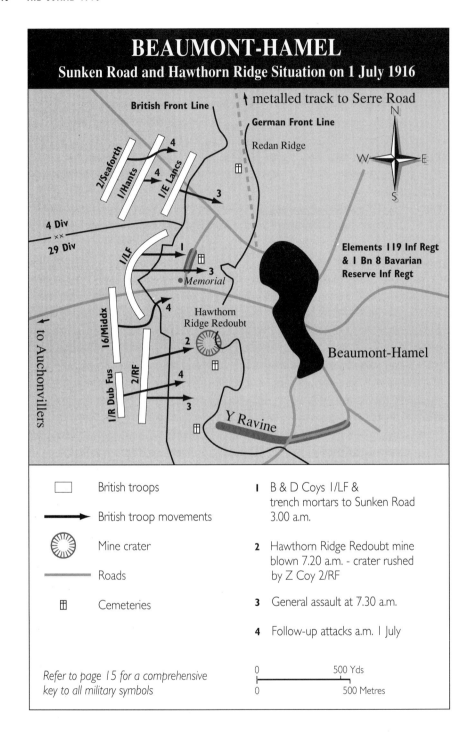

BEAUMONT-HAMEL
Sunken Road and Hawthorn Ridge Situation on 1 July 1916

British Front Line

metalled track to Serre Road

German Front Line

Redan Ridge

N
W — E
S

2/Seaforth
I/Hants
I/E Lancs
4
4
3

4 Div
××
29 Div

Elements 119 Inf Regt
& 1 Bn 8 Bavarian
Reserve Inf Regt

I/LF
1
3
Memorial

4
Hawthorn
Ridge Redoubt

16/Middx

2
Beaumont-Hamel

I/R Dub Fus
2/RF
4
3

to Auchonvillers

Y Ravine

| | British troops | **1** | B & D Coys 1/LF & trench mortars to Sunken Road 3.00 a.m. |

British troops

British troop movements

Mine crater

Roads

Cemeteries

1 B & D Coys 1/LF & trench mortars to Sunken Road 3.00 a.m.

2 Hawthorn Ridge Redoubt mine blown 7.20 a.m. - crater rushed by Z Coy 2/RF

3 General assault at 7.30 a.m.

4 Follow-up attacks a.m. 1 July

Refer to page 15 for a comprehensive key to all military symbols

0   500 Yds
0   500 Metres

cries of the wounded, sounding like fingernails being dragged down glass, as the most distressing aspect of the day.

Bravery at Serre

To trace 31st Division's attack on Serre, park in front of Serre Road Cemetery No. 1, where the Serre–Mailly-Maillet road (D919) dips south of Serre. Then walk up a long track north of the farm, following the Commonwealth War Graves Commission (CWGC) signs to Luke Copse British Cemetery, as far as the wood now known as Sheffield Park. In 1916 there were four copses here – Matthew, Mark, Luke and John. The British front line ran along the edge of the wood, and can still be seen as an unmistakable ditch. The 94th Brigade attacked Serre, just over the crest-line to the east, from this line, with two of its battalions in the first wave. The Accrington Pals were on its right, where the gates lead down to Railway Hollow Cemetery, and on its left, where the copse peters out, stood the Sheffield City Battalion.

Both battalions began to form up in no man's land at 7.20 a.m. on 1 July 1916. They were immediately machine-gunned from the German front line, about 100 yards (90 metres) beyond the small cemeteries east of Sheffield Park, and field guns bombarded the British front line. Neither counter-battery fire nor a hurricane bombardment from Stokes mortars which preceded the assault made any difference, and at 7.30 a.m. Germans could be seen running out to man their fire positions.

The Accringtons and the City Battalion attacked regardless. 'The extended lines started in excellent order but gradually melted away,' recorded Sir James Edmonds.

There was no wavering or attempting to come back. The men fell in their ranks, mostly before the first hundred yards of No Man's Land had been crossed. The magnificent gallantry, discipline and determination shown by all ranks of this North Country division were of no avail against the concentrated fire-effect of the enemy's unshaken infantry and artillery, whose barrage has been described as so consistent and severe that the cones of the explosions gave the impression of a thick belt of poplar trees.

Captain Riley led his Burnley lads into the maelstrom and was shot through the head: his commanding officer, Lieutenant-Colonel Rickman, survived the battle, although the official history reported him killed, only to be electrocuted at home in 1925.

A few men from each battalion managed to enter Serre. A gunner officer saw some of the right-hand Accrington Company disappear into the village, and when it was briefly entered in November the bodies of some Sheffield men were found in its north-west corner. The Accringtons lost 585 officers and men and the Sheffield City Battalion 512. Many are buried in the cemeteries around Sheffield Park, amongst them Private Alf Goodlad, who lies in Railway Hollow Cemetery, and whose proud parents inscribed a sentence from one of his letters on his tombstone. France was, he told them, a grand country, well worth fighting for.

A metalled track, which leaves the Serre road almost opposite the track to Sheffield Park, leads across Redan Ridge to Beaumont-Hamel. On entering the village turn right towards Auchonvillers and walk as far as a track leading north to a memorial to 8/Argyll and Sutherland Highlanders. The mound it stands on gives a good view of the defences of Beaumont-Hamel, with the German front line running along the wood edge to the east and the position of Hawthorn Ridge Redoubt marked by trees and bushes across the road to one's right front.

The Accringtons left Lancashire for Carnarvon in early 1915, and this postcard dates from their time there. The reality of the Somme had little to do with this image: most men were tired after a long march to the front the night before the battle. Yet the attack aroused great admiration. The commander of 94th Infantry Brigade wrote: 'I have been through many battles in this war and nothing more magnificent has come to my notice. The waves went forward as if on a drill parade and I saw no man turn back or falter.'

Don't be Alarmed, the Accrington Pals are on guard at Carnarvon.

Memorials and Cemeteries

The sunken road, a continuation of the track, was occupied on the night of 30 June 1916 by B and D companies of 1/Lancashire Fusiliers and eight Stokes mortars which were to fire a hurricane bombardment to cover the assault. The Germans dropped shells into the road at 7 a.m., and the explosion of the Hawthorn Ridge Redoubt mine drew heavier fire. The two leading companies were, in the words of Lieutenant-Colonel Martin Magniac, 'mown down' as they left the road, and the other two companies suffered heavily just to reach the road. Corporal George Ashurst jumped breathlessly into it: 'My God, what a sight! The whole of the road was strewn with dead and dying men. Some were talking deliriously, others calling for help and asking for water.' The second wave attacked with no better success. Some Lancashire Fusiliers lie in the cemetery which marks the front edge of the German wire, but most have no known graves. Although 2/Royal Fusiliers, across the road to the right, sent men racing for the mine-crater they were unable to secure it, and once the Germans had re-established themselves, further efforts were hopeless.

It is possible to walk up to Newfoundland Park, a large area of preserved battlefield south-west of Beaumont-Hamel or to drive there by way of Auchonvillers. A bronze caribou, bellowing out across the battlefield, commemorates the Newfoundlanders, whose front and support trenches are marked. A short walk out across no man's land, past the 'Tree of Death' which marks the limit of the Newfoundland advance, takes the visitor to Y Ravine Cemetery and, further on, to the German front line, which still gives a good impression of its former strength. The statue of a kilted soldier celebrates the capture of Beaumont-Hamel by 51st Highland Division in November 1916.

The 36th Division is commemorated by Ulster Tower, on the far side of the Ancre. It is a replica of Helen's Tower, in the Marquess of Dufferin and Ava's park at Clandeboye, near Belfast, where the division had trained, and there is a good little museum, with a knowledgeable curator, just behind it. To reach the site of the Schwaben Redoubt we must walk past Mill Road Cemetery, whose gravestones are laid flat because the ground is so unstable. There is usually a practicable route along a field edge east of the cemetery, and about 300 yards (275 metres) further on tussocks interlaced with occasional broken bottles mark the site of the Schwaben.

Thiepval is crowned by Sir Edwin Lutyens' Memorial to the Missing which bears the names of 73 412 British and South African officers and men missing on the Somme in 1916–17. Names are arranged in panels

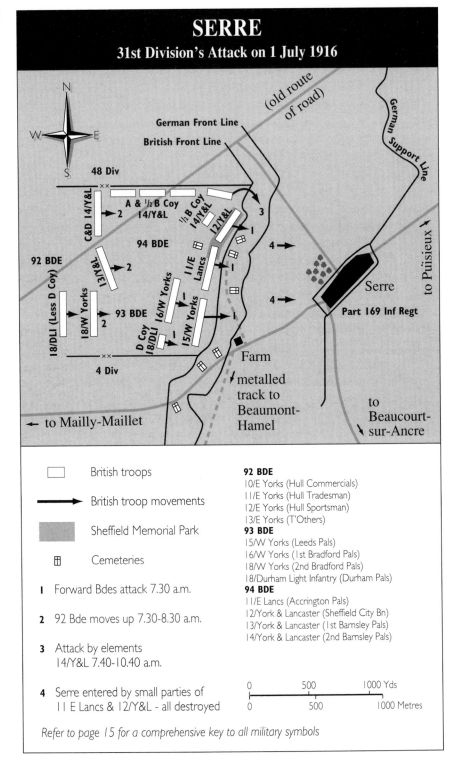

SERRE
31st Division's Attack on 1 July 1916

N W E S

48 Div

German Front Line

British Front Line

(old route of road)

German Support Line

C&D 14/Y&L

A & ½ B Coy 14/Y&L

½ B Coy 14/Y&L

12/Y&L

94 BDE

92 BDE

18/DLI (Less D Coy)

13/Y&L

18/W Yorks

11/E Lancs

16/W Yorks

93 BDE

15/W Yorks

D Coy 18/DLI

to Puïsieux

Serre

Part 169 Inf Regt

4 Div

Farm

metalled track to Beaumont-Hamel

← to Mailly-Maillet

to Beaucourt-sur-Ancre

☐ British troops

➤ British troop movements

▨ Sheffield Memorial Park

⊞ Cemeteries

1 Forward Bdes attack 7.30 a.m.

2 92 Bde moves up 7.30-8.30 a.m.

3 Attack by elements
14/Y&L 7.40-10.40 a.m.

4 Serre entered by small parties of
11 E Lancs & 12/Y&L - all destroyed

92 BDE
10/E Yorks (Hull Commercials)
11/E Yorks (Hull Tradesman)
12/E Yorks (Hull Sportsman)
13/E Yorks (T'Others)
93 BDE
15/W Yorks (Leeds Pals)
16/W Yorks (1st Bradford Pals)
18/W Yorks (2nd Bradford Pals)
18/Durham Light Infantry (Durham Pals)
94 BDE
11/E Lancs (Accrington Pals)
12/York & Lancaster (Sheffield City Bn)
13/York & Lancaster (1st Barnsley Pals)
14/York & Lancaster (2nd Barnsley Pals)

0	500	1000 Yds
0	500	1000 Metres

Refer to page 15 for a comprehensive key to all military symbols

by regimental seniority, beginning with cavalry and gunners up to the left as one approaches. It includes neither British soldiers missing in the fighting of 1918 nor Empire or Dominion missing who are commemorated elsewhere. The Anglo-French cemetery in front of the memorial contains 300 dead from each nation and symbolizes the joint effort of the Allies. It stands on the front line vainly attacked on 1 July by 16/Northumberland Fusiliers, the Newcastle Commercials.

The road south winds past the Leipzig salient and, with a left turn short of Aveluy, goes on to meet the Roman road at La Boisselle. Snaking through the village and following signs for La Grande Mine takes the visitor past craters called 'The Glory Hole', where the track for Lochnagar crater leaves the village: broken ground caused by mining can be seen on the right. Although some of the mines that exploded beneath Messines Ridge in 1917 contained more explosive, Lochnagar is the largest surviving crater. It was created by 60 000 lb (27 215 kg) of ammonal exploded beneath the German front line and was taken by the Tyneside Scottish, some of whom were hit by lumps of chalk flung into the air by the blast. An Englishman, Richard Dunning, bought the crater in 1970, having seen how farming was gradually changing the battlefield.

It makes a profound impression, and the pockmarked ground around it offers a good view of the Tara–Usna line from which the Tyneside Irish began their doomed advance.

No book of this length can hope to do justice to the whole of the 1 July front, but one remaining spot is more than worth a visit. Due south of Mametz, 8/ and 9/Devons of 7th Division attacked from Mansell Copse, on the lip of the valley south of the Fricourt–Maricourt road. The civilian cemetery of Mametz stands on the other side of the road. Captain D.L. Martin, one of 9/Devons' company commanders, had made a Plasticine model of the area and predicted that the machine-gun dug in below the base of The Shrine (the crucifix in the cemetery, replaced but easily visible) would catch his battalion as it breasted the rise and made for the German front line to its north, obliquely to the gun. He was right, and he lies with 123 other Devons, including Noel Hodgson the poet, in Devonshire Cemetery. This was a trench burial, with the dead interred *en masse* in the old front-line trench. A wooden sign, now replaced by stone, proudly proclaimed:

> The Devonshires held this trench
> The Devonshires hold it still

Mametz Wood is in private hands, but the track leaving Mametz village for Bazentin curls along its eastern edge, passing the new dragon memorial

Australian artillerymen serving a 9.2-inch heavy gun during the battle for Pozières in August. They are shirtless in the heat, but have retained their khaki fur-felt hats, the symbol of the 'digger.'

to 38th Division and then running past Flat Iron Copse Cemetery, which began as a dressing station set up shortly after 7th Division took Bazentin on 14 July. The track emerges on the Contalmaison–Longueval road, and it is possible to walk to High Wood along a track which heads off almost opposite the turning down to Bazentin-le-Grand, or to go straight on into Longueval.

Delville Wood lies east of Longueval, and amongst the divisions which fought for 'Devil's Wood' was 9th Scottish, which included a South African brigade. The South African National Memorial within the wood was built in 1987 around the original Voortrekker's Cross which commemorated the 10 000 South African dead of the First World War. The rides in the wood have stone markers recording street names given to them by 9th Scottish Division. A convenient café stands near the entrance to the wood. On the open ground between Delville Wood and High Wood is the New Zealand Division Memorial: the New Zealanders crossed this ridge on 15 September 1916, making good progress once the fall of High Wood had cleared their left flank. High Wood itself cannot be entered, but a walk around its edge shows what a commanding view its garrison enjoyed.

Pozières and Mild Trench

Two remaining spots help us to understand the Somme. Pozières, with its Australian memorials and idiosyncratic Burma Star Café, dominates the surrounding countryside, and it is easy to see why the village was important. On the northern side of the Roman road is the site of Pozières Mill, the highest spot on the entire battlefield. Just across the road the Tank Memorial, which bears Second World War damage, marks the spot from which tanks of C Company, Heavy Section Machine-Gun Corps, set off to accompany 2nd Canadian Division on 16 September.

Having seen one caribou in Newfoundland Park, we can find another north-east of Gueudecourt. He stands on a pocket-handkerchief of ground slashed by a trench. This is purportedly Hilt Trench, taken by the Newfoundlanders on 12 October, but is actually Mild Trench, captured by 2/East Lancashires two weeks later. It stands at the furthest point of the British advance. On a good day the Thiepval Memorial, almost due west, is visible with the naked eye, and to the north Bapaume, an early objective for Gough's cavalry, stands on the horizon. On a bad day the wind keens across the ridge, reminding us that by November 1916 there was sheer desolation to the west, with no metalled track or light railway until the other side of the Longueval Ridge. By the time the battle finished, soldiers up here were dying of exhaustion and exposure. Whatever historians now say about the Somme, when soldiers of a later generation sought a telling comparison it always came to mind. 'This,' they would say, 'is the biggest balls-up since the Somme.'

CHAPTER 5

Arras
1940

Background

In May 1940 the Germans rolled across the battlefields of 1914–18 with a speed which amazed them. 'It was hardly conceivable,' wrote Major-General Erwin Rommel. 'Twenty-two years before we had stood for four-and-a-half years before this self-same enemy and had won victory after victory and finally lost the war.' 'What was up with the famous French army, which in the First World War had fought against us so bravely and on equal terms?' asked Captain Hans von Luck. 'Le Cateau, then Cambrai, Arras, always far in front of everybody else,' exulted Rommel. The word *blitzkrieg*, meaning 'lightning war', summed it up perfectly.

The Aftermath of the First World War
In 1919 the Treaty of Versailles had confirmed Allied victory. Germany had already lost her imperial crown, for the Kaiser fled in November 1918, and Versailles went on to strip her of territory, returning Alsace and Lorraine to France. The German army was restricted to 100 000 men, without tanks, heavy guns or aircraft, and the general staff was abolished. Germany accepted guilt for causing and prosecuting the war, and was to pay huge reparations. France was to administer the coal mines in the Saar for fifteen years to compensate for damage to her own mining heartland. The peacemakers redrew the map of Eastern Europe, creating the new states of Czecho-slovakia and Yugoslavia, and re-establishing Poland, leaving East Prussia isolated from the remainder of Germany.

Some felt that this settlement was too harsh: others thought that it was not punitive enough. Marshal Foch, Allied generalissimo in 1918,

Men of 4/Royal Tank Regiment, in their distinctive black berets, at work on Infantry Tanks Mk I. This tank was nicknamed Matilda because of its comic duck appearance, but the nickname was soon applied to the more powerful Mk II. Tank crews carried .38 Enfield revolvers, introduced into service in 1932: this version has no hammer spur, making it less likely to catch on clothing or equipment in a tank. Most British soldiers who fought in the 1940 campaign were entitled to the 1939-45 Star, generally awarded for six months' service in an operational command – though a single day at Dunkirk qualified a soldier for the medal.

believed that it was merely a twenty-year armistice. The great powers stalked away from the peace table in a sour mood. President Wilson, who had done much to shape the settlement, could not sell it to his own countrymen. Britain speedily dismantled a war-winning instrument. In November 1918 she had $3^{1}/_{2}$ million men under arms: two years later there were 370 000. The army reverted to its traditional role of imperial policing. Public disillusionment with war combined with official attempts to reduce the burden imposed by defence. The Ten Year Rule, formulated in 1919 but slipped forward year by year until 1932, decreed that planning was to proceed on the basis that there would be no major war for ten years. As late as May 1938 a senior RAF officer declared: 'Never again shall we even contemplate a force for a foreign country. Our contribution is to be the Navy and the RAF.'

The mood in France was no more buoyant. First World War casualties had been proportionately heavier than in Britain or Germany: one-third of young Frenchmen had been killed or crippled. War memorials embodied the moral credit which France believed herself to have earned, but the sacrifice they represented counted for little. Inflation hit bourgeois and peasant alike, and former allies seemed reluctant to force Germany to pay reparations. When she defaulted in 1923 the French and Belgians occupied the Ruhr, increasing German bitterness and worsening her economic state. The Wall Street crash of 1929 plunged the Western world into crisis, and in Germany it fuelled hyper-inflation which encouraged extremist politics and permitted the rise of Hitler, who exploited resentment against Versailles and found scapegoats, internal and external, to blame for the country's plight.

France had a seat on the Council of the League of Nations and tried, through alliances with Czechoslovakia and Poland, to maintain international support. Her quest for security solidified along the Franco-German border in a barrier which took its name from André Maginot, the Verdun veteran who steered its credits through parliament. There was some logic behind the Maginot Line. Commissions had noted the relatively small amount of internal damage suffered by the Verdun forts. Tens of thousands of Frenchmen had fallen trying to expel the Germans from France. The line would prevent rapid invasion and give time for the mobilization of a mass army.

This logic collapsed under the pressure of events. In 1936 Belgium became neutral. Although money was found for some fortifications on the Franco-Belgian border, these were not on the same scale as the line proper. It was impossible to link defensive strategy with alliances in Eastern Europe. Colonel Charles de Gaulle, one of the army's most radical thinkers, warned that if war came all the French would be able to do was watch, from behind their barricades, the enslavement of Europe. The cost of the line meant that there was little left over for modern weapons and equipment. When the Popular Front came to power in 1936 and attempted to improve military preparedness, it found that French arms production failed to match that of Germany. Lastly, the line contributed to a defensive mentality and discouraged progressive military thought.

In fact, there were innovators in all the contending nations. The manoeuvres of the British Experimental Mechanized Force in the late 1920s broke new ground and Provisional Regulations of 1927 were a powerful influence on Heinz Guderian, who helped to inspire the development of German armoured troops. The apostles of mobility – men like Guderian in Germany, de Gaulle in France and Basil Liddell Hart and Major-General J.F.C. Fuller (the Tank Corps' chief of staff in the First World War and a prolific military writer) in Britain – disagreed on points of detail, but all rejected systematic attrition and envisaged a war characterized by manoeuvre. Building on infiltration tactics developed during the First World War, they emphasized the importance of achieving surprise, attacking an enemy's points of weakness, and tapping out a tempo which left him paralysed.

Many, even in Germany, regarded them as heretics. General Hans von Seekt, commander of the 100 000-man *Reichswehr*, who used a variety of measures to circumvent the Treaty of Versailles, favoured infiltration tactics; he had no particular regard for tanks, and many of his fellow officers were deeply conservative. Guderian and the 'Young Turks' made slow progress and needed high-level political support. In early 1934, a year after Hitler had become chancellor, Guderian showed him a primitive, mechanized combined-arms force at Kummersdorf. 'That's what I need,' said Hitler. 'That's what I want to have.' Yet he was no easy convert to armoured warfare. He thought that the tank would earn him prestige, and it was probably not until 1939 that he glimpsed the weapon's real potential.

Other reformers fared less well. De Gaulle was struck off the 1936 promotion list for writing a controversial book. Fuller retired as a major-general after being offered an appointment he regarded as insulting. Liddell Hart, who had left the army after the First World War, enjoyed considerable influence as adviser to the secretary of state for war in 1935–7 but was bitterly resented by the military establishment.

Germany Develops Armoured Warfare
The expanding German army gained three panzer divisions in 1933, but

the first General der Panzertruppen, Otto Lutz, was opposed by officers who hoped to use the tank to support infantry and feared these divisions would consume resources best spread across the whole army. However, experience gained in the Spanish Civil War and in the invasion of Poland in September 1939 helped the Germans to develop armoured warfare. Surprise, speed and concentration were its essence, encapsulated in Guderian's slogan *'Klotzen, nicht Kleckern'* – 'Smash, don't tap.' Their new air force, the *Luftwaffe*, not only prevented enemy aircraft from interfering in the ground battle but became 'flying artillery' for the panzer divisions.

These were not simply tank formations, but included mechanized infantry (called rifle regiments in 1940); reconnaissance; field, anti-tank and anti-aircraft artillery; and engineers. Of all their weapons, the radio was the most potent. Communications had been the single greatest constraint on First World War tactics: how different the first day on the Somme might have been in 1916 had the attackers been able to identify and reinforce their success faster than the defender could rectify his failure. General Ludwig Beck had asked Guderian how he proposed to lead a panzer division. 'From the front – by wireless' replied 'Hurrying Heinz'. 'Nonsense!' retorted Beck. 'A divisional commander sits back with maps and a telephone.' He could not do so in 1940 and hope to win.

Campaign and Battle

When Britain and France declared war in September 1939 in response to the German invasion of Poland, there was little they could do for the Poles. The French mounted an irresolute offensive into the Saar, settled down in the Maginot Line and began preparing for a long war. It was the coldest winter for years, and morale plummeted. Major-General Edward Spears had been a liaison officer in the First World War, knew the French army well, and found its condition 'horribly depressing'.

Allied Plans
The French commander-in-chief, General Maurice Gamelin, was based in the Château de Vincennes, on the eastern outskirts of Paris, within sight of the donjon in which Henry V had died. He issued orders to the North-East Front through its commander, General Georges, at La Ferté-sous-Jouarre. Georges disposed of three army groups, with General Gaston Billotte's No. 1 Army Group responsible for the Franco-Belgian border. It comprised four French armies – Blanchard's 1st, Huntziger's 2nd, Giraud's 7th and Corap's 9th – as well as Lord Gort's British Expe-

ditionary Force (BEF). In practice, Gort, a grenadier with a formidable fighting reputation from the First World War, received his orders from Gamelin via Georges. He also enjoyed right of appeal to the British government should he receive orders which appeared to imperil his force. Spears described him as 'a simple, straightforward but not very clever man … who felt above all else that orders must be obeyed.' There were to be times in the coming campaign when Gort's moral courage would stand him in good stead.

In February 1940 air zones were created to correspond with these army groups: General d'Astier de la Vigerie's Northern Zone of Aerial Operations supported Blanchard's army group. The BEF had its own air component, and there was a separate Advanced Air Striking Force (AASF), part of Bomber Command, under Air Marshal Barratt. These arrangements testified to a difference in attitude between Allied air forces and the *Luftwaffe*. The latter was geared to winning air superiority and supporting ground operations, and the system of *Luftflotte* (air fleets) enabled the Germans to concentrate air resources to match priorities on the ground. They were to commit over 3000 aircraft to the battle, and although the French had 1200 available in May 1940 d'Astier was only able to use 746 to support Billotte. The Germans were superior in tactical bombers and ground attack aircraft, and although the Allies possessed more fighters, some were retained for the defence of the United Kingdom and others were hopelessly outclassed. Ironically, the programme to replace obsolete French aircraft got under way just as the campaign started.

The Allies intended to wheel forward into Belgium when the Germans attacked. The capture of a German plan encouraged Gamelin to organize an advance on to the River Dyle, covering Brussels. He later added the 'Breda variant', which would send 7th Army to assist the Dutch. On its right the BEF would hold the Dyle between Louvain and Wavre; 1st Army would cover the Gembloux gap and Namur; and 9th Army, with a high proportion of reserve divisions, would throw its left wing forward towards Namur while its right maintained contact with 2nd Army at the end of the Maginot Line. This plan would enable the Allies to meet the anticipated thrust into Belgium but, as Georges observed, it would be hard for them to react if the Germans attacked further south.

German Plans

'Case Yellow', the original German plan, looked very like Schlieffen's scheme a generation before. General von Bock's Army Group B would make the main thrust towards Ghent; General von Rundstedt's Army

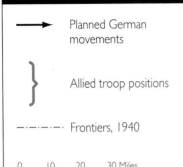

1940
The Rival Plans

→ Planned German
movements

} Allied troop positions

–·–·–·– Frontiers, 1940

0	10	20	30 Miles
0	10	20 30	40 50 Kms

*Refer to page 15 for a comprehensive
key to all military symbols*

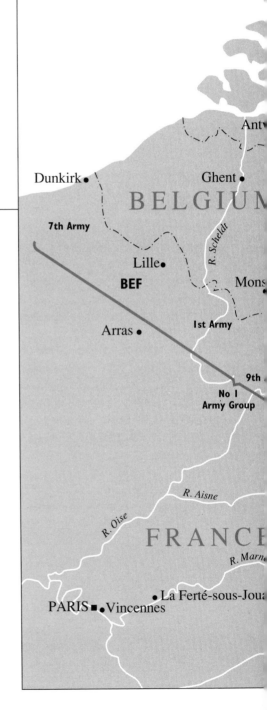

Ant

Dunkirk

Ghent

BELGIUM

7th Army

R. Scheldt

Lille

BEF

Mons

Arras

1st Army

9th

No 1
Army Group

R. Aisne

R. Oise

FRANCE

R. Marne

La Ferté-sous-Jouar

PARIS ■ Vincennes

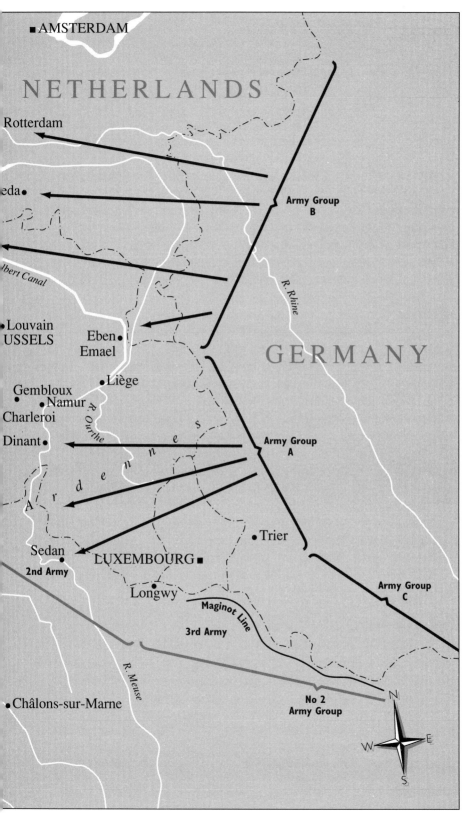

- AMSTERDAM

NETHERLANDS

Rotterdam

eda•

Albert Canal

Army Group
B

R. Rhine

•Louvain
USSELS

Eben•
Emael

GERMANY

•Liège

Gembloux
•   •Namur
Charleroi

R. Ourthe

A   r   d   e   n   n   e   s

Dinant•

Army Group
A

•Trier

Sedan
•

LUXEMBOURG ■

2nd Army

•
Longwy

Maginot Line

Army Group
C

3rd Army

R. Meuse

•Châlons-sur-Marne

No 2
Army Group

N

W   E

S

Group A would mount a subsidiary attack towards Namur; and General von Leeb's Army Group C would cover the Maginot Line. The distinguished British military historian Alistair Horne has called this plan 'manifestly bad ... so conservative and uninspiring that it might well have been thought up by a British or French General Staff of the inter-war years.'

It was no more appealing to many Germans. Lieutenant-General Erich von Manstein, Rundstedt's chief of staff, objected that it would not produce 'a decisive issue by land', and Guderian maintained that the campaign would be won by striking 'to drive a wedge so deep and wide that we need not worry about our flanks'. Hitler, lobbied by the disaffected, favoured radical schemes, for he believed that the French army was undermined by the factionalism of the inter-war years and would not withstand a single massive blow.

OKH (Army High Command) was told to think again, and its new scheme, *Sichelschnitt* (sickle-cut) was altogether more ambitious. Bock's army group would still move into Holland and Belgium, wafting a matador's cloak to draw Allied eyes to the north. Leeb's men would continue to watch the Maginot Line. Army Group A became the centre of gravity for the offensive. It was to contain forty-five divisions in three armies – 4th, 12th and 16th – and its cutting edge was formed by the seven panzer divisions of Guderian's XIX, Reinhardt's XLI and Hoth's XV Panzer Corps, the first two making up Panzer Group Kleist. The panzers were to attack through the Ardennes, the hilly, wooded area where France, Belgium and Luxembourg meet, to smash the hinge of the Allied armies on the Meuse between Dinant and Sedan. This was enormously risky. Bock pointed out that: 'You will be creeping along, 10 miles [16 km] from the Maginot Line flank on your breakthrough and hoping that the French will watch inertly! You are cramming a mass of tanks together into the narrow roads of the Ardennes as if there were no such thing as air-power.'

The Balance of Forces
In raw numbers the two sides were evenly matched with 136 divisions available for the campaign, although the Allies, with 96 French, 19 British, 22 Belgian and 10 Dutch divisions were anything but a homogeneous force. They had just over 3000 armoured vehicles, slightly more than the Germans. Most German tanks were the lightly armed Panzers Mk I and II, stiffened by 349 Mk IIs, with a 37mm gun, and only 278 Mk IVs with a low-velocity 75mm gun. The French had 311 of the heavy B1 tank, and 260 of the Somua S65 – with its 47mm high-velocity gun

arguably the best tank in the campaign – together with some 1800 lighter vehicles. The British fielded 100 infantry tanks, designed for infantry co-operation and sufficiently armoured to defeat most anti-tank weapons. The Mk I mounted either a .303 or an unreliable .5-inch machine-gun, while the 24 very heavily armoured Mk II Matildas carried a 2-pdr gun.

The Germans enjoyed no great material advantage. If they were better equipped with radios, which made it easier to fight a mobile battle, their 37mm anti-tank gun could not cope with heavier Allied tanks. They were able to use the 88mm anti-aircraft gun in the anti-armour role, although it had a high silhouette which made it vulnerable to shrapnel. The real German edge lay in training and organization. The British had no armoured division in France when the campaign began, and the French had three, with a fourth being formed. Most of their tanks were scattered amongst cavalry and light mechanized divisions or allocated to infantry support. Panzer divisions, in contrast, were flexible all-arms formations whose commanders had the experience of Poland behind them.

The Start of the Campaign
The campaign opened on 10 May with German air raids on airfields, roads and railways. Special forces attacked key points: the Belgian fortress of Eben Emael, on the Albert Canal, was taken by glider troops who landed on top of it. The Allied left wing swung into Belgium and reached the Dyle line; General Prioux's excellent Cavalry Corps of light mechanized divisions raced for the Gembloux gap, and 7th Army reached Breda only to discover that the Dutch had already been driven back on Rotterdam.

The panzers forged into the Ardennes despite resistance from Belgian Chasseurs Ardennais and French cavalry, and on the evening of 12 May Guderian's advanced guard reached the River Meuse at Sedan. Rommel's 7th Panzer Division did even better. It arrived at Dinant and, although the Meuse bridges were blown, reconnaissance troops crossed the weir at Houx, further north, and established a bridgehead. News of this reached Gamelin in Vincennes on the 13th, and there were growing suspicions that: 'The enemy seems … to be preparing to increase his pressure in the immediate future in the general direction of Sedan, where the centre of gravity of his offensive may be directed.' It was a little late for suspicions. That day, Guderian's three divisions crossed the Meuse on the heels of the heaviest aerial bombardment the world had seen. Billotte managed to move up a mechanized corps behind the broken front, but the French tried to contain rather than counter-attack and the moment passed. Guderian briefly considered his next step. One of his disciples reminded him of his dictum '*Klotzen, nicht Kleckern*', and he gave the order for a drive to the west.

Gamelin's grip on the battle weakened as the days went by. The Dutch began peace negotiations on 14 May. The BEF held firm in front of Louvain, and although Prioux's Cavalry Corps defended the Gembloux gap until 1st Army arrived it was badly mauled in the process. Corap, whose 9th Army had borne the brunt of the panzer attack, was replaced by General Giraud on the 16th, and it is symptomatic of the slowness of French reactions that when he reached his command post at Vervins, Giraud learned that there were German tanks at Montcornet, 12 miles (20 km) to the south.

The French premier, Paul Reynaud, quickly saw through the communiqués emanating from Vincennes, and on the 15th he telephoned Winston Churchill, his British counterpart, and announced: 'We are beaten;

A German Mk III tank clatters through a burning French town. The 25th Panzer Regiment, in Rommel's 7th Panzer Division, contained Mk III, Mk IV and some Czech 38(t) tanks. The campaign made Rommel's name *(right)* and he was sent to command German troops in Africa in February 1941.

we have lost the battle.' When Churchill flew to Paris the following after-noon he found things 'incomparably worse than we had imagined'. Gamelin gave a 'clear and calm' exposition of the situation, but admitted that he had no reserve to deal with the breakthrough. Churchill initially agreed to send ten fighter squadrons, but on his return to London was per-suaded that this would be unwise, for the Advanced Air Striking Force' bases were already under threat. Eventually six Hurricane squadrons, based in south-east England, were committed to the battle.

The German Advance

The panzer corridor opened out across northern France. Guderian's advanced guards were at Marle on the evening of 16 May, 40 miles (64 km) from their starting point that morning and 55 miles (88 km) from Sedan. The history of 1st Panzer Division describes the vacuum behind the spearhead: 'Hardly a single German soldier [was] to be found except for a few supply services, up to 25 or 30 miles [40 or 48 km] behind the division. Munitions and petrol were brought up over a single very thin, almost unprotected supply road. They were also, however, tanked up from petrol dumps and public petrol stations captured from the French.' Guderian passed an advancing column: 'The men were wide awake now and aware that we had achieved a complete breakthrough. They cheered and shouted remarks which often could only be heard by staff officers in the second car: "Well done, old boy" and "There's our old man", and "Did you see him? That was Hurrying Heinz", and so on.'

The speed of their advance even disconcerted some Germans. Rund-stedt grew increasingly concerned at the danger of attack into the south-ern flank of the corridor, and ordered Kleist to check Guderian's rush. On 17 May Kleist berated Guderian for not obeying Rundstedt's order to pause and allow the infantry to catch up: there was a row and Guderian was relieved of his command. When Rundstedt heard the news he sent Colonel-General List of 12th Army down to sort out the muddle. List told Guderian that the orders came from OKH and were to be obeyed. Guderian was to resume his command, and was authorized to carry out 'reconnaissance in force': his tanks were on the move again that evening.

A hint of what the Allies might have achieved came on the 17th when de Gaulle's embryonic 4th Armoured Division thudded into Guderian's flank at Montcornet. De Gaulle had only three battalions of tanks and a battalion of infantry in buses, but jabbed hard into the corridor, just as the German doubters had feared, and it was not until evening that the French drew off, short of fuel and harried by aircraft.

Rommel was on a parallel route further north. He crossed the Franco-

Belgian border at Sivry late on the afternoon of 16 May, and drove on in bright moonlight, firing on the move to discourage opposition and hampered by pitiful columns of refugees. In Avesnes he clashed with French tanks and then, travelling with the leading elements of his panzer regiment, pushed on for the bridge over the River Sambre at Landrecies. Shortage of fuel and ammunition stopped the advance just east of Le Cateau, and Rommel drove back in an armoured car to bring up the rest of his division.

The Allied Response
Behind the spearhead were shoals of French troops, many armed and some inclined to fight. A broken-down Panzer IV – its gun still in working order – provided valuable protection just east of Maroilles, and at Marbais Rommel bluffed a column of forty trucks into surrender and led it to Avesnes. He took an hour-and-a-half's rest before sending fuel and ammunition forward, and followed the supply column and its escort as it broke through a toughly defended roadblock east of Pommeroeuil, observing that: 'Our guns seemed to be completely ineffective against the heavy armour of the French tanks.' Cambrai fell after the leading panzers struck across the fields to its north-west, throwing up such a cloud of dust that the French, unable to see that many of the vehicles were soft-skinned, offered no resistance.

On the 16th the Allied left wing began to withdraw from Belgium. Troops were brought up from the south-west in an effort to block the gap left by the destruction of 9th Army – whose new commander was captured near Le Catelet on 19 May – but the Germans were moving too fast for such tactics to work. Some French instincts were sound, and on 19 May Gamelin directed Billotte to attack towards the Somme, pointing out that there was 'a vacuum' behind German armour. An attack into the flanks of the corridor might have worked, but in practice the Allied command was too dislocated to seize fleeting opportunities.

Matters were not improved by the dismissal of Gamelin. On the 19th he was replaced by the trim seventy-three-year-old General Maxime Weygand, brought back from his post as commander-in-chief in Syria. He was exhausted, but as he enjoyed some sleep the clock ticked on remorselessly. On the 20th Guderian's German tanks tore across the First World War Somme battlefield, cutting up two British Territorial divisions, 12th and 23rd, which had been sent out as lines-of-communication troops and pitchforked into a battle for which they had neither equipment nor training. That evening, tanks of 2nd Panzer clattered alongside the Somme, past the old ford at Blanchetaque and a few miles from Crécy to reach Noyelles on the coast. The Allied armies were cut in half.

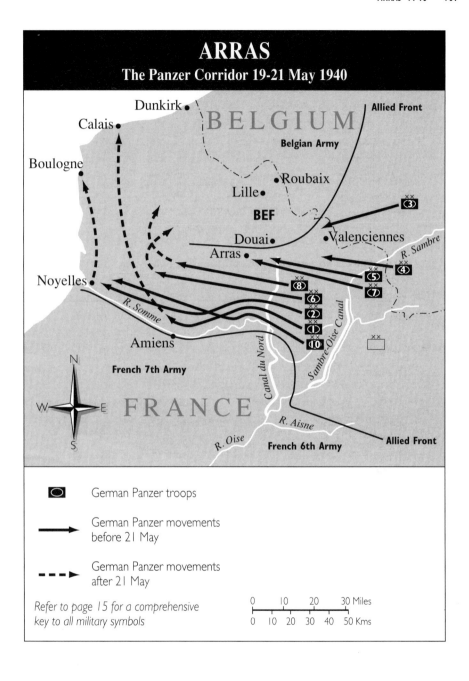

ARRAS
The Panzer Corridor 19-21 May 1940

Dunkirk
Calais
Boulogne

BELGIUM

Allied Front

Belgian Army

Roubaix
Lille

BEF

Douai
Arras

Valenciennes

R. Sambre

③

⑤
④
⑦

⑧

Noyelles

R. Somme

⑥
②
①
⑩

Amiens

Canal du Nord

Sambre-Oise Canal

French 7th Army

N

W ⬥ E

S

FRANCE

R. Aisne

R. Oise

French 6th Army

Allied Front

German Panzer troops

German Panzer movements
before 21 May

German Panzer movements
after 21 May

Refer to page 15 for a comprehensive
key to all military symbols

0	10	20	30 Miles
0	10	20	30	40	50 Kms

The Move Towards Arras

The Germans were unsure of their next move, and it was not until late on 21 May that Guderian was ordered to swing north. This pause might have given the Allies time to react but the past week's fighting had not done much for inter-Allied relations. The BEF had seen relatively little action, although 3rd Division, under a fierce little major-general called Bernard Montgomery, had fought well in front of Louvain. On the 18th the BEF fell back on to the River Escaut, and two days later General Ironside, chief of the imperial general staff, visited Gort at his headquarters at Wahagnies. There had already been discussion over the BEF's future, and word that part might be evacuated had reached Billotte. Ironside repeated the Cabinet's view that the BEF should move southwards to avoid being cut off in the north. Gort disagreed. Seven of his nine divisions were in action. Withdrawal would expose the Belgians and leave a gap which the Germans would exploit. If Weygand organized an offensive Gort undertook to use his two unengaged divisions in a limited operation near Arras on the 21st. Ironside found Billotte and Blanchard and persuaded them to support Gort's attack, but had no confidence that they actually would. 'God help the BEF,' he wrote, 'brought to this state by the incompetence of the French command.'

Weygand flew north on the 21st and met Billotte and Belgian commanders at Ypres. Gort, whose headquarters moved that day to Prémesques, on the western edge of Lille, heard of the meeting too late and Weygand had left by the time he arrived. It was agreed that the Belgians should fall back on the River Lys and there would be a combined offensive, starting not before the 26th, into both flanks of the corridor. The plan's prospects, poor at its inception, diminished when Billotte was fatally injured in a road accident later that day: it took Blanchard three days to replace him.

While tired generals were haggling at Ypres, tanks were already burning around Arras. The Arras operation was the child of more modest circumstances than the offensive discussed at Ypres. As the situation on his right deteriorated, Gort had given his director of intelligence, Major-General Mason-MacFarlane, command of the improvised Macforce and responsibility for the BEF's right rear. On 18 May he appointed Major-General Petre of 12th Division to head Petreforce and hold the Arras area. On the 20th German tanks ripped through the belly of the BEF north of the Somme, and 70th Brigade, part of the unlucky 23rd Division, was caught on the move by 8th Panzer Division just south of Arras. After a hopeless fight the brigade lost all but 233 officers and men.

Gort extemporized another formation to support Petreforce. Major-

General Franklyn, commander of the uncommitted 5th Division, was given Frankforce – 5th Division, 50th (Northumbrian) Division, a good first-line Territorial formation, and 1st Army Tank Brigade – and told to relieve French or British troops on the River Scarpe east of Arras and then, as Franklyn put it: 'to make Arras secure, gaining as much "elbow room" as possible south of the town. To the best of my memory he used the term "mopping up". I certainly got the impression that I was only likely to encounter weak German detachments.' The official history uses much the same words. Frankforce was to 'support the garrison of Arras and block the roads south of Arras, thus cutting off German communications from the east.' Evidence of German tanks south of Arras was not passed on to Franklyn, who might have had reservations about tossing a force composed largely of infantry into a whirlpool of armour.

The British Troops
The need to reinforce Arras, hold the line of the River Scarpe and maintain a reserve meant that Franklyn had only Brigadier Churchill's 151st Brigade of 50th Division and the two battalions of the tank brigade available for the attack. The men of three infantry battalions – 6/, 7/ and 8/Durham Light Infantry (DLI) – were already tired. The BEF's first-line infantry was all motorized. The soldiers travelled on trucks, and each battalion had a platoon of lightly armoured Bren-gun carriers. French and German infantry covered the ground on foot like their fathers and grandfathers before them. This contributed to German nervousness, because the panzer corridor would not be secure until infantry regiments could revet its flanks, and on 21 May they were miles back, marching bare-headed and bare-armed along poplar-lined roads. The Durhams had gone into Belgium in trucks but had returned on foot and had been on the move for days in warm weather. They were well enough trained for infantry combat, but most had never seen a tank.

The Royal Tank Regiment (RTR) was the descendant of the Heavy Section Machine-Gun Corps which had manned the first tanks to enter battle on the Somme on 15 September 1916. Its men wore a white metal image of a First World War tank on their black berets, and the regiment's distinctive colours of brown, red and green symbolized passage through mud and blood to the green fields beyond. Although most British cavalry regiments had been mechanized by 1940, the Royal Tank Regiment regarded itself as the armoured warfare professionals *par excellence*. Its units were still called battalions and its sub-units were called companies as they had been in the First World War, and a sprinkling of its officers and senior NCOs were veterans of that conflict.

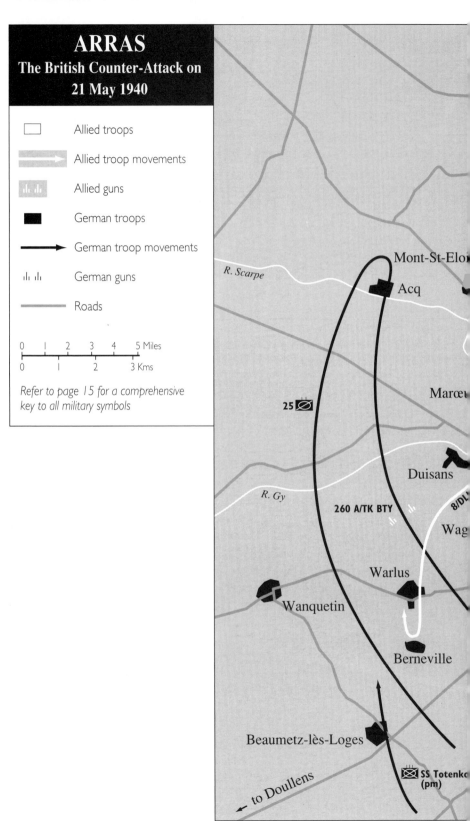

ARRAS
The British Counter-Attack on 21 May 1940

☐	Allied troops
	Allied troop movements
	Allied guns
■	German troops
→	German troop movements
ılı ılı	German guns
	Roads

0 1 2 3 4 5 Miles
0 1 2 3 Kms

Refer to page 15 for a comprehensive key to all military symbols

R. Scarpe

Mont-St-Elo

Acq

Marœu

25 ▨

Duisans

R. Gy

260 A/TK BTY

8/DL

Wag

Warlus

Wanquetin

Berneville

Beaumetz-lès-Loges

SS Totenko
(pm)

to Doullens

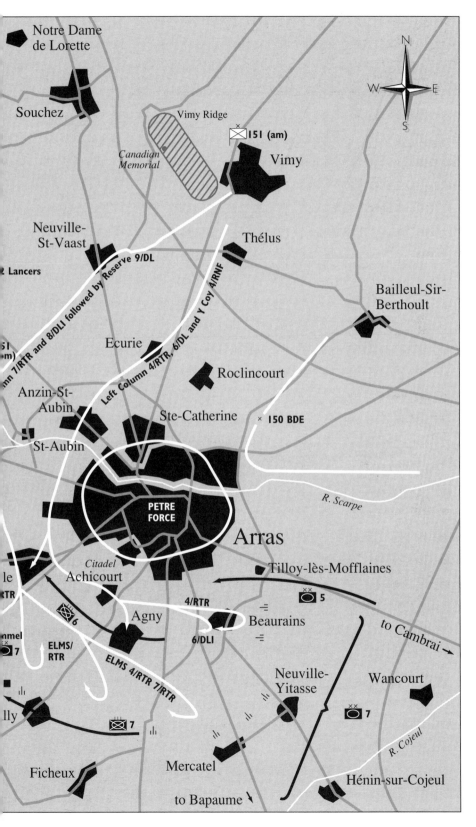

Notre Dame
de Lorette

Souchez

Vimy Ridge

⊠ 151 (am)

Vimy

*Canadian
Memorial*

Neuville-
St-Vaast

Thélus

ℓ Lancers

Reserve 9/DL

Bailleul-Sir-
Berthoult

Left Column 4/RTR, 6/DL and Y Coy 4/RNF

mn 7/RTR and 8/DLI followed by

Ecurie

51
·m)

Roclincourt

Anzin-St-
Aubin

Ste-Catherine

× 150 BDE

St-Aubin

PETRE
FORCE

R. Scarpe

Arras

Citadel

le

Tilloy-lès-Mofflaines

Achicourt

⊠ 6

RTR

4/RTR

⊡ 5

nmel

⊡ 7

ELMS/
RTR

Agny

Beaurains

to Cambrai →

ELMS 4/RTR 7/RTR

6/DLI

■

Neuville-
Yitasse

Wancourt

lly

⊠ 7

⊡ 7

R. Cojeul

Ficheux

Mercatel

Hénin-sur-Cojeul

to Bapaume ↓

Brigadier Douglas Pratt's 1st Army Tank Brigade contained 4/ and 7/Royal Tank Regiment. Both had moved into Belgium at the opening of the campaign and out of it a week later: about one-quarter of the tanks were already out of action because of worn-out tracks or lack of petrol. Lieutenant-Colonel Fitzmaurice's 4/RTR had the Mk I Infantry tank with its .303 or .5 machine-gun, and Lieutenant-Colonel Heyland's 7/RTR had, in addition, some of the bigger Mk II Matildas with their 2-pdr guns and .303 machine-guns. Before the battle, seven of the Matildas were transferred to 4/RTR. In all, the brigade had 16 Mk IIs and 56 MKIs, as well as a dozen light tanks, so lightly armoured as to be of little use except for reconnaissance and liaison.

Artillery support was provided by 365th Field Battery Royal Artillery, with 18-pdrs and 368th Field Battery with the newer 25-pdrs. The former, part of 5th Division, had not worked with 151st Brigade before, and in the last-minute hurry there was no time for liaison between observation officers, the troops they were to support and the guns whose fire they were expected to control. There were two anti-tank batteries, 206th and 260th, with 2-pdr guns. Reconnaissance was furnished by 50th Division's motor-cycle battalion, 4/Royal Northumberland Fusiliers (RNF). No air support was available. The BEF's air component and the AASF were withdrawing to bases in England, and although the Air Ministry in London sent fifty-seven Battle light bombers against targets between Arras and the coast they had no effect on the action.

Arras was held by the Welsh Guards and improvised units including Cook's Light Tanks, a handful of vehicles collected from workshops. Welsh Guards companies covered the main approaches to the town, with battalion headquarters in the Palais St Vaast in its centre, and Cook's Light Tanks and the battalion's carrier platoon in reserve. There had been clashes on the 20th as reconnaissance units of 7th Panzer Division reached Beaurains on the southern outskirts of Arras and probed towards the town. On Rommel's left, 8th Panzer, with the SS Totenkopf Motorized Regiment just behind it, made even better progress and reached Hesdin, west of Arras, by dark. The Morris armoured cars of the 12th Lancers met 8th Panzer near Beaumetz-lès-Loges and 5th Panzer on the Cambrai road, and the lancers pulled back towards Vimy Ridge, establishing their headquarters in the ruins of the abbey at Mont-St-Eloi.

The Allied Attack
In view of all this it is puzzling that Franklyn was not given fresh orders. He already knew that a larger operation was envisaged, for he had met French commanders who had asked him to co-operate in it. He declined

to do so, but the discussion was not without result because Prioux agreed to send the remnants of his 3rd Light Armoured Division – some seventy armoured vehicles – into action on Frankforce's right.

Franklyn entrusted the attack to Major-General Martel of 50th Division, telling him, at 6 a.m. on 21 May, that German infantry and tanks were moving south of Arras 'in numbers not believed to be great' and ordering him to clear the area. Martel announced that he proposed to do this with two mobile columns, and was told to attack as quickly as possible. Pratt thought that nothing could be done before 3 p.m., but Martel was persuaded to agree to 2 p.m.

The last leg of the move up to the assembly area around Vimy Ridge was wearisome, tanks completing a 31-mile (50-km) drive by dark to avoid air attack and infantry trudging up on to the ridge where some of them rested amongst preserved trenches which marked the Canadian capture of Vimy Ridge in 1917. Brigadier Churchill gave his orders in Petit Vimy, on the ridge's northern slope, at 9.45 a.m. No tank officer was present, and Lieutenant-Colonel Miller of 6/DLI was not sure which RTR battalion was to support his column: he met its commander only once, about three hours later. The tanks had established communications some days before but had preserved radio silence thereafter, and their

Men of the British Expeditionary Force on the march in June 1940. They are wearing khaki serge battledress and carrying 1937 pattern webbing equipment – not a happy combination in hot weather.

radios drifted 'off net' all too easily: few worked when the attack began. There was no radio link between infantry and tanks, and maps were in short supply. Second Lieutenant Tom Craig of 4/RTR tells how: 'I arrived at Petit Vimy in my Matilda exhausted and disorganized. I was given a map by my company commander and told to start up and follow him. The wireless was not working, there was no tie-up with the infantry and no clear orders.'

The columns set off at 11 a.m. with the aim of crossing the Arras–Doullens road, where the attack proper was meant to begin, at 2 p.m. The right column (7/RTR and 8/DLI) was to head for Boisleux-au-Mont on the River Cojeul by way of Maroeuil, Warlus and Wailly, while the left column (4/RTR and 6/DLI) made for Hénin-sur-Cojeul via Ecurie, Achicourt and Beaurains. Martel had allocated a company of 4/RNF to each column and kept the rest of the battalion, as well as 9/DLI, in reserve. As Martel's infantry began to tramp down the long, gentle slope towards Arras, Rommel was chivvying stray elements of his division around Vis-en-Artois, while 25th Panzer Regiment roared on to reach Acq, north-west of Arras, by late afternoon. Rommel's two rifle regiments, 6th and 7th, also by-passing Arras to the south, were approaching Mercatel and Agny.

The left-hand column met the Germans first. Although it had set off in good order, by the time it reached St Aubin it was evident that the British infantry could not keep up with the armour, and Lieutenant-Colonel Miller agreed that the tanks should go on ahead. They met elements of 6th Rifle Regiment in Dainville, which was cleared by Y Company 4/RNF with assistance from the tanks, and several prisoners were taken. Leaving 4/RNF to look after the prisoners, 4/RTR went on, crossing the Doullens road under sporadic shellfire. The level-crossing on the Dainville–Achicourt road was down, and it was some time before a strong-willed officer crashed through it. Some tanks negotiated the railway cutting and a few were marooned on the line. Just the other side of the railway 4/RTR ran into 6th Rifle Regiment. Second Lieutenant Peter Vaux described this:

We had come straight into the flank of a German mechanized column which was moving across our front. They were just as surprised as us and we were right in amongst them ... and for the first quarter of an hour or so there was a glorious 'free for all'. We knocked out quite a lot of their lorries: there were Germans running all over the place.

Miller, who had worked with tanks in the First World War, knew that infantry must be on hand to consolidate their success, and did his best to

Each British infantry battalion had a platoon of lightly-armoured Universal Carriers. These were usually fitted with a Bren light machine-gun, earning them the name Bren-gun carriers.

move on his 'very tired and footsore' men. German survivors had gone to ground in the villages and he sent his left-hand company to clear Agny. When he returned to battalion headquarters Major Jeffreys, the second-in-command, warned that 4/RTR was getting further away and suggested that the carrier platoon should be sent on to regain contact. Miller agreed and advanced towards Achicourt, startling a fine dog fox which Jeffreys hallooed away 'much to the delight of the men of B Company, many of whom were keen sportsmen from the Zetland country.' Many shaken Germans were taken prisoner, but Miller received a message from Martel telling him not to go beyond Beaurains as the right-hand column was making slower progress.

By now, 4/RTR was reaching the high-water mark of its advance. 'I do not know how many Germans we killed and how many German vehicles we set on fire,' recalled Peter Vaux. 'At that moment I didn't see why we shouldn't go all the way to Berlin.' But as the battalion passed through Beaurains the first tanks of 5th Panzer Division appeared at Tilloy on the Cambrai–Arras road. One tank 'with a proper gun in its turret' was close enough to 4/RTR for the commanding officer to send

Vaux on a fruitless mission to ask help from a French Somua, which was busily engaged in shelling Beaurains cemetery.

When Vaux returned to the Beaurains–Tilly road and looked westwards towards Telegraph Hill, a low ridge topped with a wood, he saw over twenty tanks from A and B Companies in the field in front of him. The commanding officer's light tank – he had transferred into it in order to get about more easily – was ahead of the others, identifiable by its flag. Vaux failed to reach Lieutenant-Colonel Fitzmaurice on the radio, and was then called forward by the adjutant. They both fired on anti-tank guns in a nearby potato clump, but Vaux realized that most enemy fire was coming from the ridge and drove forwards. As he did so he could see that the British tanks were all knocked out, crews lying beside them or crawling back through the grass. He machine-gunned the wood but was soon signalled back by the adjutant. As he returned he saw that the CO's tank had its side blown in, and 'although I didn't know it the Colonel and Corporal Moorhouse, his operator, were dead inside it.'

The damage had been done by the 105mm guns of Rommel's 78th Artillery Regiment, its 4th and 5th Batteries astride the wood on Telegraph Hill and 6th Battery south of Tilloy. Just north of the Neuville-Vitasse–Mercatel road, 1st Battery, assisted by the fire of 88mms north of Mercatel, prevented the British from outflanking Telegraph Hill to their right. Major Stuart Fernie had taken effective control of the battalion, and an officer met him on the sunken road running diagonally from Agny to Beaurains 'still in his smart service dress with his floppy jacket, on the ground, organizing the chaps since there was no wireless.'

One of those he organized was an ex-circus strong-man, 'Muscle' Armit, who held the short-lived rank of Warrant Officer Class III, Platoon Sergeant-Major. Fernie told Armit (wrongly, in the event) that the CO had been killed by anti-tank guns firing from Mercatel and ordered him to go and get them. Armit drove south, met six 37mm guns and destroyed two of them. His gun was damaged, and his tank was hit several times as he tried to repair it. He managed to reverse into cover, although he had a tense moment after he ignited a smoke discharger in the turret and then found that the hatch would not open for him to throw it out. Having repaired the gun he returned to the fray. 'They must have thought I was finished,' he reflected, 'for I caught the guns limbering up … and revenge was sweet.'

The German artillery was not only within range of Martel's batteries but could also have been hit from positions north of the River Scarpe, but British artillery fire was never effective. Miller called down the fire of his own battery, passing information to the guns by messenger because the radios had failed, but was picking his targets from the map and could not observe the fall of shot. At 8.15 p.m., with Beaurains under artillery fire and repeated air attack, Miller decided to withdraw. His two forward companies – D, in the centre of Beaurains, and C, in an orchard on the south-east edge of the village – moved back through the junction where the D919 crosses the Achicourt–Beaurains road. Y Company 4/RNF had been ordered to hold it until ordered to withdraw. The order never came, and the company fought on until well after dark when it was overwhelmed.

Miller and Fernie waited at a crossroads east of the junction as survivors of C and D Companies emerged from the flames of Beaurains. It was pitch dark when a tank approached from the east. The adjutant of 4/RTR flagged it down with a map-board to speak to the commander, who turned out to be an officer of 5th Panzer Division. There was a confused battle as the British withdrew. 'It was dark with the moon just rising,' wrote Peter Vaux. 'There was flames, smoke, our vehicles, the carriers of 6/DLI, soldiers of 6/DLI on foot; there were German soldiers, some doubtless prisoners, but others were on motor cycles – so God knows what they were doing there.' Miller eventually found brigade headquarters in Ecurie and then set about getting his exhausted men, so tired that they collapsed as they marched and slept where they fell, back on to Vimy Ridge.

The right column had also set off at 11 a.m. that morning, although without its motor-cyclists from 4/RNF who were not ready to start. Some light shelling was encountered just short of Maroeuil, and when the infantry, well behind the tanks, crossed the main road near Duisans they were heartened to see the wreckage of a 150mm battery of 8th Panzer Division which had been shot up by the 12th Lancers. The survivors had taken refuge in Duisans, which was cleared by C Company 8/DLI with the help of French tanks. Numerous prisoners were taken and handed over to the French who stripped them to their underwear and held them in the square in front of the church.

The Allied commanding officers of tanks and infantry met in Maroeuil at about 12.45 p.m., but soon afterwards 7/RTR's liaison officer, accompanying the Durhams in his scout car, lost radio contact with his own headquarters. Infantry and armour never regained touch thereafter, and Pratt cautioned Martel: 'This is going to be a shambles. The infantry are miles behind. We are going forward against strong opposition … We will be absolutely smashed and we must stop this mess, get things together and try later.' Martel, commanding from an open-topped car, told him that the attack had to go on.

Lieutenant-Colonel Heyland's 7/RTR lost direction in Duisans, edging south-east towards Wagnonlieu and Dainville and becoming entangled with the rear elements of 4/RTR. This may have happened because there were so few maps that tank commanders were told to follow a line of pylons which took them too far east, or it may be that the CO, aware that time was slipping away, decided to head straight for Wailly.

Had 7/RTR followed its intended route it would have met 25th Panzer Regiment which was heading north between Warlus and Wanquetin at exactly this time. The German regiment had far more tanks, but would have found it hard to deal with the Mk IIs of 7/RTR. As it was, 25th Panzer continued virtually unopposed, destroying a scout platoon of 4/RNF as it plunged onwards. The German tanks were spotted by the 12th Lancers at Mont-St-Eloi, and by X Company 4/RNF which had moved late but was now watching the open ground south and west of Duisans. It relayed the news to brigade headquarters and was ordered to fall back, and as it retired it passed through 260th Anti-Tank Battery Royal Artillery, its guns guarding against the reappearance of 25th Panzer.

It was with difficulty that 7/RTR swung round towards Wailly: few radios worked and orders had to be taken by officers in light tanks. The CO and the adjutant were both killed, the former by machine-gun fire as he stood outside his tank organizing the attack, and the advance became disjointed with tanks making for Wailly, Mercatel and Ficheux.

Rommel's Progress

Rommel usually travelled with 25th Panzer Regiment, often in the tank of its commander, Colonel Rothenburg. On 21 May he had intended to move with the tanks but 'the infantry regiments were so slow ... that I drove straight off back to chase up the 7th Rifle Regiment and get it to hurry up.' He could not find it, but met part of 6th Regiment near Ficheux and drove along- 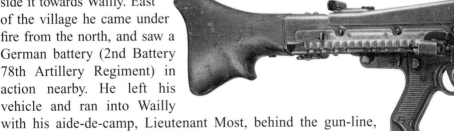 side it towards Wailly. East of the village he came under fire from the north, and saw a German battery (2nd Battery 78th Artillery Regiment) in action nearby. He left his vehicle and ran into Wailly with his aide-de-camp, Lieutenant Most, behind the gun-line, recording 'chaos and confusion amongst our troops in the village ... they were jamming up the roads and yards with their vehicles instead of going into action with every available weapon to fight off the oncoming attack.' He called up his vehicle and drove on to a prominent hillock west of Wailly where he found some anti-aircraft and anti-tank guns in hollows in a thin wood.

His position was desperate. Some British tanks (D Company 7/RTR) had crossed the Wailly–Berneville road and had already knocked out a Panzer III, while others (B Company 7/RTR) were moving up from the Doullens road. Rommel saw nearby gunners take to their heels. 'With Most's help,' he wrote:

 I brought every available gun into action at top speed against the tanks ... With the enemy so close only rapid fire from every gun could save the situation ... Soon we succeeded in putting the leading enemy tanks out of action. About 150 yards [137 metres] to the west of our small wood a British captain climbed out of a heavy tank and walked unsteadily towards us with his hands up. We had killed his driver.

Rommel dealt first with the attack from the north before engaging the tanks moving in from the west. 'The worst seemed to be over and the attack beaten off,' he noted, 'when suddenly Most sank to the ground behind a 20mm anti-aircraft gun close beside me. He was mortally wounded and blood gushed from his mouth.'

The Battle Continues

Lieutenant-Colonel Beart's 8/DLI had marched on without its tanks. Beart left B and C Companies in Duisans and continued to Warlus with A and D, sending A on through the village towards Berneville, where it came under fire from Germans on the Doullens road. D Company moved through the village to woods at its south-eastern edge. Here it was viciously dive-bombed by German Stukas. Although, as was so

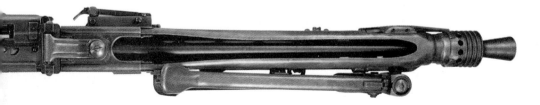

In 1934 the Germans introduced the MG 34, the first real general purpose machine-gun, which could be used on a variety of ground mounts or fitted to vehicles. The MG 42, shown above, was a wartime development which had a higher rate of fire (theoretically up to 1200 rounds a minute), giving it a distinctive buzz-saw sound.

often the case with these terrifying but primitive aircraft, few casualties were caused 'everyone was absolutely shattered. After a few minutes the officers and some of the NCOs collected themselves and said "Right, we must get on with it", but it was very difficult to get some of the men moving – we had to kick them into position and the effect was very considerable.'

Some German tanks appeared from the south-east while the air attack was in progress but three French tanks, with battalion headquarters in the area of the water tower, helped to drive them off, and other enemy tanks which threatened the Durhams' left flank were checked by the fire of part of the brigade anti-tank company. A Company had lost its commander and sergeant-major in Berneville and joined D Company, whose commander had been wounded, in Warlus. Beart pulled his men into a tight perimeter as shells ignited several houses. The French tanks left, their commander announcing that he had tasks to undertake elsewhere. Messages could not be got through to the battalion second-in-command in Duisans, and the Durhams faced the prospect of an unpleasant night.

The reappearance of 25th Panzer Regiment worsened the battalion's prospects. The regiment was cooking chickens at Acq: they were almost ready when orders arrived to return to Dainville to fall on the British rear. On the way the Germans ran into 260th Anti-Tank Battery and broke through, losing tanks in the process. They then brushed 'strong armoured forces' (probably the remnants of 7/RTR retiring northwards), losing still more tanks because of what a German officer called 'the bigger calibre and range of your tanks and stronger armour'. The regiment spent the night on the battlefield, severing communications between the two portions of 8/DLI.

Second Lieutenant Potts, 8/DLI's mortar officer, rode through the cordon on his motor bike and found brigade headquarters at 2.30 a.m. on 22 May. He received orders to withdraw and took them to the companies in Duisans but could not get through to Warlus. Just when things seemed blackest, six French tanks and two armoured personnel carriers reached Warlus. Survivors were loaded on to all available vehicles, and the little column broke out of Warlus in a squall of firing. It found Duisans deserted, and reached Vimy Ridge at 6 a.m.

The Aftermath

The day cost Rommel's division 30–40 tanks and 378 officers and men, and the British took 400 prisoners from 7th and 8th Panzer Divisions and the SS Totenkopf. According to 7th Panzer, it destroyed 43 British tanks, and credited 25 of these to 78th Artillery Regiment. The RTR battalions lost over half the tanks engaged, and the infantry returned to Vimy Ridge with perhaps half the soldiers who had left it. Not all the missing ended up as prisoners of war: some resourceful members of 4/DLI made their own way to Boulogne, assisted in the defence of the port and were safely evacuated.

The action enabled the British to tighten their grip on Arras, although Gort reluctantly authorized its abandonment late on the 23rd as part of a general withdrawal. Despite instructions from Weygand and Churchill, he saw that the projected counter-attack into the panzer corridor would never get under way. Withdrawal on Dunkirk further soured Allied relations and led some Frenchmen to argue that it was only British dereliction that had thwarted a promising plan. The Belgians, who had fought far harder than contemporaries or most historians have admitted, agreed to cease-fire terms on the 27th, persuading Gort to increase the pace of his withdrawal. Another bout of misunderstanding resulted in much of the French 1st Army fighting on in Lille, and it was only on 29 May that Weygand agreed that French troops could be evacuated from Dunkirk. Although Gort had prophesied that 'a great part of the BEF and its equipment will inevitably be lost even in the best of circumstances', 338 000 men, one-third of them French, were taken off by the time the operation ended on 4 June.

Evacuation was assisted by the fact that German armour was ordered to halt on 24 May, and it was not until the 26th that it was allowed to move again. Liddell Hart traces the halt order to shock created by the Arras counter-attack. Few historians would wholly agree with him. The attack certainly inspired what the war diary of Guderian's corps called 'nervousness throughout the group area', and General von Kluge of 4th Army admitted that 21 May was 'the first day on which the enemy has achieved some success'. There were many other reasons for a pause, not least the erosion of German armour by battle and breakdown. Yet the Arras action certainly helped to delay the German advance on Dunkirk. It not only alarmed the German High Command – the fact that 7th Panzer's situation map showed five British divisions is a measure of the concern – but it also bought time for the defence of Boulogne and Calais, which slowed down the drive on Dunkirk. The defence of Calais remains deeply controversial. The town was entrusted to the three rifle regiments of Brigadier Claude Nicholson's 30th Brigade, ordered to fight on to the end in the interests of Allied solidarity. They fought on until 26 May, and the bombardment which reduced the old town to smoking rubble destroyed many buildings which might have been familiar to Henry V's men on their way home from Agincourt.

A View of the Field

Thousands of British visitors, making the last sprint for Calais, follow the A26 which slides along the southern flank of Vimy Ridge, with the Canadian memorial to the missing of the First World War to the north and the spur of Notre Dame de Lorette to the south. An old French aphorism declared that he who held the Lorette feature held France and, although cruising the autoroute does not make the fact immediately apparent, this is vital ground. On the northern edge of Vimy Ridge the chalk downs of Artois drop abruptly on to the Flanders plain. It is a sharp geographical divide, and we should not be surprised that for centuries the northern frontier of France has run within sight of the ridge. It is a linguistic frontier too, and not far to the north Courtrai is rendered as Kortrijk and Ypres as Ieper.

In the summer of 1711 Marshal Villars held the lines of *Ne Plus Ultra* (so-called because the Duke of Marlborough was to be held there 'and no further' into France) which stretched from Cambrai to the coast. Here they ran along the River Scarpe south of the ridge, with Arras as their buttress. Marlborough unbalanced Villars first by marching from the eastern end of the lines to Vimy, the French moving parallel on their side of the lines. Then he quietly slipped his guns and baggage away behind the ridge before dashing eastwards with his infantry and cavalry – 'My Lord Duke desires the foot to step it out' – to beat the exasperated marshal to the eastern end of the lines, breaching them before the French could arrive.

A German staff car passes an abandoned infantry tank Mk I of 7/RTR. The tower and dome in the background mark the French National Cemetery of Notre Dame de Lorette.

The Town of Arras

Arras, the capital of Artois, was the birthplace of the French revolutionary leader Maximilien Robespierre. It formed an important route-centre
in Roman times, with roads running out from it like spokes from the hub
of a wheel. The medieval town grew up around the Benedictine abbey of
St-Vaast, which is now a museum of fine arts. Its considerable wealth
came from the textile industry, and the words 'arras' in English and
arazzi in Italian came to mean tapestries in general, so pervasive was the
influence of those which really originated in Arras. The town's two great
cobbled squares, the Grand Place and the Place des Héros, are fine exam-
ples of Flemish architecture, and were sensitively restored after damage
suffered in the First World War when the front line ran just east of the
town. In fact the line was so close that it could be safely reached from
the town, and the *hôtel de ville* gives access to the *boves*, a complex
system of tunnels begun in the tenth century and developed since. They
were extensively used by the British in the First World War, and contain
familiar graffiti.

Arras was fortified by the military engineer Sébastien de Vauban, and
although most of the ramparts disappeared to make way for the wide
boulevards circling the town, the citadel, finished in 1670, survives at its
south-west corner. It is still in military hands and is not open to the
public, but a lane leading off the Boulevard Charles de Gaulle between
the citadel and the British First World War memorial takes the visitor into
the ditch girdling the fortifications. Fortress ditches were convenient
spots for military executions: secure accommodation was on hand nearby
and lofty ramparts could absorb stray bullets. In 1940–4 the Arras area,
and in particular the mining belt to its north, produced fierce opposition
to the Germans, and many members of the Resistance were shot here in
the ditch. A post marks the place of execution, and plaques on the ram-
part walls commemorate the dead. The nearby British Memorial to the
Missing commemorates the First World War dead of the Royal Flying
Corps, amongst them Major Edward 'Mick' Mannock VC, DSO and two
bars, MC and bar.

Vimy Ridge

The Arras operation began on Vimy Ridge, which is an ideal spot at
which to begin any study. The Germans had taken the place during the
'race to the sea' in 1914, and in October they seized Neuville-St-Vaast,
Carency and Notre Dame de Lorette to establish a line running through
the abbey at Mont-St-Eloi. In May 1915 the French managed to wrest
Lorette from the Germans and to win a toehold on the southern slopes of

Vimy Ridge, but at an appalling cost. The cemetery at Lorette contains the graves of 20 000 Frenchmen and the ossuary the bones of another 20 000. General Frido von Senger und Etterlin was there as a young man, and remembered 'a big burial ground for the bones of those dismembered bodies that nobody could put together'. He was back in 1940 and, like so many older combatants, was struck by the absurd familiarity of the landscape. He even tracked down his former landlady: 'Unbelieving, she gazed on me, claiming to recognize again the Lieutenant von S., if that was indeed the man who stood before her.' Above the ossuary stands a lighthouse-like tower which gives a wide if distant view of the 1917 and 1940 battlefields.

Vimy Ridge was attacked by the Canadian Corps on Easter Monday, 9 April 1917. The Canadians had made good use of the tunnels beneath the ridge, some of them ancient when the battle was fought and others dug by tunnelling companies of the Royal Engineers. There were twelve main tunnels in the Canadian sector with a network of smaller tunnels and dug-outs running off them. The main shafts were 6½ feet (2 metres) high, at least 3 feet (1 metre) wide, and were lit by electricity. Grange Tunnel,

This particular 88mm gun was captured in Normandy in 1944. Its shield marks it out as an anti-tank variant of this very successful anti-aircraft and anti-tank weapon.

one of the longest, is open to the public during the season, and visitors are shown round by well-informed young Canadians.

The Canadians had taken great care to prepare the assaulting troops. Over 40 000 maps were issued, and troops were briefed on the details of German defences so they would be able to use their initiative if there was an unexpected hitch. The Germans were handicapped by the fact that the steep rearward slope of the ridge made it impossible for them to defend in depth, and the Canadian assault was an almost complete success. Preserved trenches, their sandbags filled with cement, mark the Canadian start line. They are rather neater than anything that might have been seen hereabouts in 1917 but give an excellent feel for the dogtooth layout of a First World War trench system. The Canadian memorial stands in the centre of the German line and bears the names of 11 285 Canadians who were declared 'missing, presumed dead' in France.

The memorial was only four years old when the Durhams assembled on the ridge in 1940. Their advance took them past cemeteries full of First World War dead. It must have been strange for the veterans amongst them: the forty-seven-year-old Lieutenant-Colonel Harry Miller of 6/DLI had fought in the area in his youth. The memories and memorials in the area are largely from the First World War. There is a memorial to a North African Division – 'Without fear and without pity' – on the ridge, and others, with a little museum, in Neuville-St-Vaast. The ruins of the abbey at Mont-St-Eloi are in view as one descends the slope, but they were ruined long before the 12th Lancers established their headquarters there.

The 1940 Campaign

It is not until we reach Duisans, on the route of the right-hand column, that there is evidence of the 1940 battle. German prisoners were kept in the square in front of the church, and the church itself bears the scars of shrapnel and small-arms fire.

The left-hand column's route is all but swamped by the southwards expansion of Arras. The once-distinct villages now tend to merge with one another and the construction of new roads has not been kind; the route is better driven than walked. However, the D60, which leaves Dainville and crosses the Doullens road, takes us towards Achicourt just as it did 4/RTR and 6/DLI, and ½ mile (1 km) along it is the level-crossing which caused so much trouble in 1940.

It takes adroit map-reading to strike through Achicourt and Beaurains, and it is easiest to sidestep them to the south. Stay on the D60 through Agny and zigzag, still on the same road, to meet the new by-pass connecting the N17 to the N39 Arras–Cambrai road. This goes just west of Telegraph Hill (which was held by the 4th and 5th Batteries of Rommel's 78th Artillery Regiment), and there is convenient parking on the Beaurains side exactly half-way between the N17 junction and the turn-off for Tilloy. Looking eastwards one has Peter Vaux's view of 4/RTR's last attack; the field across the road was strewn with knocked-out British tanks, and the wood on the crest-line was the one he machine-gunned. It still contains defences – a German pillbox which pre-dates the British Arras offensive of April 1917, a hopeless business enlivened only by Canadian capture of Vimy Ridge.

The right-hand column may have been less successful but its route today is more congenial. From Duisans a track leads directly along 8/DLI's line of march to Warlus, and for the car-bound the road through Agnez-lès-Duisans deviates only slightly from this route. The road crosses a gentle ridge half-way to Warlus, and it was on this that 260th Anti-Tank Battery stood, engaging 25th Panzer Regiment as it returned from the north-west. Warlus has changed little, and its water tower still stands on the road to Berneville. It was here that Lieutenant-Colonel Beart had his headquarters at the time of the Stuka attack: it is a rather bare place in which to be dive-bombed. When I was last there a rusty and battered British fuel can, known for telling reasons as a 'flimsy' and later replaced by the more robust jerry-can copied from the Germans, lay by the fence.

The general line of 7/RTR's advance can be followed from Maroeuil to Wagnonlieu and thence to the Doullens road. The wooded hillock occupied by Rommel himself is obvious from many viewpoints on this side of the road. It is surmounted by a handful of trees for which 'bushy-topped' is the only apt description: they look almost tropical. Tanks from D Company 7/RTR made straight for Warlus on the axis of the minor road which heads due south from Dainville. Others, from B Company, moved parallel with the Doullens road and then turned south-east, advancing on Rommel's position. There were others which rattled straight across the ridge towards Agny, some swinging down towards Wailly and others keeping course for Mercatel, where they encountered those deadly 88mms – the first of the many British tanks to do so during the war.

Some heavily-armoured Mk IIs bit deep into the German stop-line. Two of 7/RTR's MK 11s, commanded by Major King and Sergeant Doyle, may have got as far as the Bapaume road. They overran a 37mm battery, knocked out four tanks (they were encouraged to see that their 2-pdrs went clean through them), crashed through a barrier of farm carts and fired on another anti-tank battery. Then, turrets jammed by shell-splinters and external stowage boxes blazing, they took on an 88mm. King kept the gunners' heads down with his machine-gun and Doyle destroyed it with his main armament.

Rommel's position is on a prominent ring contour with the spot height 111 on the IGN 1:50 000 map. It is on a network of tracks, but is best approached by parking alongside the village cemetery to the north-west of Wailly: the crew of a British tank rest there. Walk up through Belloy Farm to turn right along the (usually muddy) track just beyond the farmyard. There are fewer trees now than there were in 1940, but the shallow workings of what seems to be an old quarry would have offered good protection to guns. On this piece of dominant ground Rommel demonstrated, neither for the first nor the last time, the value of forward command. But the fate of Lieutenant Most shows that it was a style replete with risks, and as we look out to the north and west, and imagine those Matildas trundling up the slope, we can see just how close Rommel came to being a promising panzer commander who was cut off in his prime.

CHAPTER 6

Operation Goodwood
1944

Background

'The battle of Normandy,' maintained Stephen Badsey, 'was the last great set-piece battle of the Western World.' An historian should never say never, but we may hope that three months of fighting amongst seaside villas, half-timbered *manoirs* and apple orchards mark the end of a barbarous dynasty of battles which had ruled Europe for centuries before Agincourt was fought. Without the great sea-borne landing of D-Day, 6 June 1944, there could have been no Allied invasion of occupied Europe: but winning a beachhead was only the campaign's first act. Surging out of it to make Normandy a stepping stone to Hitler's defeat was always the Allied aim, and for many combatants it was not the break-in but the break-out which curdles memories of this land of cream and Calvados.

Operation Goodwood was the British army's major contribution to the break-out. Historians remain divided as to whether it was meant to achieve a break-out itself, or to attract German armour from the American sector. Alexander McKee called it 'the death ride of the armoured divisions' with good reason. It was one of the largest ever British mechanized battles, and over 400 tanks were lost, more than the army's tank strength at the time of writing.

The war had been transformed from European conflict to global struggle by the entry of America, Russia and Japan and the spread of hostilities from the deserts of North Africa to the island-speckled immensity of the Pacific. There was broad agreement that Britain and the United States would enter occupied Europe, although it was less easy to agree on the time or method of invasion. At one extreme, the Russian leader Josef Stalin

The .303 No 4 Rifle shown here was approved for manufacture in November 1939, and was the most common British infantry weapon of the Second World War. It was very similar to the Short Magazine Lee Enfield of the First World War, the main difference being the new rifle's aperture backsight, hinged at the rear of the body. Soldiers laid out their equipment in a prescribed manner for kit inspection to enable an inspecting officer to see that all items were present and serviceable. The artist Rex Whistler, who served in the Welsh Guards, drew the approved layout for his regiment's No 7 Holding Company and his drawing was then reproduced as the Welsh Guards' Christmas card for 1940.

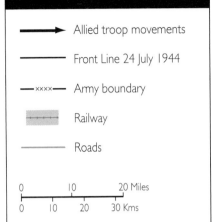

NORMANDY
Operation Goodwood and the Normandy Break-out Battles
June-July 1944

Allied troop movements

Front Line 24 July 1944

——xxxx—— Army boundary

Railway

Roads

0	10		20 Miles
0	10	20	30 Kms

Refer to page 15 for a comprehensive key to all military symbols

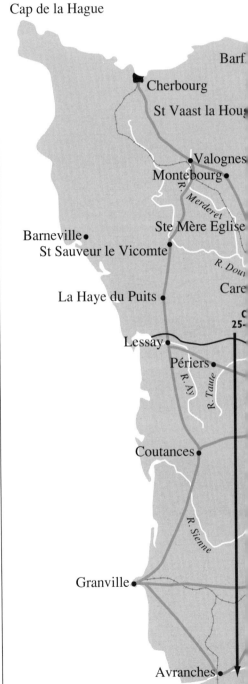

Cap de la Hague

Barf

Cherbourg

St Vaast la Houg

•Valognes

Montebourg•

Ste Mère Eglise

Barneville•

St Sauveur le Vicomte•

R. Douv

Care

La Haye du Puits •

25-

Lessay•

Périers•

Coutances•

Granville•

Avranches•

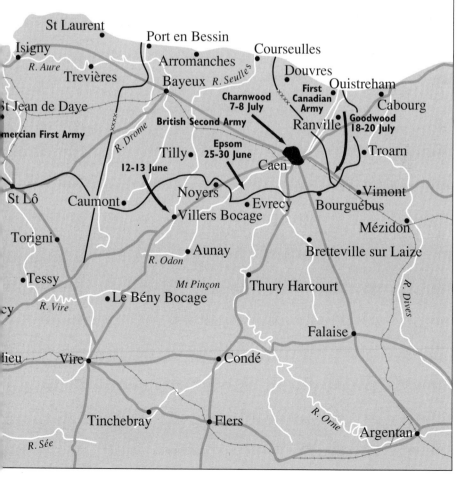

...artin de Varreville

English Channel

St Laurent

Isigny

R. Aure

Trevières

St Jean de Daye

...mercian First Army

St Lô

Torigni

Tessy

R. Vire

...cy

...lieu

Vire

Tinchebray

R. Sée

Port en Bessin

Arromanches

Bayeux *R. Seulles*

R. Drome

British Second Army

Tilly

12-13 June

Caumont

Le Bény Bocage

R. Odon

Aunay

Mt Pinçon

Noyers

Villers Bocage

Conflé

Flers

Courseulles

Douvres

Ouistreham

First
Canadian
Army

Charnwood
7-8 July

Epsom
25-30 June

Caen

Evrecy

Bourguébus

Thury Harcourt

Cabourg

Ranville

Goodwood
18-20 July

Troarn

Vimont

Mézidon

Bretteville sur Laize

R. Dives

Falaise

R. Orne

Argentan

urgently demanded the opening of a second front to divert German resources from the east. At the other, Winston Churchill was inclined to fight where British forces were already deployed because he saw the losses of the First World War as a warning of what might happen if a campaign in France turned sour. The Americans were initially persuaded to acquiesce in British-inspired Mediterranean strategy, but the Allied conference in Washington in May 1943 set a target date for an invasion one year ahead. Six months later in Tehran, the Western Allies committed themselves to Operation Overlord, the invasion of France, and at Cairo, in December 1943, the American General Dwight D. Eisenhower was appointed Supreme Allied Commander for the operation.

The German Position

The Germans had long expected invasion, and although a Canadian descent on Dieppe in August 1942 taught the Allies valuable lessons, it lent impetus to work on the Atlantic Wall, the defences along the French and Belgian coasts. The area was the responsibility of Field Marshal Gerd von Rundstedt, Commander-in-Chief West, and his two army groups. Army Group G held southern France; Army Group B defended Normandy and Brittany with 7th Army, and northern France, Belgium and Holland with 15th Army. The armoured reserve, Panzer Group West, was held back near Paris.

Rundstedt's chain of command was tangled. Field Marshal Erwin Rommel of Army Group B was also Inspector-General of the Atlantic Wall and enjoyed direct access to Hitler. Rommel had authority over three divisions in Panzer Group West, but the remainder could not be moved without Hitler's authority. Aircraft were controlled by *Luftflotte* 3, whose commander answered to Reichsmarschall Hermann Goering. Anti-aircraft guns, including dual-purpose 88mms, were the responsibility of the *Luftwaffe*, as were *Luftwaffe* field divisions, composed of redundant pilots and ground crew. The Waffen-SS maintained divisions of its own, often better equipped than their army counterparts and enjoying a great measure of independence.

The Eastern Front was Germany's overriding priority, and it burnt up troops like kindling. Most divisions in France were not fit for service in the east, many filled with unfit or over-age soldiers who could carry out only static duties: some contained 'Ost' battalions of Russian prisoners of war. The German army had become a two-tier structure as General Heinz Guderian's opponents had feared, its infantry divisions relying on horse-drawn transport. There was a conflict of opinion as to how invasion should be met. Conventional wisdom, to which most senior officers subscribed, favoured identifying the real Allied thrust (there might easily be feints) and sending massed armour against it. Rommel, who knew what Allied air-power could do, believed that the invasion had to be stopped on the beaches. Its first day would be the longest, for Allies and Germans alike.

The Allied Plan

Rommel's opponents would not have disagreed. Planners on the staff of COSSAC (Chief of Staff to Supreme Allied Commander) had decided in favour of landing in Normandy rather than the Pas de Calais, which was closer but more obvious and better defended. When General Sir Bernard Montgomery, who was to command all ground forces for the invasion, saw the COSSAC plan he demanded something bigger: five divisions were to land on a 50-mile (80-km) front, with airborne landings protecting their flanks. Montgomery briefed senior commanders on 7 April 1944. General Omar Bradley's US 1st Army would land in the west on Utah and Omaha beaches, covered by 82nd and 101st Airborne Divisions. Lieutenant-General Sir Miles Dempsey's British 2nd Army was to go ashore on Gold, Juno and Sword beaches in the east, with 6th Airborne Division securing its left flank. The Canadian 1st and US 3rd Armies would be landed later to form two army groups, Montgomery's 21st and Bradley's 12th, at which stage Montgomery would relinquish the role of overall land force commander.

Montgomery's intentions for the development of the campaign loom large in the story that follows. On 7 April his briefing map showed coloured phase lines which may be regarded as illustrative of rates of advance, useful as planning tools. However, Carlo d'Este has argued that they help to cast doubt on what was long regarded as Montgomery's master-plan for the campaign: drawing German reserves to the British sector so as to allow the Americans to break out. The briefing made no mention of a holding operation in the British sector, and a document issued a month later described 'co-ordinated thrusts towards both the Loire and the Seine, so timed as to keep making the enemy move his reserves against first one and then the other.' It was an essentially opportunistic scheme which relied on seizing and maintaining the initiative and then, as d'Este puts it, 'expanding the initial bridgehead and … seizing port facilities in whatever direction proved most advantageous.'

It would be imperative for the Allies to build up forces in Normandy more quickly than their enemy. An elaborate deception plan, Operation Fortitude, encouraged the Germans to believe that an American army group in south-east England was about to invade the Pas de Calais: long

This self-portrait of the artist Rex Whistler *(above)* in his Welsh Guards' uniform, was painted in May 1940 just as he left civilian life to join up with his new regiment. Whistler, who had studied art at the Slade in London, had a particular flair for book illustration, murals and theatre design. The elegance of the conservatory at York Terrace, overlooking Regent's Park, sharply contrasts with the rather more basic conditions of the wartime officers' mess shown in Whistler's humorous sketch *(right)*, but officers and men alike suffered far worse conditions than just the poor lighting portrayed here during wartime. Like much of the young talent of this period, Whistler was killed in 1944, aged 39, while serving with the Guards' Armoured Division during Operation Goodwood. Another Normandy casualty was the poet Keith Douglas, a Yeomanry officer, whose work stands comparison with that of the best of the First World War poets.

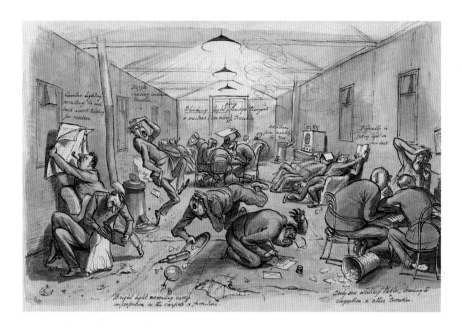

after the invasion the German High Command braced itself for the blow that never came. The Allied air forces, under Air Chief Marshal Sir Trafford Leigh-Mallory, gained superiority in the skies, crippled the French railway system and denied the Germans air reconnaissance. The Allies had an added advantage in secret information graded 'Ultra' that came from codes broken at Bletchley Park in Buckinghamshire. This gave warning of German moves and made possible the location of units whose radio traffic gave them away. When headquarters Panzer Group West at last arrived in Normandy after negotiating roads swept by fighter-bombers, it was identified by Ultra and devastated by a bombing raid which wounded its commander and killed most of his staff. It was out of action for two weeks.

Campaign and Battle

D-Day was an unquestionable but not unqualified success. The Americans ran into heavy opposition on 'Bloody Omaha', and the advance inland went more slowly than expected. Michael Carver, who commanded an armoured brigade in Normandy, went to the heart of the matter when he spoke of: 'The emphasis placed before the campaign on the expected fierceness of the battle on the beaches. There was a tendency to build up a climate of feeling that, once ashore, it would all be fairly easy and merely a matter of build-up.'

Over the next fortnight the Allies strengthened their hold on the fore-shore, taking Bayeux on 7 June and going on to link up the beachheads. Caen, a D-Day objective, remained in German hands. On 12 June, 7th Armoured Division turned the flank of its defenders by taking Villers Bocage but was rebuffed by a well-handled German counter-attack. The Americans, too, had their share of unpleasant surprises: a drive towards St Lô petered out in country that might have been made for defence. Bradley's men crossed the Cotentin peninsula to reach the Atlantic coast on 17 June, cutting off three German divisions and isolating Cherbourg.

In the second half of June the battle solidified. The Allies had bare numerical superiority, but command of air and sea meant that they could reinforce the half-million men already ashore. The Germans endured constant abrasion from the air. For example, 2nd Panzer Division left Abbeville for Normandy by rail on 9 June. It was so frequently attacked that the tanks had to finish the journey by road, and it was not until 18 June that 80 of the 120 tanks which had started reached the front at Caumont. Air-power was no respecter of persons. It killed tough old General Erich Marcks of LXXXIV Corps, whose wooden leg delayed his escape from his car when fighter-bombers swooped, and on 17 July Hurricanes strafed another German staff car near Livarot: its driver was killed and the passenger badly injured. He was Field Marshal Rommel.

Rommel had lost confidence in victory, his faith shaken as much by Hitler's wild schemes for counter-attacks as by Allied material superiority. On 23 June he told his wife that: 'Militarily things aren't at all good. The enemy air force is dealing extremely heavily with our supplies and at the moment is completely strangling them. If a decisive battle develops, we'll be without ammunition … We must be prepared for grave events.' In fact, a decisive battle in the east began that day when the Russians launched Operation Bagration, which led to the destruction of Army Group Centre and the loss of 350 000 men. Rundstedt was no more optimistic. On 1 July he assured the chief of Armed Forces High Command (OKW) that the situation was impossible. 'Make peace, you idiots,' said Rundstedt. 'What else can you do?' He was dismissed on 2 July and replaced by Field Marshal Gunther von Kluge.

'A Greater Sense of Urgency'

Allied air commanders, however, were concerned at the lack of progress: on 16 June Air Marshal Sir Arthur Coningham of the 2nd Tactical Air Force demanded 'a greater sense of urgency from the army and a frank admission that their operations were not running according to plan.' Eisenhower's deputy, Air Chief Marshal Sir Arthur Tedder, was worried by the army's failure to take the Caen-Falaise plain which could provide bases for aircraft operating from England. The landing schedule was running late. Cherbourg was still in German hands, and a gale which raged for four days from 19 June destroyed the American Mulberry artificial harbour and damaged the British one.

Montgomery did his best to break the deadlock, maintaining pressure on both sides of the bridgehead. On 18 June he directed that Cherbourg was to be taken by the Americans, and Caen by the British, before 23 June. Cherbourg eventually fell on 26/27 June; the port was so thoroughly wrecked that it could not operate at full capacity until the end of September. An American drive southwards floundered through *bocage* countryside, its chequerboard of fields blanked off with banks and hedges, and had spent itself by 11 July. On 26 June the British launched Operation Epsom, an attempt to outflank Caen from the west. It punched a salient into German lines, left Caen dangerously exposed, but did not take the city. A direct assault, Operation Charnwood, also made disappointing progress. On the night of 7 July, 460 heavy bombers pounded Caen: after fighting in rubble-choked streets, British and Canadian troops advanced as far as the River Orne but left a substantial portion of the city in German hands.

Allied Difficulties

Failure to secure Caen highlighted two difficulties. The first was the cramped state of the bridgehead. By 30 June the Allies had landed 875 000 men, 150 000 vehicles and 570 000 tons (580 000 tonnes) of stores. There were thirteen American and fourteen British divisions ashore but, although the headquarters of both follow-up armies had landed, there was no room to deploy the armies themselves, and the Americans already had nine divisions waiting in England.

The second problem was specifically British. Put simply, the army was running out of men. The Americans had suffered 37 034 casualties and the British 24 698, but while the Americans were able to replace them the British, continuously engaged in one theatre or another since 1939, could not. In August Montgomery had to break up 59th Division. Battalions were split up to provide drafts, and an NCO in 2/Hertfordshire recorded that he was 'very sorry that our Bn is being broken up in this way ... I hate leaving comrades with whom I have been for so long ... It hardly seems possible that we are all breaking up and may never see each other again.'

The problem went deeper. Three British divisions, 50th Northumbrian, 51st Highland and 7th Armoured, were veterans of the desert.

Many of their officers and men thought that they had done their bit. Brigadier James Hargest, an experienced New Zealander, said of 50th Division that 'there was a strong feeling amongst the men while in England that the Div. should *not* be asked to do the assault on D-Day ...' When Major Martin Lindsay joined 2/Gordon Highlanders in Normandy he observed 'the way in which the men's feelings are considered in this division. Twice in two days I have heard, "The Jocks don't like raids".' Major-General G.L. Verney, who took over 7th Armoured Division after its commander was sacked, was uncomfortably penetrating in his analysis:

There is no doubt that familiarity with war does not make one more courageous. One becomes cunning, and from cunning to cowardice is but a short step. The infantryman who does not want to 'have a go' and can find opportunities for lying low at the critical moment; the tank man can easily find a fault in his engine or his wireless, and thus miss taking part in the battle ... two of the three divisions that came back from Italy ... were extremely 'swollen-headed'. They were a law unto themselves; they thought that they need only obey those orders that suited them.

Brigadier Hargest argued that 'the high percentage of officer casualties is due to the necessity of them being *always* in the front to direct advances in difficult country.' Lindsay realized that 'nearly every operation nowadays is a succession of company battles' and Major-General 'Pip' Roberts of 11th Armoured Division agreed that 'casualties in Company Commanders and their equivalent were probably the most serious loss that units suffered in this phase of the war.' Brigadier Bill Williams, Montgomery's chief intelligence officer, summed up the prevailing view: 'We were always well aware of the doctrine "let metal do it rather than flesh". The morale of our troops depended on this. We always said – "Waste all the ammunition you like, but not flesh."'

War at First Hand
Sometimes Normandy was more than flesh and blood could stand. Lieutenant Geoffrey Bishop of 23rd Hussars saw a friend's tank destroyed in their first action. He was buried in an orchard: 'Suddenly and silently all the regiment is gathered round. They have all known and loved Bob, and this simple tribute brings a choking feeling to my throat.' Bishop soon discovered that death had uglier faces. He watched a self-propelled gun burn while men tried to remove ammunition: 'In a flash there are two blinding reports – I have my glasses on them and can see quite clearly – a body shoots high into the air; the others disappear

in a cloud of black smoke ... That night ... there is a lurid glow from the gun and the smell of a burnt offering to the God of War.' Trooper Ken Tout of 1/Northamptonshire Yeomanry saw that a fellow gunner had failed to escape from a blazing tank, but: 'The explosions of ammunition ... served as a humane killer before the furnace began to grill him where he sat. Something in my being revolts more against the slow grilling of my flesh after death than against the sudden swift shattering of mind and body in a massive explosion.'

Noise wore men down. The German 'Moaning Minnie' multi-barrelled rocket launcher was especially frightening. 'The actual destruction is less than would be caused by the same weight of shells,' thought Lindsay, 'but the noise, and therefore the moral effect, is much greater.' There was the buzz-saw sound of the German MG 42 machine-gun and the slower rattle of the Bren; the 'feathery shuffle' audible in the split second before a mortar bomb burst with its 'flat, grating, guttural crash'; the railway-train rumble of 25-pdr shells going one way and the sharper whiz-bang of a high-velocity shell coming the other. A barrage could be almost soporific. Ken Tout tells how 'the continuous sporadic traffic of shells overhead and the fitful jazz beat of explosions behind us have merged into our consciousness until we disregard them.' There was no disregarding the SLAM-CRASH of an 88mm, the sound of the shell's impact and the weapon's firing arriving almost together. Perhaps the most telling accompaniment to tank battle was the smack of armour-piercing shot on armour plate, like the clang of bodkin point on breastplate, obscenely amplified.

There were yells of agony and tortured desperation. The commander of a stricken American Sherman groaned that he was in the most indescribable anguish, his plight relayed to his comrades because his radio was switched to 'send'. Radios, more numerous and reliable than in 1940, gave the crews of armoured vehicles an ability to communicate which soldiers had not known since orders, exhortation and banter reverberated round squares at Waterloo. British radio procedure could snap from hunting field – '3 Baker. Good show. Move back a bit and let the hounds see the foxes ...' – to hospital: 'Oboe 4 Able. Now 4 Charlie has brewed. I think there is a nasty about ten o'clock. Can't see ... all gone dark ... all gone cold ... somebody please, please, ple ...' And yet for the infantry, the battlefield was often empty and impersonal. Lieutenant Geoffrey Picot, mortar officer of 1/Hampshires, warned that:

Those who get their picture of a battle from films where seemingly hundreds of rival soldiers are packed into a few hundred square yards may have difficulty in imagining a real battlefield. You and a couple of pals can be hundreds of yards away from anybody else; you may not have much idea where friend or foe are. You fire from a concealed position on to a hidden target.

Smells laced the landscape. There was the sickly sweet stink of corpses, human and animal: bloated cattle in fields and strafed transport horses in lanes upset some soldiers more than the sprawl of khaki or grey. Crushed apples gave platoon positions, and sometimes tank turrets, a cidery tang. Tank crews relieved themselves into empty ammunition boxes or shell-cases. Ken Tout caught the real whiff of battle inside his Sherman tank 'Stony Stratford':

The August sun beats down. The tank engine is running. Our own guns are reeking hot to the touch. Each of us is sweating from fear and exertion. We can fairly feel the heat from the burning fields and the brewing tanks. Combined with the mounting heat there is the smell of roasting flesh outside as well as the animal smells and cordite fumes from within Stony Stratford's own grimy bowels.

As the fighting dragged on the strain increased, for men could see that the odds against them lengthened by the day. Major-General Hubert Essame and Eversley Belfield affirmed: 'When judging any lack of enthusiasm displayed in action, especially by veterans of the 8th Army, it must be remembered that, for most front line soldiers, the bleak rule was that you normally continued to fight on; either until you were killed, or so severely wounded as to be unfit for further active service in the line.' An experienced infantry officer thought that: 'Everybody cracks up in the end, of course, but you hope something will have happened by then.' Nearly three-quarters of a sample of 3500 British battle casualties came from the infantry, which made up less than one-quarter of the army.

The weight of battle bore down on the Germans too. The thirty-two-year-old Major Hans von Luck had recently arrived in Normandy to command 125th Panzer Grenadier Regiment in 21st Panzer Division when the Allies landed. 'The morale of the men was still surprisingly good,' he wrote, 'although all realized that Allied success in the west meant the end.' There was a glimmer of optimism: 'The announcement of new "miracle-weapons" gave men some hope of a turn for the better.' The ever-present risk of air attack and the weight of shells delivered by Allied gunners were a constant ordeal. In July the outgoing commander of 2nd Panzer Division told his successor that the division was hit by 4000 artillery and 5000 mortar rounds a day and in the last four weeks a total of six German aircraft had been seen over the divisional area.

Yet the Germans fought well. When Martin van Creveld sought to explain why the German army consistently inflicted casualties at about a

50 per cent higher rate than it incurred, he considered that 'indoctrination with National Socialist ideas, the exalted social status of the military, and (even) some odd quirks of national character may have contributed to this result.' A study of cohesion in the *Wehrmacht*, published shortly after the war, concluded that 'the unity of the German army was in fact sustained only to a very slight extent by National Socialism.' However, when Omer Bartov examined German performance on the Eastern Front he noted that turnover amongst personnel was so rapid that there was no time for small-group loyalty to take hold. He argued that the German army in the east underwent 'a fundamental process of barbarization' in which ideology had a key role.

Although ideology was far less of a bond in Normandy, largely because Anglo-American and Russian enemies were horses of very different colours, indoctrination played its part. A good case in point is 12th SS Panzer Division 'Hitler Youth', under its thirty-three-year-old commander Kurt 'Panzer' Meyer, which enjoyed a reputation for hard combat tempered by atrocity. A British medical officer described its wounded as: 'A tough and dirty bunch – some had been snipers up trees for days – one young Nazi had a broken jaw and was near death but before he fainted he rolled his head over and murmured "Heil Hitler".' At the other extreme was a prisoner captured by 7/Somerset Light Infantry, an 'old chap of forty [who] empties his pockets including his photos of wife and kiddy and his old pipe'.

Allied and German Firepower
'The German army ...' noted van Creveld, 'regarded itself as a fighting organization above all ... So strong was the grip in which the organization held its personnel that the latter simply did not care where they fought, against whom, and why. They were soldiers and did their duty ...' Allied demands for unconditional surrender stiffened resolve: for some soldiers, death in Normandy was the lesser of many evils. Until the losses of mid-1944 destroyed the replacement system, German reinforcements were better trained than their Allied counterparts and introduced to battle with more careful preparation. The regiments within panzer and panzer grenadier divisions rarely fought as such, but were divided into *ad hoc* battle-groups containing a mixture of infantry and armour, a system which worked well in the German army but generally ran less smoothly in the British. Major Robert Kiln of the Hertfordshire Yeomanry doubted if any of his comrades 'had anything but admiration for the fighting ability of the German soldiers whether or not they hated them. In my view, as professional soldiers,

General Sir Bernard Montgomery *(left)* commanded Allied ground forces from a caravan in the grounds of the Château de Creullet. Most of his tanks were Shermans. Cromwells, seen here *(below)* waiting east of the Orne on 18 July, were used by 7th Armoured Division and the armoured reconnaissance regiments of the Guards and 11th Armoured Divisions.

they were superior to any but the very best troops in the Allied Forces.'

Some German equipment was still superior to Allied. The Panzer IV remained effective, and the Panzer V Panther with its 75mm gun was arguably the best medium tank used by either side. The angular features of the Panzer VI Tiger scowled malignantly over the battlefield. This monster weighed 54 tons (55 tonnes) and carried an 88mm gun. It was so hard to conceal and manoeuvre that its crews called it 'the furniture wagon', but it could destroy the Sherman, workhorse of British and American armoured divisions, at 2000 yards (1800 metres), long before even a Sherman Firefly, with a 17-pdr gun rather than the 75mm in most Shermans, could hope to touch it.

Allied armoured crewmen lived in the shadow of the 88mm. 'That gun will blast a shot through the co-driver's seat and through the lower turret and through my shins and through the rear of the turret on its way … into the engine space primed with fuel fumes,' imagined Ken Tout as his tank rumbled through an orchard. The Sherman had its virtues: it was cheap to produce, mechanically reliable and simple to maintain. But it caught fire easily: the Allies nicknamed it the Ronson because it always lit first time. The Germans permitted themselves a rare jest and called it the Tommy Cooker.

John Keegan defined the tank's dual nature as preserver and destroyer: Vishnu and Shiva in one. To its acolytes it was war-machine, talisman and home: they fought, and often lived, within its carapace. A Sherman had a crew of five. Its commander usually rode with his head and upper chest above the finger-chopping turret hatch. The gunner sat on his right, head close to the telescopic gunsight with its rubber eye-pad, one hand on the pistol-grip of the electrically powered turret traverse and the other on the gun's elevation handwheel, foot ready to stamp on firing buttons for the main armament and coaxial machine-gun. The loader/operator was responsible for 'netting in' the radio set to the correct frequency and keeping on net despite buffetings which would shake it off. He thrust brass-cased shells into the gun's breech, selecting armour-piercing or high explosive as required, and jettisoned empty cases, automatically ejected from the breech as it slammed backwards on recoil, through the 'pistol port' in the turret's side. In the bow, below the turret crew, sat the driver, looking through periscopes if the tank was closed down, or sitting higher, with his head above his hatch, if it was safe to do so. His co-driver, who also manned the hull-mounted machine-gun, sat beside him.

The state of the tank's interior depended on many factors, not least the pace of action and the squadron sergeant-major's zeal. Its exterior was a reflection of a unit's style and experience. Some tolerated stowage of personal belongings outside, making room in the turret but increasing the risk of fire, and others favoured the attachment of spare wheels, track-links and even sandbags, to increase protection against armour-piercing rounds or the shaped-charge projectiles fired, often at suicidally close range, from the bazooka-like *Panzerfaust*.

Crewmen might sleep beneath their tank if the ground was hard and no rain was expected – most regiments had horror stories of men stifled beneath sinking hulls – or would wrap themselves in sleeping bags or the tarpaulin covers for the engine hatches and curl up beside the tank. They were always ready for a brew, usually tea unless coffee could be scrounged from nearby Americans, its water heated on a solid-fuel

204

OPERATION GOODWOOD

The attack of the British 8 Corps
18 July 1944

→ Allied troop movements

—×××— Corps boundary

⋈ Bridge

Railway

0 1 2 3 4 5 Miles
0 1 2 3 4 5 6 7 8 Kms

Refer to page 15 for a comprehensive key to all military symbols

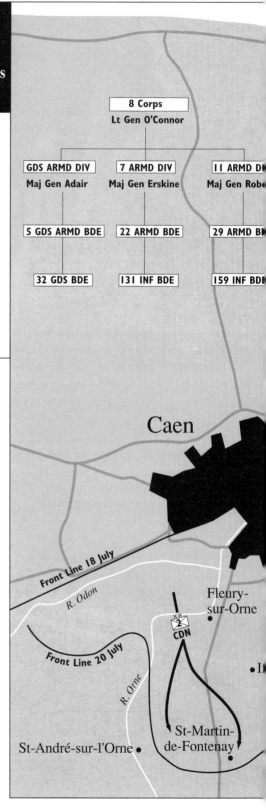

8 Corps
Lt Gen O'Connor

GDS ARMD DIV
Maj Gen Adair

7 ARMD DIV
Maj Gen Erskine

11 ARMD DI
Maj Gen Rob

5 GDS ARMD BDE

22 ARMD BDE

29 ARMD B

32 GDS BDE

131 INF BDE

159 INF BD

Caen

Front Line 18 July

R. Odon

Front Line 20 July

R. Orne

Fleury-sur-Orne

CDN

St-André-sur-l'Orne

St-Martin-de-Fontenay

I

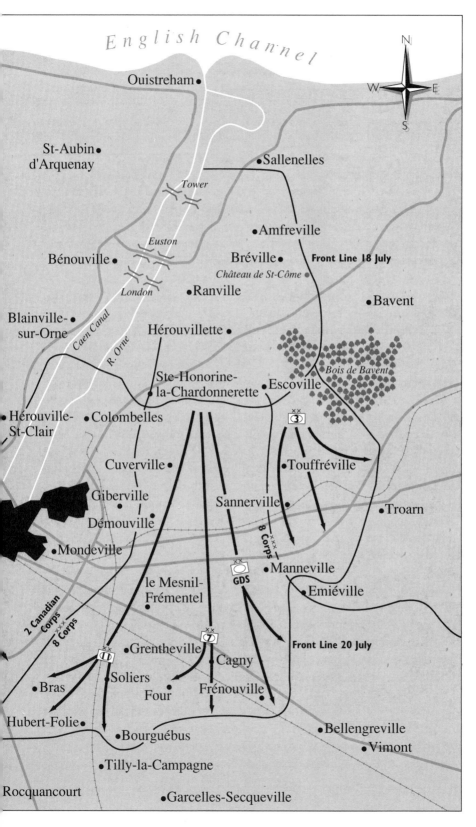

English Channel

Ouistreham

St-Aubin-
d'Arquenay

Sallenelles

Tower

Euston

Amfreville

Bénouville

Bréville

Front Line 18 July

Château de St-Côme

London

Ranville

Bavent

Blainville-
sur-Orne

Hérouvillette

Caen Canal

R. Orne

Ste-Honorine-
la-Chardonnerette

Escoville

Bois de Bavent

Hérouville-
St-Clair

Colombelles

×× ③

Cuverville

Touffréville

Giberville

Sannerville

Démouville

Troarn

8 Corps

Mondeville

Manneville

le Mesnil-
Frémentel

GDS

Emiéville

2 Canadian
Corps

8 Corps

×× ⑦

Front Line 20 July

① Grentheville

Cagny

Bras

Soliers

Four

Frénouville

Hubert-Folie

Bellengreville

Bourguébus

Vimont

Tilly-la-Campagne

Rocquancourt

Garcelles-Secqueville

cooker, primus stove or a tin of petrol-soaked sand. Tinned rations, such as Irish stew, steak and kidney pudding, corned beef and currant duff, were bulked out by hard-tack biscuits and supplemented from food bought or foraged from farms.

The Start of the Break-out

On 10 July, Montgomery outlined his plan for the final break-out. Operation Cobra would launch the Americans towards Avranches, where they would divide to plunge westwards into Brittany and eastwards towards Le Mans and Alençon. The British would mount an offensive east of Caen: Operation Goodwood. Time slippage, caused by bad weather and the American need to secure St Lô, meant that Goodwood eventually began on 18 July and Cobra on the 25th. Goodwood was always scheduled to precede Cobra, forcing the Germans to bring threadbare armoured divisions – the crack Panzer Lehr was down to 40 tanks and 2200 men – to meet it, and give Bradley's American troops a clear run.

Some hoped for much more. Lieutenant-General Sir Miles Dempsey of the British 2nd Army initially ordered Lieutenant-General Sir Richard O'Connor's 8 Corps to send an armoured division to Falaise. Major-General Roberts thought that 'Falaise was in everyone's mind as a point to be aimed for' and O'Connor discussed 'the best formation in which three armoured divisions should move once they had broken through into open country'. Eisenhower's headquarters, delighted to see Falaise mentioned, hoped for a breakthrough. Dempsey thought it 'more than possible that the Huns will break' and exploitation would ensue. Montgomery was inwardly more cautious, but encouraged high hopes in others. On 14 July he told Sir Alan Brooke, chief of the imperial general staff: 'I have decided that the time has come to have a real showdown and to loose [three armoured divisions] into the open country about the Caen–Falaise road.'

Goodwood was Dempsey's brainchild, and showed fair appreciation of those age-old determinants of battle: men, weapons and the ground. The British were short of men but had plenty of tanks, for there were now three armoured divisions, the Guards, 7th and 11th, together with five independent armoured and three independent tank brigades in the bridgehead, with some 2250 medium and 400 light tanks. Dempsey hoped to 'utilize that surplus of tanks and economize infantry'. He proposed to use the air-power that had devastated Caen to clear the way for his armoured divisions, which would advance, not into the boxy fields west of Caen, but across the rolling countryside to the east.

A crescent of jurassic limestone curves down from the landing beaches towards Alençon and Le Mans. It is topped with an open, windswept landscape of big fields dotted with woods and pierced by quarries from which pale Caen stone is still cut. Dempsey's attention was focused on the area between Caen and Falaise, bordered to its west by the River Orne and its tributary the Laize, and to its east by the marshy Dives. It was approached though a bottleneck. On its western side were the Orne, its canal, and the industrial suburb of Colombelles, marked by tall factory chimneys. To the east stood a high German-held ridge surmounted by the Bois de Bavent. Only one armoured division could form up east of the Orne and, because the Germans could observe this area from Colombelles, concentration had to be delayed until the last possible moment.

An advantage of attacking east of Caen was that it was 'good tank country'. Three years later an official publication described it as 'very much in favour of the defence and ideal for the siting of the enemy's artillery, both field and anti-tank', and observed that only after a long advance on a narrow front could 'a real break-out ... be achieved'. Although the British had ample artillery, ammunition was in short supply and most guns would be sited west of the Orne until Cagny and the southern suburbs of Caen were cleared. Montgomery and Dempsey intended to use air-power as a substitute for artillery, and the former sold the operation hard to persuade Eisenhower to extract aircraft from the bomber barons.

Between 5.45 a.m. and 6.30 a.m. on 18 July 1944, 1056 RAF heavy bombers were to drop 6000 tons (6100 tonnes) of explosive on Colombelles, a 2-mile (3-km) belt running north–south through Sannerville, and Cagny. At 7 a.m., a wave of 482 American medium bombers would hit Démouville and the surrounding villages, and from 8.30 a.m. until 9 a.m., 539 US heavy bombers were to take on the southern slopes of the Bavent feature, the ridge south of Frénouville and the Bourguébus–Bras–Soliers area. Fighter-bombers would deal with gun areas, strongpoints, and furnish 'impromptu direct air support'. Bombs were to be fitted with delayed-action fuses in areas where craters would not obstruct movement of British tanks, but in the central corridor, where cratering was unacceptable, fragmentation bombs were to be used.

O'Connor's 8 Corps was to attack on the heels of this bombardment, its left flank protected by 1 Corps, which was to hold a hard shoulder facing the Bois de Bavent and push down to Troarn, while on its right 2 Canadian Corps was to clear Colombelles and Giberville, and then move up the Orne valley. It is easy to write about 8 Corps 'driving its armoured divisions through the bottleneck' as if this was a domestic task demanding rolled-up sleeves and manual dexterity. Each division contained 2745 vehicles, which had to cross three pairs of bridges over the Orne and its canal, following routes which kept wheeled and tracked vehicles apart. They then had to move along a corridor less than 2 miles (3 km) wide, past headquarters, field ambulances and gun-lines, and through 51st Highland Division's positions before they reached the front line. This had been protected by British mines, many laid during bad weather and enemy interference, often in standing crops. Details had been indifferently recorded, shelling had moved or buried many, and clearance had to be done by night. Eighteen gaps were made through the minefield, their approaches marked with wire and white tape, but there were still many mines about. When the attack was over it took three engineer field companies, working in daylight, five days to clear the remaining mines.

As 11th Armoured Division passed through its three allocated minefield gaps its troubles were only beginning. So narrow was the front that it had to advance with 29th Armoured Brigade leading, and this in turn had to lead with 3/Royal Tank Regiment for the first 2500 yards (2300 metres), after which 2/Fife and Forfar Yeomanry could edge up into line. They would be followed up by 159th Infantry Brigade, taking Cuverville and Démouville with the help of 2/Northamptonshire Yeomanry, the division's armoured reconnaissance regiment. The division was to finish up on the right of 8 Corps' sector, on the line Bras–Verrières–Rocquancourt, with a force covering Cagny. With 11th Armoured safely through the bottleneck, the Guards Armoured Division would follow, masking Emiéville on the left, and capturing Vimont and Cagny. When the first two divisions had secured their objectives, 7th Armoured Division would advance on the line Four–La Hogue to seize Secqueville and the high ground about Cramesnil.

Early on 18 July, a grenadier, waiting with the Guards Armoured west of the Orne, was awakened by what he called 'a distant thunder in the air'. A nearby Welsh guardsman heard a 'faint and steady hum – growing into an insistent throbbing roar until the whole northern sky was filled with aeroplanes as far as the eye could see.' Some aircraft found the target area obscured by smoke and dust, but 6000 100-lb and 9600 500-lb bombs were dropped on 16th Luftwaffe Field Division, in the bottleneck, and the battle groups of 21st Panzer Division behind it.

It is no exaggeration to call the Germans' experience hellish, and that was precisely the comparison used by Lieutenant von Rosen, company commander in the Tiger-equipped 503rd Heavy Tank Battalion.

It was like hell and I am still astonished that I ever survived it … It was so nerve-shattering that we could not even think. All the tanks were completely covered with earth and the gun turrets had been torn completely out of adjustment by the shock effect. Fifty men in the company were dead, two soldiers had committed suicide during the bombardment, another had to be sent to a mental hospital for observation.

Werner Kortenhaus, a tank commander in 22nd Panzer Regiment of 21st Panzer Division, saw 'little dots' detach themselves from the aircraft. There were:

... so many of them that the crazy thought occurred to us; are those leaflets? We could hardly believe that they could all be bombs. Then began the most terrifying hour of our lives. It was a bomb carpet, regularly ploughing up the ground. Among the thunder of the explosions we could hear the wounded scream and the insane howling of men who had been driven mad.

The *Luftwaffe* division had endured the bombing of Caen ten days before, and was reduced to a handful of shaking survivors, some shocked into incontinence. In particular, 21st Panzer was hard hit: part of 1/125th Panzer Grenadier Regiment had disappeared, and a battery of 200th Assault Gun Battalion had been destroyed in Démouville. These guns were the invention of Major Becker, a German reserve officer and factory owner, who had married German 75mm and 105mm guns to French Hotchkiss tank chassis. Luck tells us that his men laughed at Becker's ungainly guns when they first saw them, but 'the assault gun companies

Shermans of the 23rd Hussars, moving up past the factory chimneys of Colombelles, on 18 July. The regiment suffered severely on the Bourguébus ridge that afternoon.

were trained to work closely with the grenadiers, and this was later a decisive aid to our defence forces.'

'"MOVE NOW." These words echoed round throughout the regiment and tanks slowly surged forward,' wrote Captain Lemon of 3/RTR. 'Then suddenly about a hundred yards [91 metres] in front of the leading tanks the earth started "boiling" all along the front as the rolling barrage from the 25-pdrs began.' His regiment and the Fife and Forfars had passed through the minefield before the bombing stopped, and Lance-Corporal Ron Cox of the Yeomanry remembered 'opening a new tin of jam and spreading it thickly on innumerable biscuits and passing them round the crew. We exchanged banter: I think the humour was a bit forced and had a slight hysterical touch to it as we were all aware that this was going to be something big ... My own emotion was a kind of numbed fatalism.'

The first railway line presented few problems. Tanks zigzagged across it to avoid exposing their bellies, and on the far side the yeomanry closed up on 3/RTR to form three waves of sixty-four tanks apiece. The infantry of 159th Brigade, Territorials from the Welsh borders, occupied Cuverville without mishap, but had to launch a formal attack on Démouville which was not cleared until mid-afternoon. The task of mopping up prisoners and pockets of resistance on the ground crossed by the armour consequently fell to the division's motor battalion, 8/Rifle Brigade, which should have had a company, mounted in half-tracks, with each of the armoured regiments. These companies were too weak to clear the villages in the centre of the battlefield, and this had unfortunate consequences.

The two leading armoured regiments, unaware of the delays behind them, found it easy going at first. Captain Lemon tells us that: 'There was very little opposition and one had a wonderful feeling of superiority as many Germans, shaken by the preliminary bombing and shelling, gave themselves up. As time passed they grew more aggressive, having overcome the effect of the bombs and shells ...' The tanks were nearing the Caen–Vimont railway line, just beyond the limit of fire support afforded by the 25-pdrs, when the plan, developing so promisingly, began to come unstitched.

The German Response

Hans von Luck's battle group comprised 503rd Heavy Tank Battalion, 200th Assault Gun Battalion, a battalion of 22nd Panzer Regiment, a rocket-launcher detachment, a battalion of 16th *Luftwaffe* Field Division and 1 and 2/125th Panzer Grenadier Regiment. Luck had established 'a graduated defence about 15 kilometres [9 miles] in depth', with his

Panzer Grenadier battalions in blocking positions behind the *Luftwaffe*, the assault guns in villages and the tanks further back. He had enjoyed a few days' leave in Paris and reached his headquarters shortly after 9 a.m. on 18 July. It was immediately clear that all was not well, and his deputy told him that the bombardment had stopped barely half an hour before and there was no radio contact with units. Luck climbed into a Panzer IV and set off down the Vimont–Caen road, telling his adjutant to pass the news to the division and to send an officer forward to the tanks. 'Slowly and without interference,' he wrote:

I approached the village of Cagny which lay exactly in the middle of my sector and was not occupied by us. The eastern part as far as the church was undamaged; the western part had been flattened. When I came to the western edge of the village, I saw to my dismay about twenty-five to thirty British tanks, which had already passed southward over the main road to Caen ... A glance to the north where my 1 Battalion ought to be, or had been, in combat positions. The whole area was dotted with British tanks, which were slowly rolling south, against no opposition.

Luck set off back down the road and was passing Cagny church when he saw four 88mms, barrels pointing skywards. Their young captain told Luck that he was part of the air-defence ring round Caen, and refused to take on the tanks, saying: 'Major, my concern is enemy planes, fighting tanks is your job. I'm *Luftwaffe*.' Luck drew his pistol and told the officer that he could 'either die now on my responsibility or win a decoration on his own'. 'I bow to force,' answered the captain. 'What must I do?' Luck ran out with him to the northern edge of the village and showed him where to post his guns, firing from an orchard across standing corn which concealed them well. Then he returned to his headquarters where he briefed Major Becker, who had a battery at Grentheville, west of Cagny and behind the railway line, and two in le Mesnil-Frémentel.

The 88mms in Cagny caught the Fife and Forfars in the flank. Ron Cox saw the tanks of his squadron leader and second-in-command hit. 'Other tanks I could see were stationary and some were beginning to brew,' he remembered. 'Dust and smoke were combining with heat-haze to make visibility more and more difficult. There were no targets. Nothing intelligible was coming over the radio. I watched through the periscope, fascinated, as though it was a film I was seeing.' His tank reversed, then there was a crash and shudder as it was hit. Sergeant Wally Herd shouted 'Bale out!' and as the crew ran, crouching, through the corn, the tank was hit again and smoke began to billow from it.

Luck's intervention destroyed sixteen of the Fife and Forfars' tanks but did not stop the regiment, and 3/RTR was already past by the time the German guns opened fire. It had lost only one tank to Major Becker's gunners in le Mesnil-Frémentel but, as it crossed the angle between the Caen–Vimont and Caen–Falaise railway lines, the battery in Grentheville hit it squarely. Major Bill Close, A Squadron's commander, saw:

Several anti-tank guns amongst the trees … the gunners frantically swinging their guns round towards us. In the cornfields around us were many multi-barrel mortar positions, which were already firing over our heads. They were quickly dealt with, in some cases simply by running over them with the tank. But the anti-tank guns were a different matter. Opening fire at point-blank range, they hit three of my tanks which burst into flames; and I could see that the squadron on my left also had several tanks blazing furiously.

After this, 3/RTR moved west of the village and advanced on Soliers, with Bras and Hubert-Folie prominent on the ridge behind it.

The Advance on Bourguébus Ridge

At 11 a.m. the battle seemed to be going well enough for the British. 11th Armoured Division was clear of the bottleneck, the Guards Armoured Division had passed through the minefield and begun to take over the eastern flank of the corridor, and 7th Armoured Division was on its way over the River Orne. A counter-attack from Frénouville had been attempted by 21st Panzer with its handful of surviving Mk IVs but they were quickly knocked out. The leading British regiments were across the Caen–Vimont railway line and had begun to ascend the ridge towards their objective.

The set-backs seemed minor. The Fife and Forfars and 3/RTR had each lost about a squadron. On the German side, Rosen's Tiger company had managed to get eight tanks into running order and had clawed the flank of the Guards Armoured around Emiéville, helping to prevent penetration between that village and Cagny. The Guards had been told that Cagny was strongly held, and had begun to swing west of it in their efforts to reach Vimont. And while 7th Armoured was indeed crossing the bridges, it was crossing them slowly. It took two hours for 1/RTR to cross, and there was a solid traffic jam between the bridges and the minefield.

Major-General Edgar Feuchtinger, commander of 21st Panzer, lacked armoured experience and was best known as organizer of the military element of Nazi party rallies. But the sternest *Kriegsakademie* instructor could not have faulted his division's response to Goodwood. The Germans were good at patching together improvised forces to meet potential breakthroughs, and by late morning the villages on the Bourguébus ridge were held by the divisional engineer battalion, stiffened by motor cyclists and scout cars from the reconnaissance battalion. The German artillery, intact behind the ridge, was out of range of batteries across the Orne, and those 88mms which had escaped the morning's calamities were ready to rake the long slopes with their fire.

Worse still, from the British point of view, Panzer Group West had been alerted by air photographs of the Orne bridges taken the previous night. The commander of 1st SS Panzer Corps, Obergruppenführer Sepp Dietrich (an ex-NCO described by the chilly Rundstedt as 'decent but stupid'), claimed to have learned just as much by putting his ear to the ground to hear the rumbling of hundreds of tanks. Panzer Group West issued a general warning to units around Caen, shuffled a battle-group of 12th SS Panzer Division to Lisieux as a backstop and ordered 1st SS Panzer Division to move from its position east of Caen against 11th Armoured Division. 1st SS Panzer Division *Liebstandarte Adolf Hitler* had served in Poland, France, Russia and Italy, and although it now had less than fifty Panthers and Panzer IVs these were crewed by men who blended long experience with the sternest resolve. The division scuttled round the southern outskirts of Caen, profiting from the scattered cover in the Odon and Orne valleys, to nudge its assault guns up on to the Bourguébus Ridge while its tanks growled around Bras, Hubert-Folie and Bourguébus itself.

'It is not ... altogether fanciful,' observed John Keegan, 'to compare the situation at Bourguébus ridge in the early afternoon of July 18th, 1944, with that at Waterloo at the same time of day 129 years and one month earlier.' The battered defenders still retained strongpoints ahead of their main position, which itself was sited on admirable defensive terrain with a reverse slope to shield reserves. O'Connor should have been able to look on to the other side of the hill, but the tank carrying the leading forward controller had been knocked out and links between ground and air were tenuous. Nor is comparison with Agincourt unreasonable. British tank crews resembled French men-at-arms: unquestionably brave; well (but not well enough) armoured; out-ranged by their most deadly opponents; and peering into periscopes as knights squinted through their visors.

'It was just as the leading tanks were level with Hubert-Folie that the fun began,' said an officer of 3/RTR. 'I saw Sherman after Sherman go up in flames and it got to such a pitch that I thought that in another few minutes there would be nothing left of the regiment.' Bill Close lost two of his squadron's tanks, and then his own. Desperate to get back into the battle, he commandeered a sergeant's tank at pistol-point, and saw 'the rest of the regiment heavily engaged, at least seven tanks blazing, and baled out crews making their way back to the embankment.' Further east, the Fife and Forfars were also in trouble, and as the 23rd Hussars approached the Caen–Vimont railway they saw pillars of greasy black smoke above this tank crematorium and were greeted by a yeomanry officer who reported, with understandable exaggeration, that his regiment had lost all but four of its tanks.

'It was no good sitting where we were,' admitted Geoffrey Bishop of the 23rd, and his C Squadron was ordered to advance on the village of Four. The squadron leader gave radio orders 'in an excited voice, but they were perfectly clear. They were to be his last.' Within minutes, five tanks were burning and another three were immobilized, and B Squadron, on the right, was losing tanks as quickly. Bishop saw that the medical officer had set up a dressing station in a signal box, 'and casualties started streaming back from the burnt-out tanks. The chaps were all blackened, their clothes burnt, and most of them had lost their berets. A tank which had survived came roaring back with a lot of wounded lying on the back of it.' The remnants of the regiment moved back behind the railway line, 'quite convinced that nothing could have been a greater failure, and everyone had seen the last of some of his best friends.' The attack fizzled out with a last charge by the Northamptonshire Yeomanry, which left sixteen of its Cromwell tanks below Bras.

The battle went on, although without the saturation bombing of Bourguébus which O'Connor had called for. He hoped to use 7th Armoured Division to join 29th Armoured Brigade in a two-pronged attack on Hubert-Folie and Bourguébus, but it was so badly delayed crossing the Orne and percolating its way through rear areas raided by the *Luftwaffe*, which threw its remaining strength into the battle, that it was not clear of the bridges until dawn on the 19th. Private Robert Boulton, in a Bren-gun carrier platoon of the Queen's Regiment, remembered that:

When we did get across, tanks and trucks were on fire all over the place. The dust was absolutely choking … There was a poor lad who had had most of the bottom of his back blown away. There was nothing to be done for him so he was just put outside on a stretcher. That poor devil screamed for about two hours; morphine seemed to have no effect. He was pleading for someone to finish him off. Our sergeant had been in the war from the start, and even he was white and shaken.

When the battle closed under cloudy skies on 20 July the charnel villages of Cagny, Bourguébus, Bras and Hubert-Folie had been taken. British penetration was at the best 7 miles (11 km) deep, and losses were great – 8 Corps alone lost over 400 tanks and 2000 men. When the losses of the flanking corps are included, 2nd Army had suffered some 6000 casualties, most of them already-scarce infantrymen. Montgomery had sent Brooke a wildly over-optimistic account of the action on the afternoon of 18 July, and over the days that followed he was assailed by a 'blue as indigo' Eisenhower and by air chiefs who accused him of having claimed their help on false pretences.

After the war Montgomery acknowledged that criticism was 'partly my own fault, for I was too exultant at the Press conference I gave during the Goodwood battle,' but went on to claim that he could not tell the press his 'true strategy' which had been to tie down German armour rather than break out. The tide of reproach was to be turned by two dramatic pieces of news. On 20 July there was an abortive attempt on Hitler's life, and five days later Bradley's American troops began Operation Cobra. Exactly a month later, all four Allied armies were level with the Seine, and the French 2nd Armoured Division liberated Paris: the battle for Normandy was over at last.

A View of the Field

The long connection between England and Normandy is summed up on the Memorial to the Missing, which stands on the Boulevard Fabian Ware, named after the founder of the Commonwealth War Graves Commission, on the western edge of Bayeux. 'We, once conquered by William,' reads the Latin inscription on its colonnaded front, 'have now set free the Conqueror's native land.' The memorial commemorates the 1537 British, 270 Canadians and one South African who fell in Normandy and have no known graves. Across the road is Bayeux War Cemetery, the largest British Second World War cemetery in France, which contains 4648 graves, including that of Corporal Bates of the Royal Norfolks, the only holder of the VC to be buried in Normandy. His headstone tells us that he was a Camberwell lad, a useful reminder that, by the end of a long war, the regimental system was not quite what it seemed to be.

Two Military Museums
Although Bayeux is off the Goodwood battlefield and a good half-hour by car from Caen, it is a sensible place to start a study of the battle because the Musée de la Bataille de Normandie, a stone's throw from the Memorial on the Boulevard Fabian Ware, is devoted to the break-out. Amongst the vehicles outside are a Sherman, an armoured vehicle Royal

Engineers on a Churchill tank chassis, and a German Hetzer self-pro-pelled anti-tank gun. The recommended route through the museum takes the visitor past cases displaying uniforms, weapons, newspapers and photographs, and a large room at the end of the circuit houses guns, one of them the powerful German 88mm that inflicted so much damage on the Allies.

The Musée-Memorial off the northern edge of the Caen ring-road (N13) is altogether different. Opened in 1988, it is a symbol of peace and takes a longer view of history. Its deals with occupation, resistance, liber-ation and reconstruction, and its concern for human rights reflects a cen-tury which seemed to offer many Frenchmen the choice between Verdun and Auschwitz.

Exploring Caen

Caen is the capital of Lower Normandy and houses the *préfecture* of the Calvados region. The town stands at the confluence of the Orne and the Odon rivers, and was fortified by the Viking leader Rollo, who secured a tract of territory from Charles the Simple of France by agreeing to con-vert to Christianity and to become Charles's vassal. In the eleventh cen-tury the Duchy of Normandy was a powerful independent state, and Norman adventurers travelled widely. The descendants of Tancrede de Hauteville established a kingdom in Sicily, and other Normans played a leading part in the crusades, ruling the Middle Eastern principalities of Antioch and Edessa.

Caen owed its rise to William the Conqueror, bastard son of Duke Robert, born to a tanner's daughter from Falaise in 1027. Its massive castle was begun by William in 1060 and improved by his youngest son Henry I. The Conqueror died at Rouen in 1087 and was buried in the Church of St-Etienne in the Abbaye aux Hommes at Caen, but his bones were scattered when the Huguenots sacked the church in the sixteenth century. A femur survives, and lies beneath the altar. In 1346, during the Hundred Years War, Edward III's men passed through Caen on their way to Crécy. They respected the Conqueror's tomb but little else: Caen was pillaged and its goods sent off to England down the Orne.

The bombing of July 1944, in the run-up to Operation Goodwood, did terrible damage to Caen. Three-quarters of the city was destroyed, thou-sands of its citizens were killed, many buried, dead or alive, beneath the rubble of their homes. When British and Canadian troops entered Caen on 9 July they were greeted with kindness but not wild enthusiasm. 'The women kissed them, the men saluted them, but with dignity, without mad exaggeration,' remembered the deputy mayor. 'We have all suffered too

The armoured divisions were withdrawn on 20 July. The weather broke, turning the ground into mud: here British soldiers struggle with a bogged motor-cycle combination.

much for our dearest ones to acclaim excessively those who have been forced by the necessity of war to do us so much harm.'

Operation Goodwood

To reach the Goodwood battlefield take the D515 northwards towards the ferry port of Ouistreham, turning westwards to Bénouville 3 miles (5 km) from the edge of Caen. Pegasus Bridge, which crosses the Caen Canal on the eastern edge of the village, was the site of the first Allied landing on D-Day and, with Orne Bridge just to the east, was secured in a brilliant *coup de main* by Major John Howard's D Company 2/Oxford-shire and Buckinghamshire Light Infantry. The original Pegasus Bridge was replaced in 1995, but markers show where Major Howard's gliders landed. The two bridges captured by the Oxfordshire and Bucking-hamshire were used by divisions moving up for Goodwood and code-named Euston Bridges. Crossings to the south, opposite the centre of Bénouville, were code-named London Bridges, and crossings further north, approached through St-Aubin d'Arquenay, were known as Tower Bridges. Marked routes took vehicles towards the front line through Ranville and Le Bas de Ranville. For an excellent overview of the bottleneck, proceed through Ranville to the western edge of Bréville, on the ridge which bears the Bois de Bavent. This area was captured on the night of 12 June by 12/Para and 12/Devons, assisted by a troop of the 13/18th Hussars, attacking from Amfreville.

Looking south from Bréville one gets a cork's eye view of the bottle-neck. Pegasus Bridge and Ranville in the British 11th Armoured Divi-sion's concentration area are easily visible, as are Colombelles on the right and the Bois de Bavent on the left. In July 1944 the low ground beneath you was strewn with gliders used to fly in the Airlanding Brigade of the British 6th Airborne Division on D-Day: Geoffrey Bishop thought that they looked like the massed skeletons of prehistoric beasts. To reach the front line, take the D37b south as far as the D513. To your left, just outside Bréville, is the Château de St-Côme, unsuccessfully attacked on 19 June by 5/Black Watch of 51st Highland Division with the loss of 200 men. Turn right on the D513, go through Hérouvillette and swing south for Escoville on the far side of the village. The minefield ran along the southern edge of Escoville: gap 14 was where the houses peter out as the road leaves the village to the south. Look westwards across the field towards Ste-Honorine-la-Chardonnerette: the front line curled north-wards between the two villages, almost touching the D513, before swing-ing back to keep Ste-Honorine as a British-held salient.

To follow the advance of the British 29th Armoured Brigade one can drive through Cuverville and Démouville, where the absence of old houses testifies to the ferocity of the bombing, as far as the northern edge of Cagny, where a track strikes south-east towards Ferme du Château and a minor road runs south-west past new industrial buildings towards the main N13. The same spot can be reached after a good hour's walk down the track which neatly bisects the angle of the D228 and D227 where they fork south of Escoville, heading due south and edging south-west for the last mile or so. The narrow-gauge railway ran between Démou-ville and Sannerville just north of the N175, and its route can still be made out. The Autoroute de Normandie, which runs parallel with it is, of course, a modern addition.

Looking west from the junction of roads and track north of Cagny we can see the farm complex of le Mesnil-Frémentel from, very roughly, the position of the four *Luftwaffe* 88mms. 3/RTR had already passed through this gap heading south, and the rear elements of the Fife and Forfars were caught in it. To understand the difficulties of 3/RTR as it crossed the Caen–Vimont railway, proceed to Grentheville by way of the N13 and the D230. The tanks went over the first railway line and then, after fighting their way past Grentheville, jinked under the second, many using the tunnel on the minor road due west of the village. They then shook out to attack Bras and Hubert-Folie, west of the railway line, and were engaged by the German tanks and assault guns of 1st SS Panzer Division as they did so.

Finally, to look at the British advance from the German viewpoint, go on through Soliers into Bourguébus, and turn right for Hubert-Folie. Stop just over the railway bridge and look north-north-east. On a clear day one can see all the way back to Bréville, with Colombelles and the Bois de Bavent defining the bottleneck as clearly from the southern end of the battlefield as they did from the north. Most of the villages have been rebuilt although some older buildings, such as the stud at Manneville, north-east of Cagny, miraculously survived. It is easy to see why this was such a killing-ground, but hard to imagine the sights reported by one British officer:

It was a scene of utter desolation. I have never seen such bomb craters. Trees were uprooted, roads were impassable. There were bodies in half; crumpled men. A tank lay upside down, another was still burning with a row of feet sticking out from underneath. In one crater a man's head and shoulders appeared sticking out from the side. The place stank.

Over 2000 British, Canadian, Australian, New Zealand and Polish soldiers, many of them killed in Goodwood, are buried in the CWGC cemetery at Banneville-la-Campagne, on the N175 south-west of Sannerville. Amongst them is the artist Rex Whistler, a lieutenant in 2/Welsh Guards, the reconnaissance regiment of the Guards Armoured Division. When his regiment was probing Emiéville he left his tank to confer with his squadron leader and was killed. Many of Ken Tout's comrades of the Northamptonshire Yeomanry also rest in this beautiful place, and the regiment's white horse runs lightly across their headstones.

Index

Page numbers in *italic* refer to
the illustrations

Abbeville 28, 196
Accrington Pals *121*, 128,
 147–8, *148*
Acheux 31
Achicourt 175, 185
Agincourt 6, 7, 10–11, 12, 14,
 16–49, *24–5*, *47*
Agincourt, Isambart d' 40
Agnez-lès-Duisans 186
Agny 175, 185, 186
Albert 31, 129, 144–5
Alençon 206, 207
Alençon, John, Duke of 28, 40,
 41
Allenby, Major-General
 Edmund 107, 110
Amiens 29, 30, 46
archers 20–1, 33, *34*, 34–5,
 38–9, *42–3*, 44–5, 50–2
Ardennes 162, 163
Armit, 'Muscle' 176
Arques-la-Bataille 28, 45–6
Arras 6, 7, 11–12, 124, 154,
 168–87, *170–1*
arrows 20–1, 44–5
artillery 56–7, 75–8
Ashurst, Corporal George 14, 149
Asquith, Lieutenant Herbert 120
Astier de la Vigerie, General d'
 159
Atlantic Wall 192
Auchonvillers 148, 149
Auchy-les-Hesdin 49
Audregnies 107, 109, 118, 119
Avranches 206

Badby, John 22
Badsey, Stephen 188
Bagration, Operation 196
Bailleul 29
Baker rifles 70
Balfourier, General 140
Ballard, Lieutenant-Colonel
 106–7, 109, 119
Banneville-la-Campagne 219
Bannockburn 18
Bapaume 31, 129, 132, 153, 186
Baring, Major 70, 80, 84
Barratt, Air Marshal 159
Bartov, Omer 201
Bascule 105
Bates, Corporal 215
Bates, Lieutenant E.G. 143
Bayeux 196, 215–16
bayonets 56
Bazentin 151–2
Beart, Lieutenant-Colonel 179,
 180, 186
Beaumetz-lès-Loges 172
Beaumont, Private Harry 98,
 106
Beaumont-Hamel 129, 134–5,
 143, *146*, 148, 149
Beaurains 172, 175, 176, 177,
 185, 186
Beck, General Ludwig 158
Becker, Major 209, 211, 212
Belcher, Lieutenant Robert 79
Belfield, Eversley 200
Bennett, Matthew 28, 30, 31
Bénouville 217
Berneville 179, 180
Bernhardt, Prince of
 Saxe-Weimar 68, 70

Berry, Duke of 28
Berthier, Marshal 65
Bethencourt 30, 46
Billotte, General Gaston 158,
 159, 163, 166, 168
Bishop, Lieutenant Geoffrey
 198–9, 214, 218
Bismarck, Otto von 90
Blackman, Captain John Lucie
 85
Blanchard 158, 159, 168
Blanchetaque 27, 28, 46
Blangy 31, 46–8
Bloem, Captain Walter 105–6
Blücher, Field-Marshal 64–5,
 68, 69, 81, 83
Bock, General von 159, 162
Bois de Bavent 207, 218, 219
Bois la Haut 104–5
Boisleux-au-Mont 174
Bonaparte, Prince Jerome 71,
 72, 74, 83, 85
Boucicault 28, 30, 36, 37, 40
Boulogne 181
Boulton, Private Robert 214
Bourbon, John, Duke of 28, 36,
 41
Bourguébus 207, 213, 214, 219
Boves 29, 46
Bradbury, Jim, 34
Bradley, General Omar 193,
 196, 206, 215
Bras 207, 212, 213, 214, 215,
 219
Brébant, Clignet de 36
Breda 163
Bréville 218, 219
Brewster, Joseph 72

Bridges, Major Tom 107, 109, 115, 118
British Expeditionary Force (BEF) *94–5*, 97–114, 122, 158–9, 164, 168, 169, 172, *173*, 181
British Experimental Mechanized Force 157
Brooke, Sir Alan 206, 215
Brunswick, Duke of 69, 82
Bülow 79, 83
Burgundy, John, Duke of 22, 28
Burne, Lieutenant-Colonel Alfred 14, 33–4
Butt, Lieutenant Tom 112
Butterworth, George 120–2
Bylandt 70, 74, 87

Caen 21, 196, 197, 206–7, 209, 211, 213, 216–17
Cagny 207, 208, 211, 212, 215, 218
Calais 22, 27, 31, 44, 49, 181, 182
Cambrai 166, 182
Canadian memorial, 185
Carency 183
Carrington, Charles 7
Carver, Michael 195
'Case Yellow' 159–62
Casteau 98, 103, 115
Caumont 196
cavalry 56, 75–8, 90, 106–9
cemeteries 116–18, 151–2, 185, 215, 219
Chance, Lieutenant Roger 107–9, 118
Charles V, Emperor 46
Charles V, King of France 22
Charles VI, King of France 22–3, 28, 44
Charnwood, Operation 197
Château Gendebien 116
Château de St-Côme 218
Cherbourg 196, 197
chevauchées 19, 22, 28
Churchill, Brigadier 169, 173
Churchill, Winston 164–5, 181, 192
Clarence, Thomas, Duke of 26
Clay, Private Matthew 71, 72
Close, Major Bill 212, 213–14
Cobb, Lieutenant-Colonel C.H. 125
Cobra, Operation 206, 215
Colborne, Colonel John 81, 93
Colombelles 207, 209, 218, 219
Commonwealth War Graves Commission 14, 116, 118, 147, 215

Coningham, Air Marshal Sir Arthur 196
Connolly, Sergeant Michael 64
Corbie 29
Cornwall, Sir John 27
COSSAC 193
Cotentin peninsula 196
Cotton, Sergeant-Major Edward 84, 85
Courtrai 182
Cox, Lance-Corporal Ron 210, 211
Craig, Lieutenant Tom 174
Cramesnil 208
Crécy 7, 10, 19, 20, 21–2, 216
Creevey, Thomas 64
Creveld, Martin van 200–1
Crowe, Lieutenant Bert 122
Cuverville 208, 210, 218

D-Day landings 188, 195–219
Dainville 174, 180
d'Albret, John 28, 30, 36
de Gaulle, Charles 6, 156–7, 165
de Lisle, Brigadier-General 107
Dean, Lieutenant Archie 122
Dease, Lieutenant Maurice 104, 115, 117
Delville Wood 140, 141, 142, 143, 144, 152
Démouville 207, 208, 209, 210, 218
Dempsey, Lieutenant-General Sir Miles 193, 206–7
Demulder, Lieutenant Augustin 85
d'Erlon 69, 71, 74, 75, 79, 81
Dernancourt 144
Dieppe 192
Dietrich, Obergruppenführer Sepp 213
Douie, Lieutenant Charles 125
Doyle, Sergeant 186–7
Dugmore, Captain Wilfrid 107
Duhesme, General 83
Duisans 177, 178, 179, 180, 185, 186
Dunbar 18
Dunkirk 181
Dyle, River 159, 163

Easton, Corporal Harry *89*, 107, 109
Edgington, Sergeant William 97
Edmonds, Brigadier-General Sir James 13, 143, 147
Edward, the Black Prince 22
Edward I, King 18, 20

Edward II, King 18
Edward III, King 19, 20, 21–2, 46, 49, 216
Eeles, Major 75–8
Eisenhower, General Dwight D. 192, 206, 207, 215
Elouges 107, *108*, 118
Emiéville 208, 212, 219
Engell, Lieutenant J.S. 133
Epsom, Operation 197
Erpingham, Sir Thomas 35, 36
Escoville 218
Essame, Major-General Hubert 200
Estuteville, John d' 26
Eu 28, 46
Euston Bridges 217
Evans, Major George de Lacy 64, 75
Evry, Colonel Henri d' 15

Falaise 197, 206, 207
Falkenhayn, General Erich von 123–4, 141, 143
Falkirk 18
Farrar-Hockley, General Sir Anthony 134
Fécamp 28, 45
Fergusson, Major-General Sir Charles 106–7, 113, 119
Fernie, Major Stuart 176, 177
Feuchtinger, Major-General Edgar 212
Ficheux 178
First World War 10, 11, 13, 185, 192; casualties 156; Mons and Le Cateau 12, 88–119, *100–3*, *109*; The Somme 12, 120–53, *126–7*, *139*
Fitzmaurice, Lieutenant-Colonel 172, 176
Fitzpatrick, Regimental Quartermaster Sergeant 105, 114
Flers-Courcelette 142–3
flintlock muskets 53–6, 71
Foch, Marshal Ferdinand 93, 154–6
Foncquevillers 145
Forceville 31
Fortitude, Operation 193
Fougières, Gallois de 49
Four 208, 214
Foy 72, 74
Franco-Prussian War 90–1, 92
Franklyn, Major-General 168–9, 172–3
French, Sir John *96*, 97–9, 114, 116, 123

Fressin 49
Fricourt 31, 129, 138
Froissart 20, 33, 34
Fuller, Major-General J.F.C. 157

Gaffikin, Major George 135
Gam, Davy 23, 41
Gamelin, General Maurice 158, 159, 163, 164, 165, 166
Garrod, R.G. 93
Gaucourt, Raoul de 26
Gembloux 159, 163, 164
Genappe 82–3
George V, King 97–8
Georges, General 158–9
Gerard 68
Giraud, General 158, 164
Gloucester, Humphrey, Duke of 23, 27, 35
Gneisenau, August Wilhelm von 64, 65, 69, 79
Godley, Private Sid 104, 115
Godsell, Lieutenant Kenneth 98, 99
Goering, Hermann 192
Gold beach 193
Gommecourt 129, 134, 144, 145
Goodlad, Private Alf 148
Goodwood, Operation 10, 12, 188–219, 190–1, 204–5
Gordon, Brigadier-General 132
Gordon, Colonel Sir Alexander 85, 86
Gort, Lord 158–9, 168, 181
Gough, Lieutenant-General Sir Hubert 124, 132, 140, 142
Graham, Corporal James 72
Grange Tunnel, 184–5
Graves, Captain Robert 141
Green, Captain J.L. 145
grenades 132
Grenfell, Captain Francis 107
Grentheville 211, 212, 218–19
Grierson, Sir James 97
Griffith, Lieutenant Wyn 141
Gronow, Ensign 14, 78–9
Grouchy, Emmanuel de 65, 68, 69, 74, 79, 81
Guderian, General Heinz 157, 158, 162, 163–4, 165, 166, 168, 181, 192
Guesclin, Bertrand du 22
Gueudecourt 153

Haig, Sir Douglas 97, 110, 123, 124, 132, 140, 142
Haldane, R.B. 92, 93
Halkett, Colin 69, 80, 81, 82
Harclay, Sir Andrew 19

Hardinge, Colonel 65
Harfleur 23–7, 31, 45
Hargest, Brigadier James 198
Harris, Rifleman 61
Harwood, John 128
Hawthorn Ridge 129, 133, 134, 146, 148, 149
Hénin-sur-Cojeul 174
Henry I, King 45
Henry IV, King 22
Henry V, King 10–11, 16, 17, 22–49, 129, 158
Henry of Navarre 45–6
Hérouvillette 218
Hesdin 172
Heyland, Lieutenant-Colonel 172, 178
High Wood 140, 141, 142–3, 152
Hill, Lieutenant-General Lord 60
Hitler, Adolf 156, 157, 162, 188, 192, 196, 215
Hodgson, Lieutenant 'Clarrie' 113
Hodgson, Lieutenant William Noel 120, 151
Holland, Sir John 26, 27, 33
Home, Major 'Sally' 107
Horesfield, Private 64
Hornby, Captain Charles 115
Hougoumont 62–3, 70, 71–4, 78, 81, 85, 86
Howard, Major John 217
Hubert-Folie 212, 213, 214, 215, 219
Hugo, Victor 83, 84, 90
Hundred Years War 7–10, 16, 21–3, 44, 216
Hungerford, Sir Walter 31

infantry 53–6, 75, 90, 103
Ironside, General 168

Jardine, Brigadier-General 138
Jeffreys, Major 175
Joffre, General Joseph 11, 97, 98, 123
John II, King of France 19, 22
Juno beach 193

Keegan, John 32, 203, 213
Kellermann 69, 82
Kiln, Major Robert 201–2
Kincaid, Lieutenant John 64
King, Major 186–7
Kitchener, Field Marshal Lord 97, 114, 124–5
Kleist 165

Kluck, Colonel-General Alexander von 102–3
Kluge, Field Marshal Gunther von 181, 196
knights 18, 33
Kortenhaus, Werner 209

La Boisselle 129, 138, 141, 151
La Haie Sainte 84
Lambert, Major-General Sir John 80
Lancaster, Duke of 19
Landrecies 110
Lanrezac, General 98–9
Le Caillou 69, 83
Le Cateau 6, 7, 12, 96–7, 99, 110–14, 111, 118–19
Le Havre 45
Le Mans 206, 207
le Mesnil-Frémentel 211, 212, 218
Leeb, General von 162
Leeke, Ensign 64
Legros, Second Lieutenant 72, 78
Leigh-Mallory, Air Chief Marshal Sir Trafford 195
Leipzig Redoubt 138
Lemon, Captain 210
Lesboeufs 143
Lewis, Lieutenant C.S. 133
Liddell Hart, Basil 124, 157, 181
Ligny 68, 69
Lille 181
Lindsay, Major Martin 198, 199
Lion Monument 82, 83, 84
Lisieux 213
List, Colonel-General 165
Lloyd George, David 140
Lobau 65, 71, 74, 79
Lochnagar crater 138, 151
London Bridges 217
longbows 20–1, 44, 50
Longueval Ridge 140, 141
Lorette 182, 182, 183–4
Louis, dauphin 27, 28
Louis XVIII, King of France 50, 57
Luck, Major Hans von 14, 154, 200, 209–12
Lucy, Corporal John 13, 88, 93, 109–10
Ludendorff, Erich von 143
Luftwaffe 158, 159, 192
Lutyens, Sir Edwin 149
Lutyens, Lieutenant Lionel 113, 119
Lutz, Otto 158

Macdonnell, Lieutenant-Colonel 72
machine-guns 90, 102, 130–2, *179*
McKee, Alexander 188
Macleod, Lieutenant Rory 112, 113
Macready, Lieutenant Edward 79
Maginot Line 156–7, 158, 159, 162
Maisoncelle 31, 41–4, 48
Maitland 71, 81, 84
Malplaquet 116, 118
Mametz 31, 130
Mametz Wood 140–1, 144, 151
Manning, Frederic 12
Mannock, Major Edward 'Mick' 183
Manny, Sir Walter 19
Manstein, Lieutenant-General Erich von 162
Marcks, General Erich 196
Marlborough, Duke of 7, 118, 182
Marmont, Marshal 60
Maroeuil 177, 186
Marsden-Smedley, Lieutenant George 120
Martel, Major-General 173, 174, 175, 176, 177
Martin, Captain D.L. 151
Mary I, Queen 49
Mash Valley 138
Mason-MacFarlane, Major-General 168
Materne Lake 82
Mauberge 97
Maurice of Nassau 52
Maxse, Major-General 128, 138
Memorial to the Missing 149–51, 215
memorials 82, 149–52, 185, 215
Mercatel 176, 178, 186
Mercer, Captain Cavalié 78, 79, 84–5
Meyer, Kurt 'Panzer' 201
Mild Trench 153
Miller, Lieutenant-Colonel Harry 173, 174–5, 176–7, 185
Milton, Fred 93
Moltke, Helmuth von 11, 90, 92, 123
Mons 6, 7, 12, 98–110, *100–3, 109*, 114–19
Monstrelet, Enguerrand de 36
Mont-St-Eloi 172, 178, 183, 185
Mont-St Jean 69, 83–4
Montauban 130, 138, 140

Montgomery, General Sir Bernard 168, 193, 197, *202*, 206, 207, 215
Mormal, forest of 6, 118
Mortier, Marshal 65, 118
Morval 143
Most, Lieutenant 178, 179, 187
Mouquet Farm *139*, 142
Müffling, Baron 65, 80
Munro, H.H. 120
muskets 53–6, 70, 71

Namur 159, 162
Napoleon I, Emperor 12, 50, 53, 57–60, 65–9, 71, *73*, 79, 80, 81–3
Napoleon III, Emperor 90
Napoleonic Wars 50, 53
National Socialism 201
Nesle 30
Neuville-St-Vaast 183
New Zealand Division Memorial 152
Newfoundland Park 149, 153
Ney, Marshal Michel 57, 65, 68, 69, 71, 74, 75, 78, 79, 80, 87, 90
Nicholson, Brigadier Claude 181
Nicholson, William 93
Niemeyer, Private 104
Nimy 99, 104, 115
Normandy, Operation Goodwood 188–219, *190–1, 204–5*
Northampton, Earl of 19
Notre Dame de Lorette 182, *182*, 183–4

Obourg 99, 103, 104, 115–16
O'Connor, Lieutenant-General Sir Richard 206, 207, 213, 214
Omaha beach 193, 195
Ompteda, Baron 80, 84
Orange, Prince of 60, 68, 69, 74, 80, 82
Orleans, Duke of 22, 28, 36, 41
Orne, River 197, 207, 208, 212, 213, 216
Overlord, Operation 192
Ovillers 129, 138, 141, 144
Oxford, Earl of 40

panzer corridor 166, *167*, 169
panzer divisions 157–8, 163
Papelotte 83, 84
Pas de Calais 193–5
Pegasus Bridge 217, 218
Pennycuik, Lieutenant James 98

Péronne 7, 29, 30, 31, 46
Petre, Major-General 168
Picot, Lieutenant Geoffrey 199–200
Picton, Sir Thomas 68, 69, 74, 79, 82, 87
Plancenoit 79, 83–4
Plowman, Lieutenant Max 141, 143
Poitiers 19
Ponsonby, Sir William 75
Potts, Lieutenant 180
Pozières 132, 140, 141–2, 144, *152*, 153
Pratt, Brigadier Douglas 172, 173, 177
Prestwich, Michael 19, 33–4
Prioux, General 163, 164, 173
Public Record Office 13

Quatre-Bras 68, 69, 82
Querrieu 144

radio 158, 173–4, 199
Ranville 218
Rawlinson, General Sir Henry 124, 132, 133, 140, 141, 144
Rebecq, Constant de 68
Reille 68–9, 71, 83
Reynaud, Paul 164
Richard II, King 22
Richards, Private Frank 97, 119
Richmond, Duke of 68
rifles 90, 102
Riley, H.D. *121,* 128
Robbesard, Lewis 23
Roberts, Michael 52
Roberts, Major-General 'Pip' 198, 206
Rommel, Major-General Erwin 11–12, 154, 163, *164*, 165–6, 174, 176, 178–9, 186, 187, 192, 193, 196
Rosen, Lieutenant von 208–9, 212
Royal Air Force (RAF) 207
Royal Artillery 64
Royal Engineers 64, 184
Royal Flying Corps 98, 134, 183
Royal Fusiliers 104
Royal Garrison Artillery 112
Royal Tank Regiment 169–72, 180–1
Rundstedt, Field Marshal Gerd von 159–62, 165, 192, 196, 213

Saigneville 46
St Aubin 174

St-Aubin d'Arquenay 217
St Ghislain 105
Ste-Honorine-la-Chardonnerette 218
St Lô 196, 206
St-Pierre, Eustache de 49
St Symphorien 117–18
Saltoun, Lieutenant-Colonel Lord 71
Sannerville 207, 218, 219
Sartel Wood 145
Sassoon, Lieutenant Siegfried 7, 140–1, 144
Saveuse, William de 37
Schlieffen Plan 91–2, 159
Schwaben Redoubt 135, 149
Schwalben Nest 145
Second World War 158–67; Allied plans, 158–9, 160–1; Arras 11–12, 154, 168–87, 170–1; balance of forces, 162–3; German plans, 159–62, 160–1; Operation Goodwood 10, 188–219, 190–1, 204–5
Secqueville 208
Sedan 163
Seekt, Major Hans von 157
Senger und Etterlin, General Frido von 184
Serre 129, 134, 147–8, 150
Shaw, Corporal 74
Sheffield Park 147, 148
Shephard, Sergeant-Major Ernest 12–13, 96
Sherman tanks 202–6, 209
Short, Ensign 70–1
Siborne, Captain William 13
Sichelschnitt scheme 162
Smith-Dorrien, Sir Horace 96, 97–8, 99, 104, 106, 110, 112, 113–14, 119
Soignies 115
Soliers 207, 212
Somme 7, 114; Agincourt campaign 29–30, 46; battle of the Somme 6, 10, 11, 120–53,

126–7, 139; in Second World War 166
Soult, Marshal 65, 69
South African National Memorial 152
Spears, Major-General Edward 98–9, 158, 159
Stalin, Josef 188–92
Sword beach 193

Tank Memorial 153
tanks 142–3, 153, 157–8, 162–3, 175, 202–6, 202, 209
Tedder, Air Chief Marshal Sir Arthur 196–7
Telegraph Hill 176, 186
Tennant, Lieutenant Edward 120
Tertre 105–6
Thielmann 79
Thiepval 129, 135–8, 140, 142, 143, 149–51, 153
Thomas, Corporal Edward 115
Tilloy 175, 176, 186
Tout, Trooper Ken 199, 200, 203, 219
Tower Bridges 217
Tramecourt 35, 48
trench warfare 130–2, 131, 136–7

Ulster Tower 149
Ultra 195
Umfraville, Sir Gilbert 27
Utah beach 193
Uxbridge, Lord 60, 74, 87

Vandamme 68
Vauban, Sébastien le Prestre de 53, 183
Vaux, Lieutenant Peter 174, 175–6, 177
Vendôme, Count of 36, 41
Verdun 124, 140, 156
Verney, Major-General G.L. 198
Versailles Treaty (1919) 154–6, 157

Villars, Marshal 7, 118, 182
Villers Bocage 196
Vimont 208, 212
Vimy Ridge 7, 124, 172, 173, 177, 180, 181, 182, 183–5, 186
Vis-en-Artois 174
Vivian, Sir Hussey 80
Voyennes 30, 46

Waffen-SS 192
Wagnonlieu 186
Wailly 178–9, 186, 187
Walsingham, Thomas 19
war graves 116–18, 151–2, 215, 219
Ware, Fabian 116, 215
Warlus 178, 179, 180, 186
Wars of the Roses 50–2
Waterloo 10–11, 12, 13–14, 50–87, 58–9, 62–3, 66–7, 76–7, 88
Watson, Corporal W.H.L. 99
Wavre 81
Wedgwood, Ensign 72
Wellington, Duke of 7, 10–11, 12, 51, 56, 57, 60–87
Wells, Private 107
Welsh Guards 172
Weygand, General Maxime 166, 168, 181
Wheeler, Private William 70, 78
Whistler, Rex 194, 195, 219
White, Robert 20
William II, Kaiser 92, 154
William the Conqueror 215, 216
Williams, Brigadier Bill 198
Wilson, Major-General Henry 92–3
Wilson, Woodrow 156
Worrell, Private Ted 115
Wounded Eagle monument 83

York, Duke of 27, 40, 41, 49
Ypres 123, 124, 168, 182

Ziethen 79, 80